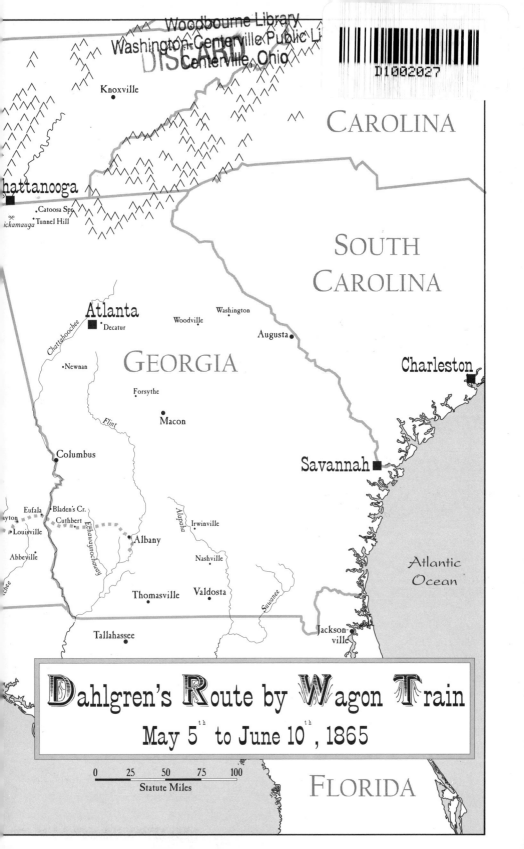

Knoxville

CAROLINA

hattanooga
.Catoosa Spr.
ickamauga .Tunnel Hill

SOUTH
CAROLINA

Atlanta
.Decatur

Woodville

Washington

Augusta

Charleston

•Newnan

GEORGIA

Forsythe

Macon

Columbus

Savannah

Eufala   Bladen's Cr.
ayton   Cuthbert
.Louisville

Irwinville

•Albany

Abbeville

Nashville

Atlantic
Ocean

Thomasville   Valdosta

Tallahassee

Jackson-
ville

Dahlgren's Route by Wagon Train

May 5th to June 10th, 1865

0   25   50   75   100
Statute Miles

FLORIDA

CHARLES DAHLGREN
of Natchez

Also by Herschel Gower

Pen and Sword: The Life and Journals of Randal W. McGavock

Jeannie Robertson: A Biography of the Scottish Folk Singer

Editor, *The Hawk's Done Gone and Other Stories by Mildred Haun*

Editor with Robert L. Welker, *The Sense of Fiction*

Editor, *Beersheba Springs: A History*

Faces in a Nashville Arcade (Novel)

CHARLES DAHLGREN

of Natchez

THE CIVIL WAR AND
DYNASTIC DECLINE

HERSCHEL GOWER

BRASSEY'S, INC.
Washington, D.C.

Library of Congress Cataloging-in-Publication Data

Gower, Herschel.
    Charles Dahlgren of Natchez : the Civil War and dynastic decline/Herschel Gower.—1st ed.
        p. cm.
    Includes bibliographical references (p.   ) and index.
    ISBN 1-57488-394-1
        1. Dahlgren, Charles Gustavus, 1811–1888. 2. Plantation owners—Mississippi—Natchez—Biography. 3. Natchez (Miss.)—Biography. 4. Natchez (Miss.)—History—Civil War, 1861–1865. 5. United States—History—Civil War, 1861–1865—Biography. 6. Natchez (Miss.)—Social conditions—19th century. 7. Reconstruction. 8. Dahlgren family. 9. Philadelphia (Pa.)—Biography. 10. Brooklyn (New York, N.Y.)—Biography. I. Title.

F349.N2 G68 2001
976.2′26—dc21

                                                                    2001037786

ISBN 1-57488-394-1 (alk. paper)

Brassey's, Inc.
22841 Quicksilver Drive
Dulles, Virginia 20166

First Edition

10 9 8 7 6 5 4 3 2 1

For
Alma Kellogg Carpenter of Natchez
Bruce R. Allardice of Chicago
Daniel E. Sutherland of Fayetteville
Three stalwarts who aided, abetted,
and survived the making of this book

❦ Contents ❧

❡ Preface ❡

In the summer of 1987, at Beersheba Springs, Tennessee, my friends the Howells marked the centenary of the family's ownership of the Dahlgren cottage on the Cumberland Plateau, about 100 miles southeast of Nashville. Howell cousins from Maryland, Connecticut, and Germany joined their Nashville kin to celebrate one hundred summers in the big log and clapboard house dating from the 1850s. Reminiscences ran rife as three generations clustered on the porches shaded by pine and hemlock. Memories stretched back to earlier generations; stories brought presences again to the wide front hall and the kitchen wing and down the flagstone steps leading to the two-room cabin for the overflow of teenage boys.

There was a lot of storytelling, a lot of eating and singing, and, at times, some confusion. This last was occasioned by references to Cousin Lou or old Cousin Flavill or Papa's Virginia kin. The youngest of the wives struggled to keep the degrees of cousinship sorted out and generations straight when names so often had been duplicated. A child was heard asking, "What's a first cousin twice removed?" The young mother, ten years in the family, replied, "Remember, Julia, I've told you to ask your father questions like that."

The celebration ended with a Saturday brunch for two hundred people that included an aluminum canoe filled with ice for drinks and 50 pounds of pork barbeque from Pope Taylor's stand near Murfreesboro. Beersheba Springs (altitude 2,000 feet, population 420) had seldom seen such gatherings as the Howells' during the twentieth century. One had to look back to the flush times of the 1850s for greater gatherings and more spectacle at the columned antebellum hotel and its cluster of cottages. The Civil War had had a lingering effect. The summer of 1860 was never to be repeated because it had outdone, outshone, and outlasted all other summers since 1833 to the present.

Before the Howells could stage their celebration, they had to put house and grounds in order for the visitors. After all, Charles G. Dahlgren had bought the property in 1859, and some housekeeping was always necessary. By 1987, the pine grove on the south side, where the children liked to play, needed a lot of attention because it had become a thicket of scrub oak, running vines, and tangled briars.

The Howells contracted with Josephine Eubanks and her family of Beersheba for clearing the scrub and bushes from the grove. On fair days all that spring, Mrs. Eubanks worked to tame the wilderness. She hewed, cut, pulled, whacked, and sawed. She grubbed up poison ivy and poison oak by the roots and threw them on the brush pile. Her grandson, Nicholas King, too young to be of much help, carried sticks and branches. He was always impatient to start a bonfire.

To put Nicholas where she could see him and keep him out of the briars, Josephine cleared off the moss on a small, rounded boulder that rose about two feet from the ground. She chopped away the vines. "You stay there, young man, till I tell you. Set." Nicholas minded.

Some months later, Josephine reported that she had noticed some initials when she set about clearing the years of accumulation on the slanting sides of the little sandstone boulder. "I never paid 'em any mind. Thought it was prankish boys carving their names, with nothing better to do." Then she added, "I did notice marks that looked like they went way, way back, but it didn't mean a thing to me." Nicholas was sitting on a date, August 31, 1860.

Three years later, in the summer of 1990, I was first shown the rock with the initials and was propelled back 130 years. Questions rushed to my head and were loath to leave. Who were these people who had left their initials on the stone in 1860? Who could identify them? Were they all lost to time and memory? Although about half of the initials ended in *D* and others in *G* and *V*, there were no other clues but the date. From Isabel Howell's monograph, *John Armfield of Beersheba Springs* (Beersheba Springs Historical Society, 1983), I knew that the owner of the property in 1860 was a planter from Natchez, Mississippi, by the name of Charles G. Dahlgren, who was later a brigadier general of Mississippi volunteers. But during all the years that we had known her,

Isabel had never mentioned the boulder in the thicket; surely, she would have pointed it out if she had known it was there.

After seeing the rock and puzzling over the initials that first time, I kept taking walks that ended in the pine grove. I went silently, gnawed by curiosity, pulled back to the summer of 1860. The irony had moved in. It had been the last summer of fencing lessons for the teenage boys in the courtyard of the hotel, a French chef from New Orleans had presided over the kitchen, and a string orchestra had played waltzes for dances and masquerades in the ballroom. I was piqued by what little I knew and by what I did not know at all. I was conscious of what I knew in 1990 that *they* could not possibly have foreseen 130 years earlier.

As the season of 1990 closed with Labor Day, I wrote down the initials and went back to Dallas. I already knew there was little chance of ignoring, for very long, fourteen sets of letters on the sandstone. What I know now is that their owners rose up and began stalking me. Each time I opened my briefcase, they seemed to say, "Tell them who we are."

Dallas has a fine public library and its eighth floor has superior resources for genealogical and historical research. With the generous help of the library staff and the referrals they provided—including loans from the Fort Worth branch of the National Archives—I began my pursuit of Charles Dahlgren, the "C.G.D." on the rock. I began plotting his movements and raising a man who had dropped from sight one hundred years before. And, through him, I met and identified and came to know his large and often elusive family. Slowly, all of the initials began to turn into names, the names turned into people, and members of Charles's family gave me a portion of their lives.

Of this I am certain—if the Howells had not planned their centenary celebration in 1987, if Josephine Eubanks had not cleared the pine thicket and anchored Nicholas King to the rock, and if curiosity had not continually plagued me, the people occupying the pages that follow would not exist in the state and condition you find them here.

All of the initials are identified in the footnote on page 215. The appendix contains genealogical tables that clarify the family relationships.

ও Acknowledgments ৩

I have been fortunate in having from the earliest version of this book a number of friends and colleagues who read the manuscript and offered valuable suggestions. I am indebted to the scrutiny of Bertram Wyatt-Brown, Bruce Allardice, Alma Kellogg Carpenter, Daniel E. Sutherland, Mimi and Ron Miller, Nathaniel C. Hughes Jr., Robert J. Schneller, Jr., Ridley Wills II, and Grady Howell.

I extend continuing appreciation to the directors and their helpful associates of the following libraries and depositories: Ann Alley and Marilyn Bell Hughes, Tennessee State Library and Archives; Lloyd Bockstruck and Staff, Dallas Public Library, in particular Lee Markoff, Ed Boehringer, Sally Peden, Judy Williams, and Paul Oswalt; Elbert Hubbard, Clinton Bagley, and the Staff of Mississippi Department of Archives and History; Kent Carter, Fort Worth Branch, National Archives.

Friends have volunteered for and carried out research when I was unable to travel beyond my desk: Samuel H. Howell, Jr., Dabney Adams Hart, Jeanne Oglesby, Daniel Beatty, Richard Kilbourne, Richard Chenoweth, Marguerite Harrison, Betty Bridgewater, Donald Estes, Carolyn Cole, Bertram Lippincott III, Tim Burgess, Jeffrey Alan Owens, Joan and Thomas Gandy, and June Dorman.

Those individuals who generously placed family papers at my disposal are Julie Ann Young Johnson, John E. Berg, Virginia Wilson Severs, Bernardine Avdek, William E. Berg, and Ulric Dahlgren IV.

Five editors at Brassey's gave the manuscript much attention and the author good counsel: Rick Russell, David Arthur, Julie Wrinn, Terry Belanger, and Don Homolka.

Karen Cantu cheerfully transcribed many pages of rough copy over a period of six years. The final draft was completed with the editorial skills and devotion of my wife, Dona Spawn Gower.

❧ *Introduction* ❧

Charles Gustavus Dahlgren was one of three sons born to Bernard Dahlgren, a Swedish adventurer, and his American-born wife of Irish descent, Martha Rowan. Dahlgren and Rowan were names the boys were taught to honor, and did honor, as their lives spanned nearly all the years of nineteenth-century America.

As young men, Charles, John Adolphus, and William Theodore Dahlgren went to sea, either in ships of the U.S. Navy or in the merchant fleet. Their apprenticeships were rigorous and sometimes harsh, but the sea challenged their manhood, their fortitude, and their ability to excel and survive. The sea was a way of confirming their descent from lines of Viking warriors, real or imagined. From the Irish side, they inherited a gift of gab and a wiliness that stood them in good stead when they wished to impress their superiors or widows of recognized means.

John, the oldest, rose to the rank of rear admiral through his discipline as an officer and his skill as the inventor of the Dahlgren 11-inch naval cannon. By 1861, he enjoyed a close relationship with Abraham Lincoln. His second wife, Madeleine Vinton Goddard, was a Washington socialite, writer, and woman of influence.

Charles won the favor of the powerful financier Nicholas Biddle as a young man and became Biddle's protégé in Philadelphia. He was soon dispatched south to a post in the Natchez branch of the Bank of the United States. Driven by a compulsion to get ahead, Charles became a landowner in the hierarchy of cotton planters and slave owners in Mississippi and Louisiana. He courted and married the wealthy widow Mary Routh Ellis in 1840, built two mansions in Natchez, and became a general with his own brigade of Mississippi troops in 1861. As a go-getter whose aims were typical of many "men on the make" in nineteenth-century America, Charles Dahlgren emerges as the central figure of this narrative because of the variety of roles that he tackled and the pitfalls that he encountered in a long and turbulent life. A fine biography of John Dahlgren by Robert J. Schneller Jr. was published in 1996, but no biography of Charles exists and no study has charted the tangled relationships of Charles and his brothers John and William in a house divided.

William broke with both brothers but kept alive the seafaring tradition. Under the alias de Rohan, he was a ship's captain and mercenary with revolutionary commanders in South America and Italy. In 1860, he joined Giuseppe Garibaldi and his Red Shirts in their fervor to unite the Italian states as a modern nation. William helped, by deceit and cunning, to put Victor Emmanuel of Sardinia on the throne of Italy.

Only in retrospect and across the chasm of years can a later generation look at players like the Dahlgrens and attempt to judge their performances. In opening the curtains that have obscured them, we become aware that each brother, with no small self-esteem, would be quick to express the heft of his role in the tumultuous affairs of nineteenth-century America.

The Dahlgrens attract our interest today because their actions reflect the tempestuous times during which they walked with bold strides. Each brother courted danger—from street fights and duels in Natchez to rebellions in Italy, from filibuster campaigns in Central and South America to the Atlantic blockade against the South. The Dahlgrens were virile and impetuous glory seekers who played dangerous games for the sport.

Other such families flourished in America during the nineteenth century and have been portrayed in both biography and fiction. In his novels, William Faulkner of Mississippi chronicled actual families of the Old South under the fictional names of Compson, Sutpen, and Sartoris. Faulkner's own great-grandfather was the model for Colonel John Sartoris in *The Unvanquished*. William Cuthbert Faulkner was a Mississippi planter and Confederate colonel. A short, gallant man, he was sighted among his men by the large black feather in his cap. After heroic action at Manassas, Faulkner was commended by Gen. Pierre G. T. Beauregard and dubbed "The Knight of the Black Plume."

To the prudent in their society, the stalwarts like Faulkner went out of their way looking for an opportunity to brandish their sabres. In *The Unvanquished,* one finds little rational delineation between John

Sartoris's acts of heroism and his moments of recklessness. These acts extended from the first and second battles of Manassas to the theft of a ballot box during Reconstruction in Mississippi when Sartoris killed two carpetbaggers in cold blood. The fictional Sartoris reckoned that valor was achieved from the demands of the times. "Honor was accorded on the basis of community decision," as Bertram Wyatt-Brown points out in writing about Southerners (*Honor and Violence in the Old South*). That is, honorable acts reflected the time and the place. Honor was not a matter of addressing such abstract concepts as freedom or democracy. Ultimately, Wyatt-Brown adds, "one had to improvise."

But Sartoris brought distress to his family, especially his sister Jennie. She suffered from his escapades because she feared for his life. He had gone too far with all his killing. Could he ever respond rationally again with all the blood on his hands?

At the end of *The Unvanquished*, Jennie has a word with her nephew Bayard at the time of his father's death. She expresses anger, frustration, and dismay at all the escapades through which Bayard's father has put the family. In love and grief and pity and helplessness, she lets go of her pent-up feelings to Bayard: "Oh damn you Sartorises. Damn you. Damn you."

Bayard's Aunt Jennie had found words for the vagaries of valor and the skewed honor in her clan. Sister Martha ("Patty") Dahlgren Read and the Dahlgren wives might have used the same words about the chances taken by John, Charles, and William, and especially her nephew Ulric. "Damn you Dahlgrens. Damn you. Too long we've put up with your recklessness and conceited honor."

It takes two or three generations to put into perspective such protagonists as Colonel Faulkner and the Dahlgrens. At the distance of a few years, their descendants are more charitable than were their contemporaries. Thus, Charles Dahlgren and his brothers catch the attention of readers today because of their vagaries and because they left a legacy of tales to be remembered and passed down the years.

❧ One ❧

Young Charles Dahlgren:
A Heritage of Adventure

Born in Philadelphia in 1811, the boy was given the name of Charles Gustavus Ulric Dahlgren. The Swedish side of his family had prevailed again, as it had two years earlier when Charles's brother was born and named John Adolphus Bernard Dahlgren. The immigrant Swedish father, Bernard, had won out over any wishes of the Irish mother, Martha Rowan, and her side of the boys' bloodlines. Both parents had sufficient reasons to assign the names of their forebears, but for their sons the father insisted that the names reflect the Nordic warriors in his past and the royal rulers of Sweden. Another set of ancestral names was given a third son, William Theodore, who was born in 1820, also in Philadelphia. William was later to repudiate the Dahlgren name for de Rohan, an adaptation of the Irish Rowan.[1]

When Bernard Dahlgren died in 1824, Charles wrote to his mother from school in Arbor Hill: "I received your letter on the second. You cannot imagine my grief on hearing of my Father's death, but why should I weep, was he not in pain and misery and did not God in his mercy take him from us to live with him? And is he not now basking in the Sun-shine of eternal bliss?"[2] The letter suggests a young stoic brought up in Christian concepts, with a firm belief in immortality. He would find comfort in having an admired older brother in whom he could confide and with whom he could share adventures at sea, like those of their Viking ancestors.

That same letter suggests that Charles was already a regular visitor

1

on board ships docked in Philadelphia. Charles asks his mother to send someone "aboard the *Philadelphia* and ask if my riding-whip is there."

Two years later Charles was corresponding with brother John, the midshipman. One letter is full of family news and reports on neighbors and school friends. It reveals again the close ties between the brothers. Before John sailed, the boys had exchanged watches as a token of brotherly affection. Charles reported: "I have lately had your watch done up which cost $2 and now keeps elegant time. . . . Do tell me if mine keeps good time." The watches seem to have symbolized a way of participating in each other's experiences.

But Charles was still landlocked, as his humorous verse at the end of the letter indicates. He tells John to direct his letters thus:

> This will go by my desire
> To Charles Dahlgren Esquire,
> Who lives as I repeat
> Philadelphia, 22 Pine Street.[3]

Even though Charles could not, in fact, be sailing with John, he was at one in his thoughts with his brother and wanted to talk about the sea, sails, rigging, quadrants, and telescopes. Even when their relations broke down in later years and they were literally at arms against each other, they kept before them the image of the sea and themselves as companions standing up to the challenges and perils that it offered.[4]

When Charles was fourteen years old, he took part-time employment as a scribe to help with the support of his mother, sister Martha Matilda ("Patty"), and brother William. "[The job] was secured by Hon. John Vaughn, copying the writings of George Washington at ten cents per hundred words."[5] This was the effort to assemble Washington's papers so that Professor Jared Sparks could prepare the first president's biography. The family clearly stood in favor with the Honorable Mr. Vaughn; Charles's younger brother William also reported having done his turn at copying the papers while he was in school. His early experience as a scribe helped to equip Charles with a fine writing style that would serve him well in later years as businessman and litigant.

In 1827, at age sixteen, Charles followed his older brother to sea. John recorded in his diary that while aboard the *Macedonian* in Brazil he was pleased to see the arrival of the American brig *Satona* from Rio de Janeiro: "My brother Charles arrived in her. I went aboard and brought him on shore: we spent the evening very agreeably with Doña Joaquina." Eleven days later, on 24 March, John and Charles had another visit. On 26 March, John wrote: "Charles, on *Satona*, about to sail for Philadelphia. Took with him letters to Ma, Mr. [John] Vaughn, and Judge King."[6] Quite likely, Charles also kept a diary as a seaman and recorded his own impressions of Brazil and his happy meeting with John, but no such record has come to light.

ℚ ℗

Charles's and John's romantic notions and adolescent musings were enhanced by the knowledge that their father had spent his early life as an adventurer. Bernard was the son of Dr. Johan Adolphus Dahlgren (1744–1792), who won honors as a physician and was a protégé of the renowned naturalist Carolus Linnaeus. After graduation from the University of Uppsala, Bernard took a post in Ulesborg, at the head of the Gulf of Bothola, a wild and frozen region in Lapland. At six feet four inches, Bernard accepted the challenge of surviving in the Arctic Circle and made a reputation for himself as an explorer of the North Cape and Alten.

He was also a political liberal and zealot of republican reform in monarchial Sweden. In 1804, he became such an active partisan of democratic principles that he was forced to flee the country at the risk of his life. The Crown confiscated all of his property, and Bernard wandered about the European Continent for the next few years. He reached Spain when Napoleon was waging war against the Bourbons and narrowly escaped death on several occasions.

Bernard's wanderings in early nineteenth-century Spain intrigued his sons. His adventures were certainly kept alive in their memories. In one episode, Bernard told how highwaymen plotted to rob and kill him at a hostel in Seville in the dead of night. Pretending to be asleep as his attackers entered his room by a hidden passage, he rose up and shot at them with two of his pistols and then escaped through a second-story window. After reporting the incident to the local police and getting little satisfaction, he concluded that "the police and robbers were at that time nearly identical in Spain."[7]

On another occasion, Bernard was furnished wine with his supper by a charming young girl from the kitchen. As she set down the tray, she gestured in sign language that he should not drink the wine. Understanding her warning, Bernard emptied the vessel into the fireplace and made an excuse to the hotelier to go outside for a few moments of fresh air. His report to the police was so convincing that officers were sent to investigate the tavern's owner and interrogate the maid servant. According to the story remembered by Bernard's sons in later years, the police discovered in the cellar several recently buried bodies of travelers who had been first put to sleep by drugged wine and then murdered.[8]

Many of Bernard's stories were akin to the bizarre tales associated with nineteenth-century Romanticism. That movement manifested itself in England in works by Coleridge, Byron, and Shelley, and later in America by Washington Irving and Poe. About the same time, Sweden, under the influence of such writers as Immanuel Kant, Johann Wolfgang von Goethe, and Johann Christoph Schiller, developed its own Romantics: B. Höijer, F. W. J. von Schelling at Uppsala, and Amadeus Atterbom. These writers retold ancient tales from the folk tradition, explored and adapted the Gothic sagas from Sweden's past, and became spokesmen for nationalistic ideals.[9] These were the literary currents that young Bernard Dahlgren met with while a student at Uppsala. Then, the success of the American Revolution caused him to look for adventures in the New World. His first step was to negotiate a way across the Atlantic to that democratic refuge sought by other young men with the same zeal for freedom and excitement.

During this period in his life, Bernard kept a diary in which he detailed the hardships and frustrations that beset him. Selling his guns and most of his personal effects, he raised eighty dollars to pay for his passage to New York, where he arrived as a stranger with a knowledge of French but limited English. He took menial jobs at any work that came to hand.

In 1807, he went to Haiti as a cashier for Thomas Lewis and Co. at a salary of eight hundred dollars a year, but the heat and fevers of the Caribbean were not the climate for a North European. He returned to the United States and settled in Philadelphia. Quickly, as his English improved, Bernard became a figure in international commerce at the busy port city. Later, in a happy reversal of fortune, he was appointed Swedish and Norwegian consul in charge of international trade between the two countries and the United States.[10]

In 1808, at age twenty-four, Bernard met, courted, and married Martha Rowan, daughter of a revolutionary soldier and descendant of the Mortimers of North Ireland. The happy marriage would produce three sons, John, Charles, and William, and one daughter, Martha Matilda.[11] Despite the early death of Bernard Dahlgren at age forty in 1824, his children would never forget their father's many spellbinding escapades amid the turmoil of Napoleonic Europe.

Although Charles Dahlgren was only thirteen years old when his father died, Charles passed the family lore on to his sons: "My father refused to desert his King Gustavus to the interest of Napoleon, who placed Bernadotte on the throne, and was driven from Sweden and his property seized, but afterward triumphed in the return of his possessions when Sweden became hostile to Napoleon & received full amnesty from Bernadotte and was made Consul General for Sweden and Norway [in the United States]." Although the sequence became scrambled over the years, Charles pointed out to his son John Adolph, eighteen years old at the time, how individuals and families are called on to suffer "by adherence to their truth and principles." Thus, his sons should be prepared to take a stand and make sacrifices for the family's honor at whatever cost.

Dahlgren also told his son about their Rowan forebears in Ireland and their part in a rebellion against English rule in the eighteenth century: "[My grandfather] James Rowan lost his estate and was expatriated in 1765 for attempting to make Ireland free. He escaped to Phila., took arms with Gen. Washington in 1776, and lived to see his principles triumph at the peace of 1783."[12] As a son and grandson of revolutionaries, Charles took pride in his descent from such men. He knew full well the losses that they had sustained, and he wanted to pass their values on as a legacy for his son. Later, as the father of sixteen children by two wives, he became an Old Testament patriarch, strict, demanding, and expecting not only full obedience but honor as well from his children.

ʘ∝

Exactly how many years Charles spent in the pursuit of a formal education and how he came to the notice and employment of financier Nicholas Biddle are matters of conjecture. The record is silent about details. As a young man, tall, gray-eyed, and of good bearing, however, Charles won the confidence of Biddle and became his private secretary in Philadelphia. A businessman and president of the Second Bank of the United States, Biddle had stabilized the currency by increasing the note issue of the federal bank and by forcing the state banks to redeem their issues in specie. These transactions alienated Andrew Jackson, who was politically opposed to the bank and who was successful in preventing the renewal of its charter in 1836. One result was the turbulent financial panic of 1837.[13] Charles Dahlgren was on the sidelines of these developments because Biddle had sent him, at age twenty-four, to New Orleans and then to Natchez to look after his interests in the cotton states.

Through his association with Biddle, Dahlgren acquired a firm grasp of banking; he also had the grit and stamina to do business with the frontier clientele of a bustling river town like Natchez. There he learned about the wealth to be got in cotton and sugar, the tobacco trade from upriver, and rafts piled high with timber floating downstream. Biddle had chosen well. Dahlgren remained in Natchez and began to prosper. He had discovered his calling and had also found the place to put it to work.

❧ Two ❧

Banker, Planter, Husband, and Dynast

ppointed teller on January 2, 1835, by the Board of the Natchez Branch of the Bank of the United States, Charles Dahlgren gave a bond of $5,000. All of his securities, except one, were family members. Then, on 9 October 1835, Dahlgren resigned from the position and left honorably, with only a minor incident: "The Board being informed by the Cashier that a part of the Deficiency in the Cash reported above was lost when Mr. C. G. Dahlgren was Teller. . . . Resolved that claim against C. G. Dahlgren for Ninety-four Dollars nine cents . . . by cash deficiencies be remitted and that the cash be balanced by profit and Loss." Blameless, Dahlgren left the bank, as did his friend John Sims, whose deficit was $100. The board believed "that their general good conduct while in office entitled them to the favor of the Board."[1]

Because President Andrew Jackson had rallied his forces successfully against Nicholas Biddle and prevented renewal of the bank's charter, the demise of the Bank of the United States was imminent. Dahlgren, having learned by now to be aggressive in a new country, switched to the Commercial Bank in Natchez. He was an employee there on March 14, 1836, when there was a rush on its stock. William Johnson, a black diarist in Natchez, recorded the pandemonium:

There was the Greatest Rush made for it [stock] by the people that was Ever Known in this place before. A very Greate many Persons did not get any shairs. . . . Mr Dalhgreen [sic] & Mr

7

Dillon has a fight at Mr Bells Tavern about Bank Stock. Dalhgreen gave Dillon a Black Eye. . . . [2]

So the scrappy young banker from the City of Brotherly Love—claiming bloodlines to Nordic warriors—retired Dillon to the sidelines with a shiner that Johnson and the town would remember.

◌ఠ

The Natchez in which Dahlgren settled in 1835 was in many respects a frontier town with characteristics of the Old Southwest. Mississippi had become a state in 1817, only eighteen years before Dahlgren's arrival. Easterners looked upon Alabama, Mississippi, Tennessee, and Arkansas as territories where the unwritten laws of the frontier took precedence over the laws of the legislatures. The half century from 1800 to 1850 produced volatile frontiersmen like David Crockett, Andrew Jackson, and Sam Houston. Their local counterparts cropped up in every village and were notorious in all the frontier settlements. When society got too tame, or the sheriff too ornery, or the neighbors too close, frontiersmen set out for the endless stretches of freedom awaiting them in Texas.

The major source for the description of Natchez as a city typical of the Old Southwest is William Johnson's substantial diary. A mulatto barber and free man of color, Johnson was also a farmer, horse breeder, merchant, moneylender, slaveholder, and recorder of events in Natchez from 1835 to 1851. His daily entries of town news and the people involved are colorful. What he presents is an array of characters and events in a river town clearly western in tone but cosmopolitan in its upper strata. It was a society that Hennig Cohen and William B. Dillingham, in the introduction to *Humor of the Old Southwest*, cite as developing and fostering certain sports and games typically associated with frontier America: "the hunt; fights, mock fights, and animal fights; frolics and dances; games, horse races, and other contests; militia drills; steamboat races; gambling. . . ."[3] Johnson also reported such sports, as well as duels, deaths and funerals, catastrophes on the river, violent exchanges, and murders. (Johnson himself was murdered in 1851 after a heated dispute over a property line.)

One might suspect that Charles Dahlgren, the young banker from Philadelphia with a good education and Eastern upbringing, would be aloof to the rowdy elements of Natchez. But like John A. Quitman and Sargent S. Prentiss, also from the North, Dahlgren had a temper and was quick to resort to arms when crossed.

Johnson recorded another incident concerning Dahlgren on 28 November 1836. The twenty-five-year-old banker became involved in an altercation with one Charles Stewart. The fight began at Mrs. Mary Rowan's boarding house, where Dahlgren and other young bachelors lived and took their meals. The boarders were discussing a recent duel in South Carolina. Because the newspapers had reported no bloodshed, Dahlgren wagered that the participants were pretenders, had gone soft, and had fought with paper bullets. Stewart, a loyal South Carolinian, responded hotly that the bullets were real and "if any man would say they fought with paper Bullits that he is a Damed Lyar and a Dd Scoundrel & a Dmd Coward—this was at the supper table."

Dahlgren jumped up and slapped Stewart hard on the cheek and the fight began. Friends parted them, but Stewart promised to settle the argument next morning. According to Johnson:

> . . . [Y]oung Stewart took a stand up at Carpenters Drug Store for the purpose of making the attackt upon Dahlgreen as he was going to the Bank . . . and as Dalhgreen past the Door Stewart steped up to him and told him that now was [the time] to Settle their Dispute and at the Same time Struck Mr Dalhgreen with his stick, Mr D then Struck him Back with an umbrella—Stewart Struck him with the Stick again—Mr. D. then steped Back and Drew a Pistol and Fired at Mr. S. and missed Him—Mr. S. then Drew and Fired and the Ball Lodged under the arm in the Left Side of Mr. Dalhgreen, Mr. D. then steped in at Throckmortons Store. S. steped in at the Door but finding that D. had another Pistol he steped Back and stood in the caseing of the Door. . . .

After a year and a half in Natchez, Charles Dahlgren had fully expected Stewart to be a man of his word. So, he carried an extra pistol as he made his way to the bank that morning.

Johnson continued: "D. then advanced on him, shot Him on Left Side of the face on the Temple or upper hinge of the Jaw Bone and the instant the Ball took Effect he Droped on his Knees and Fell over on the pavement as Dead, so Dead that he Barely Breathed." Then, Elick Stewart, Charles's brother, took up the fight with Dahlgren and struck him with his fist. By this time, Dahlgren's pistols were empty. Next Elick Stewart advanced with a bowie knife and Dahlgren began to fight with naked hands: "It was one of the gamest fights that we have Ever had in Our City before—E.S. cut him twice over the Head and cut his Little Finger nearly off and split his hand pretty Bad. . . ."[4] This story has come down in Dahlgren family lore, which says that Dahlgren almost lost the end of his little finger and kept the bullet in his chest and the tip of the bowie knife in his skull for the remainder of his life.[5]

Two days later, William Johnson was called to the office of Dr. Hubbard to shave young Charles Stewart's head so that bandages could be better applied. Stewart was reported hovering between life and death. On 30 November, Johnson was asked to shave Dahlgren's beard but noted that "he was very Comfortably Situated and in a thriving condition."

Charles Stewart, attended still by Dr. Hubbard, got worse before he got better. He was recovering slowly, head and scalp disfigured by Dahlgren's bullet, when he summoned William Johnson on 14 December to take measurements of his head for a wig to cover the wounds. One supposes haste was important. The Christmas season was close at hand and cotillions would be in progress. The young ladies of Adams County would expect the gallant young men to attend their balls and bring with them their scars along with the manners of gentlemen.

Another version of the same attack on Charles Dahlgren was remembered years later by his son John Armfield Dahlgren. In this version two disgruntled depositors in the bank set upon Dahlgren in the street and planted the tip of a bowie knife on the left side of his head; the tip broke off and remained in his skull. Dahlgren was rescued by his friend John

Armfield, a prosperous slave trader (for whom Charles would name his son). Armfield sent "a servant to be in constant attendance."[6] This courtesy was responsible for a long friendship of mutual regard and confidence between Dahlgren and Armfield.

Many years later, in 1879, the street fights were dramatized still again when a Philadelphia newspaper reporter interviewed the aging Dahlgren:

> Gen. Dahlgren has a deep, long scar on both sides of his left hand, where in fighting a duel with bowie knives, he clasped the keen edge of his antagonist's weapon to prevent a thrust into his bowels, and held it so hard that the blade cut through his hand and severed his little finger. He carries two pistol balls, received in duels, in his body, one lodging against his ribs. . . . Two other balls, fired to kill him, have been removed by surgeons. On top of his head, toward the left side, beneath the scalp, is the broken tip of a bowie knife, which is fastened into the skull bone, and was left there in a duel.[7]

The scars still spoke for themselves and propelled Dahlgren's listeners backward to a fading frontier era.

Johnson reported yet another incident on 6 December 1837: "Mr. Dalhgreen and a Mr. [John] Hagan from New Orleans Crossed The river last night for to fight a Duel Early this morning but the parties interfeared and the mater was Settled and they both Came Over this Morning with out having a fight, I am truly Glad it Ended in that way. . . ." Johnson gave no explanation as to why Dahlgren and Hagan crossed the river to fight their duel on the Vidalia sandbar. Actually, there was a very good reason to shoot it out on the Louisiana sandbar rather than on Mississippi soil. Although laws against dueling had been passed in both states, they were seldom enforced. Then, in 1835, the Mississippi Legislature passed a law that made a sobering difference: *The survivor in a duel fought on Mississippi soil was legally liable to pay the debts of his victim.*[8] Having shown the seriousness of their intentions by going to Louisiana, Dahlgren and Hagan soon settled their differences and shook hands. That time Dahlgren returned to Mrs. Rowan's boarding house with increased notoriety but without a wound.

☙☜

Similar confrontations and challenges marked the career of brother John Dahlgren. During the long months aboard ship John kept precise diaries of his travels and recorded incidents involving his honor. In 1829, while serving on the *Ontario,* he criticized a midshipman, Henry Walker, on the *Constellation.* Walker, chafing under the supposed insult, challenged Dahlgren to a duel. Before the details could be formally arranged, however, the *Constellation* sailed. Dahlgren's shipmates felt that the affair was over and that they had heard the last of Walker. But, still bearing his grudge, Walker renewed the challenge when the two were in port again. Fortunately, the friends of both men interceded and convinced them that the honor of neither had been questioned. Again, bloodshed was prevented by friendly counsel.

Several years later, Lt. John Dahlgren felt that he had been slighted when he failed to receive an invitation to a supper on board the *Cumberland.* To him, the entertainment "had the appearance of a general affair" and he should have been invited. Dahlgren announced that he could not ignore the breach in protocol, which to him "wore the aspect of intentional uncivility." Confronting the other officer face to face and expressing his grievance, he expected "a mortal quarrel." But, when the officer came forth with apologies and a satisfactory explanation, Dahlgren, who had been ready to uphold his honor with arms, accepted his explanation, and the two officers shook hands.

Dahlgren wrote later to his wife and children about the affair: "I know you would not have me tamely to submit to an insult, wherever I might be compelled to appeal for redress. What indeed can be so degraded as a man without courage, unless it be a woman without virtue?"[9]

Their years at sea taught all three Dahlgren brothers the code expected of the nineteenth-century naval officer. "Dueling was the ritualistic expression of honor, the code of the gentleman," as John Dahlgren's biographer observed.[10] The cramped, often suffocating conditions on board ship inevitably caused tempers to flare up. A chance remark could be blown out of all proportion. Honor would take unsettling strides above and below deck. It was trigger-ready from prow to stern.

 formula

One early incident relative to brother William Theodore Dahlgren and the sea has come to light. The letter is dated 26 November, but the year is omitted. The addressee is "Sir" and sometimes "General," but he is not further identified. From the content and tone, one can deduce that the person addressed is an older Natchez friend of brother Charles, probably John A. Quitman, a planter and general in the Mississippi militia. William is writing to this man of influence to plead for his intercession with brother Charles. He needs cash and thinks that Charles will deny him if approached directly. "Now, Sir, will you not do me the favor to call on my brother and persuade him to furnish me with $15.00 for a quadrant, $12.00 for a watch, and $8.00 for a telescope, so I shall be able to prosecute my voyage on the ship *George Evans* from New Orleans on December 3 as Chief Mate."[11]

Although the letter does very little to answer several questions, it suggests that William might have squandered his wages in New Orleans, hocked or had stolen from him his "tools of navigation" and was willing to swallow his pride and accept a gift from the hand of his estranged brother Charles, who had bailed him out before. He admits still owing the "General" himself $20 on a loan "when I stood imperatively in need of it having at the time not a stitch of clothes to go to sea with and that in the dead of winter. Since that time I have stuck to the sea but a fit of sickness together with a fine of $250 to which I was unjustly condemned for punishing a refractory seaman on board the ship of which I was an officer, have placed it wholly out of my power to repay the sum you so kindly and promptly loaned." William's temperament had been responsible for a succession of woes, and he was pleading for help and forgiveness.

Surmise suggests a date circa 1838, but the exact time is probably less important than the content of the note. William was eighteen years old in 1838. If Charles could be persuaded to make him another loan, William would take his berth and steer the *George Evans* to ports in Central America. Trickster that he was, the youngest brother knew that he could not be tracked by footprints on the open sea.

If Charles and William had come to a breakup, the rift was even more severe between John and William during the late 1830s. Their altercation took place in the Washington Navy Yard. John, then a lieutenant, "saw fit to take William severely to task for something, and that brought on a storm of angry words," as reported in *The Washington Post* many years later. The exchange "resulted in the younger man knocking the older brother into a corner of the room." Because William had violated the naval code by striking an officer, "[d]ignity forbade a personal altercation." Lieutenant Dahlgren sent for an aide, and William was promptly taken to City Hall and charged with attacking a superior in uniform. There the feeling between the brothers mounted. "William was sullen and unrepentant . . . and Dahlgren pressed the case." After the court levied a fine of $100 for the offense, John relented and "told the magistrate that if William would make a public apology . . . he would be willing that the penalty be set aside." But William remained stubborn and refused to make amends. "Never! Never!" he said. "I will never apologize nor even speak a word to you while God lets me live; and more, while you live I will never again bear the name that you do."[12]

From that day until his death, William took de Rohan as his surname (an adaptation of Rowan, their mother's maiden name), by which he was known as a ship's captain and soldier of fortune in two hemispheres.

Recent historians agree that Natchez was early marked with a stratum of ambitious, wealth-pursuing young men from the North who would influence its social and political life.[13] A large percentage of them had descended from the Northeast, a circumstance that made the area a haven for "naturalized" arrivals born outside Mississippi. William Banks Taylor calls them Southern Yankees and lists Dahlgren among the many who accumulated fortunes in cotton in both Mississippi and Louisiana. Their hard-driving enterprise started the young men upward on the economic scale; many were ultimately to achieve rank through socially proper marriages. For the most part, they voted as Whigs, were politically conservative, and were finally confirmed Unionists during the late 1850s. By 1840, Charles Dahlgren of Philadelphia had acquitted himself well and was moving in a proper direction as banker, businessman, and landowner. Socially, he had joined other young men in the Hussars, a local unit of the home guard, where he consorted with such surnames as Minor and Pollard during drills and at fancy balls on holidays.

Charles Dahlgren took a keen interest in the militia drills staged by the several companies of these home guards. They were select groups of volunteers who wore colorful uniforms, marched to fife and drum in the streets, staged drills on the esplanade overlooking the river, and challenged each other in target practice. Besides the loud, noisy parades with fife and drum that brought the town to the streets, the companies staged sumptuous dinners at Mr. West's tavern (all male) and Christmas balls at the City Hotel (printed invitations, ladies).

The Natchez Fencibles were organized in 1824 under John A. Quitman, who was to achieve recognition as a politician and commander in Mexico. Joseph Holt Ingraham, a visitor to Natchez and author of *The Southwest* (1835), pronounced the Fencibles "the finest looking body of men west of the Alleghanies." By 1841, Natchez could also boast the Hussars, the Guards, and the Adams Light Guards.

On 23 June 1838, Charles Dahlgren was made a second lieutenant in the Hussars. He ranked third in the company, just below Capt. William J. Minor and 1st Lt. Edmund P. Pollard.[14] The militia companies were like a fraternity and a *sine qua non* for ambitious young men who sought standing in the community. The Hussars attracted all eyes with their polished swords hanging from their belts and uniforms adapted from the Hungarian Hussars: a bushy or high cylindrical cloth cap, jacket with heavy braiding, a dolman or pelisse, and a loose coat hanging from the left shoulder. It was understood that Dahlgren—tall and fair-haired, with a virile stride—could put on the uniform and charm every lady in attendance. The scars he wore became permanent marks of distinction.

The Hussars captured the spring social news when they flooded Adams County with printed invitations to their ball on 4 April 1839 at Parker's Southern Exchange. Eight "managers" were named, including Minor,

Pollard, and Dahlgren. There would be quadrilles, cotillions, lancers, and the Old Virginia Reel to test the fortitude of every beau and his belle. A single card, addressed to "Miss Sprague," survives among the Ephemera of the Natchez Trace Collection, Austin, Texas. For what reasons did Miss Sprague save her card as a memento of the Hussars' Ball that spring? Did she become the bride of one of the managers the following June?

♂♀

It would appear that Charles Dahlgren began to think seriously about marriage at the age of twenty-eight in 1839, particularly after his friend, Thomas George Ellis, a man of property and a captain in the Fencibles, had suddenly died during a trip to buy more property in Tensas Parish, Louisiana. After Ellis was buried, Dahlgren was seen less and less at Bell's tavern and Natchez under-the-hill and the quarter races. Instead, he was observed riding south on Woodville Road to the Routhland estate. There, he put the art of eloquence to work in paying his respects to Ellis's widow, Mary Routh, and consoling the four fatherless children at her knee. Dahlgren was adept at these proprieties when the occasion presented itself. He soon made a formal proposal of marriage to Mary Routh Ellis and, in turn, received a formal acceptance.

Dahlgren's bride was born in 1813, the youngest daughter and ninth child of Job and Ann Madeline Muller Routh. Mary's father came west during the Spanish period and took up hundreds of rich acres in Mississippi and Louisiana. He died in 1834 as a man of recognized wealth. His children married well and his son John, Mary's older brother, was dubbed "Cotton King" because his last crop before the war yielded 8,842 bales. If *Goodspeed's Biographical and Historical Memoirs of Mississippi* (1891) can be trusted, "He owned so many negroes he did not know them all. His silver dinner service cost him $35,000."

Fifteen years older than his little sister Mary, John Routh had kept her under his protective wing until she fell in love with Thomas Ellis and married him in 1828 when she was fifteen years old. Ellis was also of prominent planter stock, the son of John Ellis and Sarah Percy, names of power recognized on both sides of the lower Mississippi.[15] Between the Rouths and Ellises alone, not to say the marriages of two Rouths to two Williamses and two to the Lanes, there was wealth in abundance. The boom years were at hand, cotton was king, and the South was not only prosperous but "invincible."

Year by year, the considerable investment in slaves was multiplied by natural increase; managers and overseers were in great demand; the immense acreage of Rouths, Ellises, Percys, and finally Charles Dahlgren was enough to keep all help busy in the fields, commissary, gin, and at the loading dock. When several of the owners retreated north to Saratoga Springs, Newport, and Beersheba Springs in summer to escape the heat and fevers, the overseers were left to keep order and see that the slave drivers applied the whip to surly work gangs. Cotton grew fast in the semitropical sun by day and during the still, hot nights. Chopping it, that is, constantly weeding it, was believed to be a labor that an African could perform and survive.

Unfortunately, when Thomas Ellis died in 1838, he left a number of debts for his wife. His disgruntled creditors soon demanded settlement from Mary Ellis, his administratrix. She was forced to give a note to the bank for $60,000 in 1839, presumably as security for debts that Ellis owed the bank. Mary and her brother John personally guaranteed the note; that is, they stood sureties—if the estate did not pay, they personally pledged to do so.[16]

By 1840, Charles Dahlgren, after his employment with the Bank of the United States in New Orleans and with banks in Natchez, had learned to seize opportunities for investments. The extent of his holdings in 1840 cannot be easily determined, but it is likely that he had his eye on the alluvial land across the river in Tensas Parish.[17] He was judged a suitable husband for Mary Routh Ellis and a proper surrogate father for Sarah Ann, age eleven; Stephen, age nine; Thomas, age five; and Inez, age two. The union pointed to advantages for both Charles and Mary and, during the next eighteen years, would give Mary and her children some relief from the debts left by Thomas Ellis. The marriage would also produce seven children, four of whom would reach manhood.

Now that he was the master of Routhland and a planter with social position, Charles invited Patty Dahlgren, his spinster sister, to live with him and Mary Routh as a member of the family. This was a hospitable gesture. Moreover, every household with children needed an "old-maid" aunt in residence. Patty accepted their invitation in 1841, and her stay in Natchez is recorded.[18] She was welcomed in some of the wealthiest homes in Mississippi. After five years under the roof of her unpredictable brother and observing the excesses of the planter aristocracy, however, Patty grew petulant. By 1846, the arrangement had soured and Charles refused her a home any longer. As she left Natchez, she voiced her condemnation of him and of the South. At the same time, their dispute served to set John Dahlgren against Charles. John was Patty's protector, and he took her to live again in his less affluent household in the East.

⁜

At the time of her marriage to Dahlgren, Mary Routh Ellis was plagued by her late husband's debts, estimated at $300,000 at the time of his death. In her prenuptial agreement with Dahlgren, recorded on 19 October 1840, in the Adams County Courthouse, Mary Ellis acknowledged responsibility for Ellis's debts, payable out of his estate. But she would have, after her union with Dahlgren, "the power and authority . . . to devise and bequeath by will or writing testamentary, any and all of her estate herein secured to her, in the same manner as if she were a *femme sole*."[19] Her marriage, therefore, would not prevent her from selling or exchanging all or any part of the property, real or personal, that she possessed at the time of the union. Her Routh inheritance after Job Routh's death in 1834 was thus duly considered and protected. The Routhland house and property where she and Ellis had lived, and where Dahlgren was to move, were part of the dower that Mary Routh had brought to the second marriage. She was twenty-seven years old, and Dahlgren was twenty-nine when they signed the agreement and made their vows.

Dahlgren tried at once to secure the Ellis holdings, including approximately 140 slaves who had been offered as collateral by the estate. They were about to be sold at a loss when Charles began bidding to buy them back with his own means. Other bidders, some of whom were Thomas Ellis's creditors, saw what was happening and challenged Dahlgren by running up their bids. The sale turned out to be a free-for-all, with Charles borrowing $90,000 to rescue his wife's property,[20] a gamble that drove him deeply into debt. Other moves by the Ellis creditors necessitated signing a mortgage on the Ellis household goods, field horses and thoroughbreds, carriage horses, and seventy head of cattle. Mary Dahlgren finally found a little help with the $5,000 that she borrowed from her father's estate in 1841.[21] (William Johnson, the barber, was perhaps correct in implying that Thomas Ellis had let the princely sport of horse racing divert him from plantation business.) With the Ellis debt hanging over the Dahlgrens, Charles made an offer to the bank to secure the Ellis debt by a mortgage on the 140 slaves—in essence, to substitute the mortgage for Mary's 1839 note and that note's surety of guarantees— but the bank refused the offer. In 1842 and again in 1843, Dahlgren began to pay on Mary's note in U.S. Bank notes from an account in Philadelphia. After 1843, he could make no more payments.

John L. Goddard, acting as agent for the trustees of the Bank of the United States, went to Natchez to collect debts assigned to Mississippi and the upper part of Louisiana. In a summary letter to agent Joseph L. Roberts marked *private and confidential,* Goddard wrote in 1852, ten years after Dahlgren had made only two payments: "Dahlgren and his wife had property in Louisiana, but as they avoided being caught there, we could not get service on them, and to attach their property it was necessary for me to give security in double the amount of the debt—I could not do so—but had suit brought against Mr. John Routh, who is one of the securities [along with Dr. Elias Ogden]."[22] Routh, it turned out, was burdened with mortgages himself.

Added complications had arisen over statutes of limitations in Mississippi and Louisiana and differences in the laws of each state. John L. Goddard continued to Roberts: "Somewhere Dahlgren got a copy of the Note & with his family left privately [for Washington and the East]. Dahlgren gave Mr. [Daniel] Webster $1000 to obtain if possible a reverse of the decision of the case of the Grand Gulf Bank vs. John R. Marshall . . . but he failed. . . ."[23] The accusations, in Goddard's capacity as an agent of the bank, were scathing. His tirade against Dahlgren intensified: ". . . [T]his case of ours, & other instances in which he has attempted to evade and evaded payments has sunk him materially in the honest & honorable part of the community. . . . If I can obtain the note when our Vice Chancery Court meets say on the 28th June next, I wish to send it on to proceed vs. him & his wife in New York or Rhode Island, or catch him as he comes through Ohio. . . ."[24]

The bank was more anxious than ever to overcome all legal technicalities and collect the remaining $75,000. Written exchanges among Roberts, lawyer John Bacon, and the clerk of the Supreme Court in New Orleans took place in June, July, and September. Roberts had J. S. Yerger, a Mississippi colleague, draw up a list of states where the statute of limitations did not apply and where Dahlgren could be served papers if apprehended. There were thirteen such states in all, ranging from Maine to Alabama and Arkansas. Local agents were busy throwing out their nets.

Then in September 1852, Goddard reported to Roberts: "Dahlgren we have reason to believe is removing all property out of his hands. We are informed that all their cotton is being shipped in the name of Sarah A. Ellis (Mrs. D's daughter) and that a store house in the town is now in the name of another child, Stephen Ellis."[25] Sarah Ann was twenty-three years old and Stephen was twenty-one; therefore, both were of legal age to transact business.

The chase after Dahlgren proceeded to Cincinnati with the hope of finding him on board one of the steamboats on the Ohio River that was headed for the lower Mississippi. Goddard wrote again to Roberts: "I much regret to learn of D's escape. . . . [If Dahlgren and his wife] come to New Orleans, even under assumed names & disguised [they will be apprehended by Mr. Ferguson]. My impression is, he would take Steamer or Ship at New York for Charleston, Mobile, or New Orleans. I sincerely hope it may be so, & that we catch him. . . ."[26] Dahlgren had outwitted his pursuers all summer in 1852 and led them on an extended chase. They had refused his offer in 1841 with a mortgage on the slaves that he had made in good faith. Now he felt justified in invoking the statute of limitations to cancel the debt.

On 20 October 1852, John L. Goddard reported to Messrs. John

Bacon and Thomas Robbins, as surviving trustees of the U.S. Bank, that he was still without clues: "I do not know where the Individual is, or his family, but wherever he is I have no doubt he is at some develry [sic] . . . his family residence [Routhland] in the immediate vicinity of Natchez has been undergoing a cleaning, painting & doing up. I have no doubt by conveyances, if not already done, he will make way with all his property."[27]

At this point in his life, Dahlgren, the planter, stood in poor repute with the bankers, but he had managed to outwit them for a dozen years. On 26 October 1852, Goddard wrote: "Mr. Dahlgren's family I understand have got home, but he, *it is reported*, is in Philadelphia prosecuting the Trustees for damages as to the extent of $150,000 for persecuting him. After suing him here & his own state clearing him. For the last two weeks there has been all sorts of stories circulating."[28] The bank had lost the case when it sued Dahlgren in Mississippi and Louisiana. Dahlgren was seeking damages in Philadelphia for defamation. The rumors soon flew back to Natchez. There, the gentry found the gossip too choice to withhold from circulation. It was the kind that the sewing circles would also take up, ladies chattering in their parlors, or on their piazzas, as they thrust their tiny lances through the checkered canvas of needlepoint.

It is of some interest here that Goddard refers to Dahlgren and his family as absent in the East. In 1852, Mary Dahlgren probably had with her Charles ("Charlie") Routh, age eleven, and two younger boys, Bernard, five, and John Adolph, three. It is possible to deduce from the Dahlgren genealogy that a son, Adolphus Eric, died that same summer in Pittsburgh on the way home to Natchez. In spite of the physical demands on the mother that travel with children can make, Mary Dahlgren was apparently happy to accompany her husband. There is a barely legible note on the flyleaf of the genealogy stating that her last son, Austin Mortimer Dahlgren, was born "on a steamboat at 12 M. in Kentucky." The date was 3 October 1856, and Mary was forty-three years old.

Hoping to settle his troubles with the banks, Dahlgren was rumored to have hired Daniel Webster to represent him; for years Webster had been on the payroll as counsel for the U.S. Bank. In the South, the continuing legal dispute also involved high-priced talent—Gen. Thomas Sparrow was a leading lawyer in Louisiana; the defendants were represented by the law firm of future Confederate Attorney-General Judah Benjamin. Each side was determined to show its case to be legal and to prove its cause just.

Finally, on 17 November 1852, Goddard wrote again to Joseph L. Roberts and conceded: "Dahlgren individually is worth very little and would be hard to come at. . . . The property is mostly the property of the late T. G. Ellis . . . Dahlgren married that widow & has managed the property & I understand from hearsay that within the last 18 months or 2 years Dahlgren has caused to be paid over (or part over) to the two eldest children of Ellis (they being of age) their proportion of the estate and profits."[29] Even this adversary indicated Dahlgren's softer side when it came to acting in behalf of his stepchildren. By questionable ploys, he salvaged some of the inheritance belonging to them and rationalized that what he did was for their gain, not his, and that the maneuvering was a benevolence. He knew that he was not a rich man in his own name in 1852. The alternative left to him was to be a clever man.

∾∻

After buying a choice commercial lot from W. W. Cochran in Natchez, Charles Dahlgren published a broadside announcing his new venture in March 1851:

> Sir:
> Having entered into the Produce and Commission business, I will be glad to furnish any supplies you may require of Pork, Corn, Bagging, Rope, and Western Produce generally, Wholesale or Retail.
> Respectfully, etc
C. G. DAHLGREN
Corner of Main and Broadway streets [30]

This was a plantation supply firm that would provide russet shoes for the slaves, hats, blankets, barrels of salt and bacon—items necessary for the operation of plantations on either side of the river. Because of his marriage to Mary Routh Ellis and her wide family connections, Dahlgren expected a thriving business. Clustered around Lake Saint Joseph in Tensas Parish, Louisiana, not far upriver from Natchez, were Routh or Routh-connected holdings running into thousands of acres: Elkridge (Hollings-worth-Walker-Routh); Evergreen (Williams-Routh); Winter Quarters (Routh and Nutt); Raritan (Odgen-Routh); Hollywood (Routh); Cypress Grove (Routh); Kenilworth (Routh); Routh-Wood (Routh); Verona (Routh-Gordon); Blackwater (Routh); and Franklin (Routh-Bowie).[31] Seldom, perhaps, has a forty-year-old started a business with such a ready-made clientele as Dahlgren had in 1851. His venture prompted author D. Clayton James to remark that, while operating the supply business, Dahlgren also had under his management or control some 6,100 acres in Tensas Parish. Thus, "like a number of other nabobs, he could be classified with both the commercial and agricultural elements of the Natchez aristocracy."[32] It had taken Charles Dahlgren fifteen years in business to predict his next windfall and to grab the profits as soon as it hit the ground. In spite of his battles in the courts, he had become a power to watch among the planters.

⊘⊘

Like many Southerners of his class, Dahlgren received illustrated catalogues each year from Eastern manufacturers of carriages and wagons. He could choose those vehicles that suited his needs and request shipment via Charleston, South Carolina, or New Orleans. One such supplier was G. and D. Cook of New Haven, Connecticut, who advertised its offerings as "greater than any other establishment in the world."[33] The Cooks went after Southern business by giving a number of their models such names as "Pride of the South," "Georgia No Top," "New Orleans Jump Seat," "Crescent City," "Alabama Six Seat," and "Mobile Top." The company also touted its reputation for work "so arranged, divided, and sub-divided, that each workman devotes his whole time and capacity to doing a single thing, and incidentally to devising new ways of doing that thing simpler, better, and *cheaper*."[34]

Ira Smith and Co. of 19 Dey Street, near Broadway, New York City, did a brisk business with Charles Dahlgren by shipping him fancy groceries and dry goods. One invoice survives from December 1852 when Routhland was laying in special provisions for the Christmas season. Listed are festive goods ranging from a keg of almonds to twelve boxes of lobster to seasoning spices and cheeses. Also included were kits of salmon and sardines, drums of Sultana raisins, macaroni, and vermicelli. In another order, Smith supplied the Dahlgrens with Farina, wheaten grits, Oolong tea, bottles of Picollili, and glasses of "best" prunes.[35]

There was also the catalogue of luxuries imported by Thomas and Co. of New Haven. Among them were London Porter, St. Croix Rum, Swan Gin, Old Scotch Whiskey, and Pale Brandy, along with ales, cordials, and cigars. The commerce between Northern suppliers and Southern consumers during the years prior to 1861 indicates what a profitable market the South had become, where the latest carriages and exotic luxury items for the table were in great demand.

Francis Horsfall, bookseller, of 777 Broadway, sent an invoice to Dahlgren for a shipment of ten volumes on 1 July 1853. The titles included the works of Shakespeare, a biography of John Randolph of Roanoke, *Russell's Life of Fox, Cooper's Naval History, Carey on the Slave Trade,* and *Collier's Notes and Emendations.* Among the adventure stories were *Old Forest Ranger* and *The Old House by the River.* Listed on back order were *Cobbet's French Grammar* and *Walton's Angler* (with Bethune's Notes). The selections reflect not only Dahlgren's interest in a variety of subjects but also include books chosen for his growing sons.[36]

From June to October 1853, Bailey and Company of Philadelphia sent several shipments of table silver to the Dahlgrens. The items included a silver coffee urn "with Roman border" at $200, three silver cups at $11.50 each, a pair of butler's knives at $7.50, and two Sheffield waiters at $23. There were also a silver decanter label, a patent corkscrew, and a gold thimble. The total came to $534.12, and it is likely that several items had been chosen for the dowry of Sarah Ann Ellis.[37]

☙❧

On 19 January 1853, the Dahlgrens gave their hesitant approval to the marriage of Sarah Ann Ellis to Samuel W. Dorsey. The oldest of the Ellis children, Sarah Ann was twenty-four years old and the bridegroom forty-two. Her stepfather had seen to it that she had had all of the advantages—tutors, private school in the East, a sojourn in Europe in 1850. He lavished expensive wedding gifts on her, and the Dahlgrens presented a brilliant fete at Routhland for three hundred guests following the nuptials presided over by the Reverend Joseph Buck Stratton.[38]

Dahlgren, like many fathers, however, had his misgivings about bridegroom Dorsey, who was of good Maryland stock but had hardly met his family's standards. Although a competent plantation manager, he was an unsuccessful lawyer in a family of distinguished solons. Mentally, he was no match for the lively, spirited Sarah Ann. Feeling the chill of Dahlgren's reluctant approval, the Dorseys went to live at Elkridge on Lake Saint Joseph and put the Mississippi River between them and Routhland for most of the year.

That same summer, the Dahlgrens made their annual trip to New York ahead of an onslaught of yellow fever that struck many families and left Natchez paralyzed. One memento of that journey to the East is an elegant portrait, which Dahlgren commissioned Charles Loring Elliot of New York City (1812–1868) to paint of Mary Dahlgren at age forty. It is a half-length oil of a "middle-aged" woman, seated facing left. She wears a black dress with elaborate white lace, V-shaped collar and cuffs, and a black lace piece partially covering her brown hair. She is holding a multicolored feather fan. Her hair, thick and luxuriant, is parted in the middle and falls in loose waves to her shoulders. The eyes are large, luminous; the lips are full and poised for a smile.[39]

Evidence of the strained relations between Dahlgren and his stepchildren is a bill that he drew up and sent the Dorseys on 23 December 1854. When pieced together, the story seems to be as follows: Sarah Ann and Samuel Dorsey honeymooned in the North and went to many fashionable places—Niagara, Toronto, and New York. They were accompanied by Sarah Ann's younger sister Inez and her brother Thomas LaRoche Ellis. Among affluent families of the era, a groom required the company of a man on such prolonged journeys and the bride needed the attendance of another young woman. The bills received by Dahlgren were enormous. The party of four had lived gloriously, far beyond the means that Dahlgren felt he could afford, so he itemized the account and sent all four of them bills.[40] No records of payment have survived.

The year 1855 brought serious troubles to the Dahlgrens at Routhland. A dependency caught fire in June when the family was away. Fortunately, the blaze was detected early, the fire brigade was alerted, and serious damage to the house was avoided. Then, a lightning fire occurred on August 7, and the house itself suffered a major conflagration that rendered it uninhabitable.[41] The Dahlgrens returned to blackened walls, stark chimneys, and mounds of ashes. Again, the fire brigade had been on the scene and was able to rescue whatever could be snatched up and carried off ahead of the flames. One surviving item was the Elliot portrait of Mary Dahlgren. Its present owners in Savannah report that when they received it the portrait bore tell-tale marks of the fire.[42]

With the destruction of Routhland, plans for a new edifice were soon drawn up and construction began under the direction of builder John Crothers. The ultimate in Greek Revival structures in the South, it is the only house in Mississippi with columns standing on four sides. The neoclassic age had reached its zenith and perhaps final expression. Mary Dahlgren moved into the imposing edifice with her husband and children in 1856, but the combination of four young sons, fires, housebuilding, and a chronic heart condition made her an invalid by the time she was forty-five years old. She was never well enough to share fully the amplitude and appointments of the new mansion with her husband and the growing boys.[43]

❦

Charles Dahlgren was a vigorous participant in the building of the new Routhland and worked daily with Crothers, "one of the best and ablest mechanics" of the Greek Revival mode. Although Dahlgren wrote in his old age that the design was adapted from a plan of A. J. Downing, he probably meant Alexander Jackson Davis, who designed "temple buildings," whereas Downing stuck to the Gothic and was anticlassical.[44] Dahlgren's enthusiasm was diminished only by Mary Dahlgren's steady decline in health. Even with a number of servants, she had had too many family responsibilities while the construction was going on. Her four Dahlgren boys were still young and troublesome, and her Ellis children were also a concern because they criticized her husband. The refusal of each side to make peace added to her despondency.

Hoping to make a final plea to all of them for reconciliation, Mary wrote her will in a weak hand at Routhland on 16 January 1858. The tone is one of uneasy hope. She asked that her Ellis children be paid for their interest in the Routhland property on which the new house had been built; she thought the value of the land was between $3,000 and $4,000. Mary wanted her husband to be fully compensated for his direct contribution of about $100,000 to the recovery in 1841 of the 140 slaves and other expenses. She left her silver pieces acquired during the Ellis years and a few other items saved from the fire to the first set of her children. She acknowledged Dahlgren's good deeds to them all. Finally: "I do not wish any bitter or evil feeling or words between my children & Mr. Dahlgren, but desire peace and kindness & kind inter-course. My children I wish to love each other, let no difference of name separate them. I wish those who are strong to help & aid the poor & weak and to cling to each other thru the trials of life. . . ." She had lived through a succession of trials herself, and they had been heavy even in the best of times. Praying that her last wishes would be honored, Mary died on 4 March 1858. She was buried in the walled family cemetery across the road from Routhland.

Neither had the flowers faded nor the earth settled on her grave before Charles, on March 25, advertised the sale of Routhland in the Natchez *Daily Courier:*

For sale. My residence Routhland, including 50 acres of land. Apply on Premises. C. G. Dahlgren

With the sale, the stepchildren would be able to collect their Routh inheritance and Charles would be free of their complaints. Maybe the earth would finally settle on the grave of his beloved Mary.

On 4 January 1859, Dahlgren accepted $30,000 from planter Alfred Vidal Davis of Louisiana for the Routhland property and, in turn, handed over $10,000 to his stepchildren.[45] Even with the death of his wife and the loss of his home, he was resolved to recover. He began studying plans for a new home for himself and his four boys. The young were his best reason to be sanguine about the future. With them, he had reason for trust—his name would be recalled and his memory kept alive. Yet, what Charles must have wanted most during the spring of 1859, imagined often during sleepless nights, and told himself that he must soon find was a young wife who would manage his household, bring up his boys, and share his bed. As the intolerable heat of summer descended on Natchez, he resolved to look for a companion among the genteel company at Col. John Armfield's mountain resort at Beersheba Springs in Tennessee.

~ Three ~

Riding the Crest

From 1830 to 1860, bankers and planters in Natchez became increasingly aware that much of their prosperity was closely tied to the plantations across the river in Louisiana. From the beginning of the nineteenth century, when Job Routh took up thousands of low-lying acres in a vast domain named for the Taënsa Indians, a rush of planters grabbed up the alluvial tracts, cleared and drained them, and cultivated miles of cotton rows. Tensas and three other parishes, Concordia, Carroll, and Madison, were developed by owners who either lived across the river in Natchez or banked and transacted their business there. Although relatively late on the scene, Charles Dahlgren was a member of this connection between the planter establishment of Tensas Parish and the town of Natchez.

A profitable year for the two hundred plantations in Tensas meant prosperity for Natchez as well. Louisiana cotton, often floated across a bayou to a small river and then to the Mississippi, finally reached the markets in New Orleans and brought profits back to Natchez. By 1860, as one historian observes, "sixty-three of Tensas's plantations belonged to absentee proprietors, including . . . Charles Dahlgren of Routhland."[1] With the hiring of overseers, who in turn selected the stock tenders and slave drivers, the owners were not tied to their remote plantations all year.

There were also bad years with heavy losses when operations in "The Cotton Kingdom" of Louisiana seemed impossible of recovery. Natchez proper was high enough to be out of danger of the rising torrents from the Mississippi and its tributaries, but the lower town, Natchez under-the-hill and other areas, was subject to devastation. Historian D. Clayton James points out: "Beginning in 1809, the great river hurled widespread floods upon the bottom lands west and south of Natchez every second year with disastrous regularity for the next two decades. The worst . . . came in 1811, 1815, 1828, and 1840."[2] There was always the need in Tensas to divert slave labor to the building of levees; petitions went to Congress and state legislatures for flood control measures. During the bad years, homes of the resident planters were threatened, livestock was swept away, and crops were so ravaged by the floods that as many as three plantings would be attempted during a single spring.

Natchez and its adjacent districts, like much of the Deep South, were also under siege by yellow fever during the summer. In 1853, there were 750 casualties recorded in the city area; the numbers in the swampy stretches across the river were not recorded. In a sermon reminding his Natchez congregation of the deaths that year, the Reverend Stratton recalled: "The portion of the population which could escape fled, as from an invading foe, to such places of shelter as they could find in the country. [Charles and Mary Dahlgren had gone to New York City and probably Saratoga Springs.] For nearly four months the places of business were closed. The grass literally sprung up in our untrodden streets; and the silence, not of a Sabbath, but of a funeral hour, hung over our usually bustling city."[3] The last victim, Stratton recalled, succumbed as late as December, "a beautiful and gifted young lady."

Natchez, as a busy port city, was also hit with cholera, often brought by the hapless crews of visiting riverboats. No respecter of rank, the scourge felled Bishop John M. J. Chanche in 1853, a year before the scheduled completion of St. Mary's Cathedral, which became his great monument for Catholic parishioners.[4]

◎◇

Three families with extensive holdings in Tensas Parish were the several descendants of Job Routh, members of the Ellis clan, and Charles Dahlgren and his sons by Mary Routh Ellis. In fact, Mary was the link— born a Routh, married first to Thomas Ellis, and then married to Charles

Dahlgren. Although Dahlgren had sold Routhland to satisfy the step-children, Sarah Ann Ellis Dorsey pressed him even further for her mother's "personal effects, paraphernalia, wardrobe, apparel, and the like." She took him to court to hand over the "tenements and appurtenances" from Routhland. Although she had already collected a check from him for $10,600 on 29 May 1859,[5] she also lodged petitions in Adams and Wilkinson Counties, Mississippi, as well as in Tensas, to be sure Dahlgren was held to the letter of his late wife's intentions for her heirs.

After handing over Routhland to Alfred Vidal Davis, Dahlgren arranged temporary quarters for his four boys, ranging from ages eighteen to three, until the new house on the South Bluff in Natchez could be completed. Then, in March 1859 when urged by his sons, Charles invited his nephew Ulric Dahlgren, brother John's son, to come south for a visit. Charles Dahlgren's sons, Charles Routh, age eighteen, and Bernard, age twelve, made plans for hunting, camping and fishing expeditions, fencing, rowboat races, horseracing, and visits with the Routh kin around Lake Saint Joseph. They found this Eastern cousin, standing at 5 feet, 10½ inches and weighing 129 pounds, a lively companion ready to join them in whatever sport they fancied, including wrestling and shooting.[6] His Uncle Charles put Ulric to work as his surveyor at Marydale and The Oaks. In such a vast domain, property lines were often in dispute and boundaries not easily defined.[7] Marydale was divided into four large tracts; they included "Slough S. of J. R. Road, Indian Lake Field, Grave Yard Slue [sic], Gin Ditch, Old Dividing Ditch, Sassafras Road, and Mound Bayou Tract." Smudged and tattered though they became, the survey books are testimony to the vast property of Charles Dahlgren at the height of his prosperity.

Extracts from Ulric's letters to his father in 1859 and 1860 give specific details of life in Tensas, Natchez, and Beersheba Springs: "[At Tensas] Very busy surveying. . . . Went hunting. . . . Knocked over a splendid buck. . . . Have a bay colt . . . just broken . . . gaiting him . . . am on horseback the whole time. . . . I carry the compass on horseback at full speed and jump a large ditch with ease . . . the alligators plenty . . . bellow like bulls. . . . "[8] To avoid his father's disapproval, Ulric added: "I am going to swim the lake when it is warm enough, where there are dozens of alligators. They won't touch white men, but eat negroes whenever they catch them." Surely, the well-traveled father was not deceived by his son's promises.

Ulric also addressed his father from Natchez and assured him that he was in excellent health. In Louisiana again on 5 June, he was studying French and reporting that "the old stock minder killed three deer and a bear yesterday." He told his father that he rode horseback every other week from Natchez to Marydale to look at the work on the levees. He would leave Natchez at 5 A.M. and arrive at the plantation at 3 P.M., a distance of 48 miles. He sent word to his younger brother Paul that he must learn to swim: "I would have been drowned today if I had not learned. My horse gave out in swimming a bayou. I tried to cross the bayou two hours ago on Charlie's [Cousin Charles Routh's] horse 'Derrick' and when I had got half way over he sank right down from under me, so I had to strike out and swim to shore, and directly I saw him rise and come across, but he is such a rascal that I could not catch [him], being wet I could not run fast and so I had to swim back to get home." The summer was spent in work, adventure, and "party excursions of ladies and gentlemen—very pleasant." Ulric hastened to assure his father that his surveying and French lessons had not been neglected.

By July, there was "much sickness" at the plantation and Uncle Charles kept Ulric in Natchez. He saw a lot of activity there because his uncle was busy with the construction of the new home for himself and the boys. Built in the Italian, or Tuscan, style, the house was adapted from a design by A. J. Downing, whose book, *The Architecture of Country Houses* (1850), combined Gothic-revival with Italianate details. It was built on former Routh property and christened Llangollen from the town in North Wales where Job Routh, Charles's late father-in-law, had been born. There were galleries with columns on three sides of the raised first floor, a central hall with stairs leading to the second level, and another small flight to the rectangular belvedere with ten windows. When the house was finished, the boys would be able to climb to the roof for views of the river and watch the traffic of steamboats, barges, and ferries.

When Ulric wrote again to his father on 12 August, he and the family had left Natchez for the Dahlgren Cottage at Beersheba Springs. Ulric described the resort as "a beautiful place on the height of a mountain top" and reported that he and his cousins had started fencing lessons and the study of French at the resort. At this time, Beersheba Springs boasted a new two-story hotel and several rows of cabins for guests, most of them Southerners, and ample quarters for their servants. The visitors came to escape the fevers and enjoy the cooler climate and chalybeate water, which was thought to be medicinal. The resort was highly praised in brochures and newspapers, including an advertisement in the Natchez *Daily Courier*.

Ulric obliged his uncle again by surveying in Beersheba Springs, now that Charles had bought a cottage and nine acres across from the hotel on 27 July.[9] He gave Colonel Armfield a note for $4,000, and the Dahlgren family felt at home. Then, joining thirteen other gentlemen of wealth, Charles became an incorporator of the Beersheba Springs Company, which was capitalized at $45,000."[10] He felt it to be a sound investment; it was also a guarantee that he and his descendants would have a summer home free of the plagues common to the Deep South. They would no longer have to make long journeys to Saratoga Springs and Newport, where Southerners had begun to encounter misunderstanding and criticism. At Beersheba Springs, they found genteel company, healthy air, a French chef, an orchestra for balls and concerts, and some relief from debates brought on by sectionalism. They did not feel the need for a daily defense of their way of life at Beersheba. Charles Dahlgren liked the retreat even more when Miss Mary Edgar Vannoy, a guest at the hotel with her parents, caught his eye in the ballroom and accepted his invitation for a waltz. All told, 1859 was a summer to remember, and the next one, 1860, would be even busier and happier for the Dahlgren family and their guests.

ℂ℞

Cool weather brought the usual exodus from Beersheba. On his way to Natchez, Charles stopped in Nashville to pay further court and to propose to Miss Vannoy. During this era, the ages of individuals were not openly discussed, although finances were arranged in prenuptial agreements between people of means. If Charles Dahlgren and Mary Edgar Vannoy knew the other's exact age, neither was apt to reveal it in a society given to other considerations for marriage. At the time, he was forty-eight and she had just turned nineteen. They set a wedding date of 19 December, and Charles hurried back to Natchez to put Llangollen in readiness for his bride.

Meanwhile, at Marydale, Ulric and Charlie Routh had been inseparable—running lines and hunting game for Thanksgiving. They were later joined by the younger boys, Bernard, John Adolph, and Mortimer, at Christmas and made the rounds of open houses among the Routh kin in Tensas.[11]

Dahlgren and Mary Edgar were married on 19 December in the Edwin Gardner parlor on Vine Street in Nashville. There they spent the Christmas season and sat for their portraits by Washington Cooper.[12]

⋐⋑

Ulric continued to report his adventures to his father: "[1 January 1860] We hunted all the week and killed four deer . . . one weighed 205 lbs. *cleaned*. Charlie killed two and I two. Yesterday in crossing a little lake my horse bogged and I had to take to a tree that was leaning over in the water, but by firing my gun over the mare's head, I scared her out and caught her." He also reported that his weight had increased from 129 to 136 pounds and that he was never in better health.

In March, Ulric decided to return to Washington for counsel with his father about a career, even though his Uncle Charles had made him an attractive offer to stay in Mississippi and read law. He was therefore with his father in April to mark his eighteenth birthday. In a letter dated 3 February, before leaving Natchez, he had dutifully assured his father, "[Y]ou know what's best for me and I will cheerfully and willingly follow your advice."

It is quite likely that Charlie Routh accompanied Ulric to Washington, had a visit with Uncle John, and then sailed for Europe. Charlie had left Oakland College in Rodney after a dispute with the college president and did indeed go abroad at this time. The evidence is a letter directed to his father in Natchez from Harry Emanuel of London, a goldsmith and diamond merchant, dated 4 January 1861:

> 21 Hanover Square &
> 70 & 71 Brook St.
>
> I beg to enclose an Account owing by your son C. R. Dahlgren, Esq. hearing that he has left England and not knowing his address I am induced to write, as from all I have heard, your high sense of honor will not allow me to remain a loser. The articles were all supplied at Cash prices, and I await your kind favor of a remittance in settlement of the amount, or am prepared to take back the articles if you can return them to me.
>
> I remain, Sir,
> Yours obediently
> H. Emanuel[13]

The itemized bill has not survived, but one can assume that Dahlgren met the jeweler's demand and gave Charlie his proper chastisement.

In May 1860, Ulric returned to Natchez at his uncle's bidding and considered "a very liberal offer to study law and be admitted in 18 months."[14] Meanwhile, he would earn a salary of $25 per month for services such as "writing, fixing papers." He again sought his father's advice before making a decision and continued to run lines. On 18 June, he finished a painting of his uncle's new house and presented it to the family.

With the return of the heat and threat of malaria, Dahlgren and his new wife left Natchez that June for Beersheba Springs. The change was especially welcome to Mary Edgar because she was expecting her first child in September. The four boys accompanied their father and step-mother, and Cousin Ulric also returned with them to the mountain.

૭૪ૐ

About the time the Dahlgrens arrived at Beersheba, William Dahlgren, known by the alias de Rohan, was very much involved in ferrying Red

Shirts for Garibaldi in the liberation forces swarming to Sicily. William's machinations in 1860 show a daredevil flouting of international law, which brought him close to causing a breach of relations between the United States and the Kingdom of the Two Sicilies. Using funds provided by the Causa Nationale, de Rohan made a surreptitious and hasty purchase of three ships from France for Garibaldi's second convoy of armed troops to Sicily. The money was handed to de Rohan from a fund established for the *Risorgimento*. As the American owner of the ships, he could fly the American flag on the three transports loaded with insurgent men and arms. The ploy was of serious concern to the American consuls at Turin, Genoa, and Naples. They feared retaliation from the government of the King of Naples, whom the United States had supported, and their official dispatches reflect their skittish states of mind. Yet, they could not disguise the fact that hundreds of recruits were flocking to Garibaldi's call. Ship movements toward Sicily were public knowledge.

"Days before the vessels set out, their proposed departure, the force that they will convey, and even the hour of their leaving Genoa or Leghorn is known to everyone here and sometimes announced in the newspapers."[15] William de Rohan's exploits as a ship's captain and soldier of fortune under Garibaldi were also noted in press dispatches to American newspapers, where sympathy for the liberation forces was indeed strong. Although William had often troubled his brothers and behaved badly toward them, Charles might have looked with sibling envy on these latest international escapades and the notoriety they brought to his younger brother.

ℝ™

The U.S. agricultural census of 1860 for Tensas Parish is a rough indicator of Charles Dahlgren's holdings. Marydale, originally Saddletree and renamed when he honored his wife Mary Routh, was the largest: 1,500 improved acres and 4,600 unimproved acres. The cash value was $183,000, and the farm implements and machinery were valued at $3,500. A total of 187 slaves lived in forty-two slave houses. The livestock, valued at $11,595, included 8 horses, 64 asses and mules, 250 sheep (an extremely large flock for Tensas), and 300 swine.

Marydale also produced 8,000 bushels of Indian corn, 700 bales of cotton at 400 pounds per bale, 1,000 pounds of wool, 100 bushels of peas and beans, 750 bushels of sweet potatoes, and 750 pounds of butter. Although not as extensive or productive as some of the Routh holdings in Tensas, it was nevertheless an enviable operation.

The ages of the male slaves at Marydale ranged from seventy-five years to one year and the females from eighty-five years to one year and under. The census taker noted that no slaves had been manumitted and there were no fugitives. Charles Dahlgren was listed as an absentee owner.[16] His overseer, David Richardson, was in charge and answerable to Dahlgren. To get the cotton to market, his hands floated it down Mound Bayou to Dahlgren's Landing on the Tensas River and thence to the Mississippi.

The Oaks was considerably smaller: 150 improved acres and 850 unimproved acres. It had a cash value of $30,000, with equipment and machinery worth $1,000. Two horses, six asses and mules, five milch cows, and eight working oxen had a total worth of $1,200. The Oaks produced 50 pounds of butter per annum, the only separate product noted; the other yields were added to those of Marydale. Twenty-three slaves occupied five slave houses. Thirteen males ranged in age from eighty-five years to a few months and ten females from twenty-five years to two years.

There were no references to the overseer Richardson or to the slaves in Ulric's letters to his father. What we do find is the reason for his decision not to stay in the South, even with his uncle's patronage. The Deep South, Ulric wrote, as contrasted with Texas, Arizona, or Kansas, was "too civilized" and there was "no room to move ahead in these wealthy cotton states" without ownership of vast acreage and a number of slaves. So Ulric left Natchez in 1860 with his uncle and cousins for Beersheba Springs, remained there for about a month, and then headed north to Washington.

While enjoying his uncle's hospitality, Ulric and his cousins hunted, fished, fenced, played billiards, and danced in the quadrilles and cotillions at the Beersheba Hotel. Mary Edgar Dahlgren told how they played tricks on the summer visitors by dragging a dead fox in and around the courtyard and setting the dogs loose to howl during the dark hours of night.[17] McMinnville novelist and poet Lucy Virginia French remembered young Ulric that summer because of the condescending remarks he had made about a young mountain girl named Darl: "He had said to me one morning as she [Darl] passed us on the plank walk, 'Heavens! What magnificent eyes! What ten thousand pities they should be wasted on a mountaineer! I know many a belle who would give thousands of her dollars and some years of her life for such a set of living diamonds!' "[18] It is clear that Mrs. French could not forgive Ulric's remarks; she remembered him as an arrogant young man with patronizing ways toward the people in the little mountain community. He doubtless echoed his father, who had a reputation of feeling superior to ordinary sailors, Latin Americans, and Arabs.

In August, the Dahlgrens were joined at Beersheba Springs by Mary Edgar's mother and father, Mason and Jane Ward Vannoy of Nashville. They had brought her to Beersheba Springs the year before when they had met Charles Dahlgren for the first time. Also visiting was Robert McEwen Vannoy, Mary's older brother, a farmer and lawyer living in nearby Manchester. With the Dahlgren cottage overflowing, the Vannoys probably stayed at the hotel and took their meals there, as did Mary Edgar's older sister, Ellen Smith Vannoy Gardner, and her daughter Laura. They were all dedicated to the care of Mary Edgar during her last weeks of confinement. Mrs. Gardner saw to it that Dr. John Waters, in the cottage next door, was kept on the alert, and she admonished him to perform as well for this baby as he had for the baby's mother twenty years earlier. They all felt a sense of family and continuity, took comfort in it, and could not imagine ties like these ever being broken.

Toward the end of their stay, the restless boys spotted a small rounded boulder rising in the pine thicket at the side of the Dahlgren cottage. Because Ulric was soon to return to Washington, they decided that the smooth sandstone rock would be a way of marking the summer of 1860 and perpetuating their time on the mountain. With chisel and hammer—and probably the help of a local mason—the members of the house party carved their initials on the top and sloping contours of the boulder. A total of twelve sets of letters represented Dahlgrens, Vannoys, and Gardners. They also carved the date to mark the occasion: "August 31, 1860." It was, without their knowing it, the last house party of the *D, V,* and *G* families and the last brilliant season at the Beersheba Hotel. Most of the large cottages would be in the hands of receivers within five years; the two Episcopal bishops, James Hervey Otey and Leonidas Polk, would be dead and their houses plundered; the hotel and its dependencies would stay idle without guests; the ravages of war would take their toll for four years and sow bitterness throughout the land. But no one, even the most prophetic, could have divined the dissolution and bloodshed that was to begin the following year.

There was a brief postlude to summer and cause for rejoicing on 22 September when Mary Edgar, with the help of Dr. Waters and Ellen Gardner, gave birth to her first son.[19] There was indeed cause for celebration at the successful entry of Gustavus Vannoy Dahlgren, a healthy infant whose birth marked the beginning of Charles Dahlgren's second family. The event also signaled another step toward Dahlgren's ambition for a dynasty in the Deep South—one that he confidently hoped would place his name alongside the Rouths, Surgets, Ellises, and Percys and the hierarchy of planters who had built their fortunes in the twists and bends of the Mississippi.[20]

✑✎

While Charles and Mary Edgar Dahlgren were packing for their return to Natchez with the new baby, a special dispatch arrived at the *New York Herald* from its London correspondent. Brother William de Rohan was in the news again on 27 September as "the sailor, captain, pilot, traveller, linguist, merchant, French, English, American—everything in all lands— commander-in-chief of an expedition which he has got up himself. . . ." William was forty years old and in command of the steam frigate HMS *Emperor.* His passengers were volunteers, English and American, sailing from England to join Garibaldi in Italy. Among the motley adventurers was a gentleman-soldier from Tennessee, the red-haired Roberdeau

Wheat, a hard-drinking revolutionary and the son of an Episcopal minister. He had fought for pay with Lopez in Cuba, with Carvajal and Alvarez in two Mexican revolutions, and with William Walker in Nicaragua. He would die leading the Louisiana Tigers in Virginia at the Battle of Gaines Mill in 1862.[21]

Opinions ran high about de Rohan's troops on the *Emperor:* "Never was there such a boldfaced act," the correspondent wrote, "men, money, guns and ammunition, and in broad daylight."[22] And never a brother like William, who was winning the battle of sibling rivalry and attracting the attention of the world press at the same time.

While Charles chose to perpetuate his name as a grandee in the South and John looked for international recognition as an inventor of arms, William boldly transported volunteers to Sicily for the Risorgimento that eventually saw the birth of modern Italy. There was no halting the three Dahlgren brothers in their rush for acclaim during the autumn of 1860.

❧ Four ❧

A Civil War, a Family War

When Charles Dahlgren became a secessionist in Mississippi and adopted the political stance of states' rights, his brother, Commander John Adolphus Dahlgren, U.S. Navy, tried to maintain the views of a Union moderate who was willing to make concessions and compromises in order to preserve the Union. The commander wrote to his son Ulric from Washington on 18 December 1860, a few weeks after the election of Abraham Lincoln as president of the United States and as South Carolina threatened to secede from the Union:

> In the North there is no personal servitude, but there is the Slavery of the classes, so well understood that when a man does rise from it, so much is made of it, as when copper approaches the White level. But however this may be, what right has the Northern man to infringe on the admitted duty to the White man in order to discharge a factitious & gratuitous duty to the Negro? Let him see the starving laborers in Kansas and elsewhere at hand. The mischiefs of this unconstitutional interference are not far from wrecking this Union. At this very time it is about to cost our Constellation one of its stars, and more will drop out if the evil is not staid by patriotic hands.[1]

South Carolina, one of the Union's "stars," would officially secede two days later. Dahlgren hoped that good will and statesmanship in the North—"patriotic hands"—would prevent the other Southern states from withdrawing. In fact, he closed the letter by hoping that "a convention as prescribed by the Constitution and the 'Missouri compromise' amended will settle the trouble. And the proposition of Mr. [William Henry] Seward's organ [newspaper] to pay for fugitives rescued will take away all bitterness."[2]

These were the thoughts of a father writing to his son, not those of a high-ranking naval officer who soon would be called to direct his cannon against naval craft belonging to the Confederate States of America (CSA). Dahlgren soon saw several of the senior officers at the Navy Yard including its commandant, Franklin Buchanan, resign and turn south, and he accepted command of the Yard when Buchanan handed his resignation to Lincoln. A stern, mature officer of fifty-two, Dahlgren had experienced long voyages in American ships, had later been recognized for his skills in perfecting the smooth-bore naval cannon that bears his name, and in past months had held hope for the Union. Now he was suffering disillusionment.

At the time that John Dahlgren was expressing his concerns to Ulric, his brother Charles was writing letters from Llangollen to the *Free Trader* and the *Natchez Courier* about the purchase of the Dahlgren cannon for the defense of "our Southern Country." The letters were published in January and February 1861, after Mississippi had seceded. Charles called for the immediate acquisition of "the rifle musket of my brother . . . one of the most effective weapons in use." After outlining the merits of John's brass twelve pounder, he added: "I hope our Southern Confederacy will take measures to have some made for us in this section."

Hopeful, as well, that he and John could agree about the right of the Southern states to withdraw from the Union, Charles went on to suggest that John, along with other Navy officers, might soon turn to the South because "the arrangement would be as valuable to them, as agreeable to C. G. Dahlgren." So both Dahlgrens were trying to reach a meeting of minds in early 1861, as did thousands of other brothers.

But at every level of enlistment and in every branch of service, brothers pledged their lives on opposite sides. At the top rank, besides John and Charles Dahlgren, were Thomas Crittenden, a Union major general and his brother George, a Confederate major general. They were the sons of John J. Crittenden, a U.S. Senator from Kentucky. The Terrill brothers of Virginia, William and James, were both brigadier generals. William was killed in action in 1862 while fighting for the Union. His Confederate brother James died two years later from wounds in combat. The McIntosh brothers from Florida were also brigadier generals. John survived fighting for the Union, but James died in action against the Union in 1862.

The brother-in-law of Mary Todd Lincoln was Brig. Gen. Ben Hardin Helm, CSA. Gen. Robert E. Lee's cousin was Union Rear Adm. Samuel P. Lee. Brig. Gen. Thomas F. Drayton of South Carolina, CSA, had a brother, Percival Drayton, who was a captain in the U.S. Navy and head of its Bureau of Navigation.

At Llangollen, his fine home in Natchez overlooking the Mississippi, Charles Dahlgren believed that the South had a right to secede, form an independent government, bear arms, and protect its borders from invasion. As a young man, Dahlgren had been quick to address an insult or supposed slight. Now, at age fifty, he was ready to defend his cotton plantations in Louisiana, his ownership of two hundred slaves, and his hard-won social position in Natchez. He was willing to protect his investments to the point of military action. He would not hide under "neutrality," as would some of the other Northerners who had grown rich in Southern soil. The South had given the emigrant's son an opportunity to rise in the world and put his foot on the path to fortune. He would not forsake the South when his domain in Louisiana had produced one thousand bales of cotton in 1860. With those convictions, he acquired a Confederate uniform and began recruiting men and officers for the 3d Mississippi Brigade. He kept busy by lamplight devising plans for the defense of the South, outlining schemes for arms and supplies, and urging Governor John J. Pettus to launch a fleet of gunboats to patrol the Mississippi.[3]

Brother William vowed at the opening of the war that he was a patriot and that his sympathies were with the Union, but he would not seek service in the U.S. Navy. He gave as his reason the likelihood of being assigned to the command of his despised older brother John. Instead,

William spent part of the war in England spying on Confederate agents sent abroad to buy supplies and arms for ships to run the Yankee blockade of Southern ports.[4]

When Lincoln was elected president on 4 November 1860 by defeating three opponents—Stephen A. Douglas, John Bell, and John C. Breckinridge—the Southern reaction had been immediate. South Carolina passed the Ordinance of Secession on 20 December and was followed by Mississippi on 9 January. By May 1861, eleven states had left the Union and formed the Confederate government with Jefferson Davis as president. Dahlgren had declared his allegiance to Mississippi and offered his services in support of the new nation. These included recruitment, military leadership, and strategies for defense. Although he had turned fifty and was fifteen years past "the meridian of life," he maintained a stubborn determination to see the seceding states flourish as the Confederate States of America.

∂♭

Charles Dahlgren reminded his fellow Confederates that he had been a military student all his life and that his chief mentor was Napoleon I.[5] He referred to his famous "model and authority" when he offered defense stratagems for the South to the leaders in Richmond. He made broad, sweeping proposals for acquiring warships from Europe, arms through Mexico, and a labor force of slaves working to feed the army. He was a visionary urging schemes that already were beginning to prove impossible of attainment. Although his assertive style received attention, his subscribers were few.[6]

After the Confederates fired on Fort Sumter, South Carolina, and the fort surrendered to them on 14 April 1861, President Lincoln had called for seventy-five thousand volunteers to quell the "Rebellion." In turn, the Confederate Congress in Montgomery, Alabama authorized the placing of one hundred thousand men under arms to defend the South. Volunteers on both sides rallied to the call. They included Ulric Dahlgren in Washington, age nineteen, and his cousin Charlie Routh Dahlgren, age twenty, in Natchez.[7] Each received the blessing of his father and like their fathers, the young men marched in different uniforms.

Bernard, the second son of Charles Dahlgren, age fourteen, wrote a petition on 17 April 1861 to join the Natchez Cadets. Because he was under the age of sixteen, Bernard was refused membership and told "we have some members who are not of the requisite age but their height of stature and manliness of appearance deceived us."[8] His father and stepmother were probably relieved because of the boy's immaturity and uncertain health.

On 18 May 1861, Bernard's older brother Charlie Routh enlisted in the Adams Troop of the Mississippi Cavalry, which later became part of the Jeff Davis Legion. His service record shows that he rode a horse valued at $225 and carried his own equipment worth about $40. Writing to his father from Memphis, where his company stopped for a few days before setting out for Richmond, he complained that the Tennesseans had made no proper provisions for their arrival and kept them without food for "the whole day." But, he assured his father, "I have signed for the whole war, however long it may last. . . . It may be that I may fall in the coming contest but if I do, be sure I will not disgrace the name I bear, all the wounds will be in front."[9] Here, he took his stand with the South and pledged a valorous fight. He also asked his father's forgiveness for some youthful escapades that had strained their relationship. He was probably referring to his dismissal from Oakland College and his unpaid bills in Europe. But for the next four years Charlie Routh would bear arms in the Virginia theater of operations and try to live up to the heroic stories he had heard of his forebears in Sweden.

Charlie Routh wrote his father again in August, a few weeks after First Manassas, and gave him a detailed report on his movements in northern Virginia. The letter is laced with bits of Charlie's humor, even though the circumstances were grim.

Manasseh 1861 August 29th

Dear Father

Here We are at last at Manasseh after six days hard marching. We left Ashland last Thursday and marched twenty miles through one of the hardest rains I ever saw. We bivouacked that night beneath the trees and a greater part of the Troops slept under the trees in the rain. I fortunately had carried the flag that day and some young ladies who lived about a quarter of a mile from the encampment extended an invitation to me to bring the flag in the house out of the rain. After getting in the house I made myself so agreeable I received an invitation to sleep in the house and you may depend I accepted it. We left there the next day about ten o'clock and on the third day out from Ashland We entered Fredricksburg. We were three days marching to this place. Our Troop will remain here four days. From here We will march to Fairfax (Court House) to join our Regiment (Col. Stuart's Black Horse). As soon as We get there Gen. [Joseph E.] Johnston has assured us we shall have the post of honor. We will act as scouts three miles in advance of our army. It is a post of great danger. The Yankees have advanced to Falls Church five miles from Fairfax. I think We will have a fight now before long. Gen. [G. T.] Beauregard left here last night at two o'clock, and several regiments received orders today to march without baggage. In the next battle that is fought our Troop will be engaged and it may be You and I may never meet again. If so I hope you will forgive me all the trouble and anxiety I have caused you. If I do fall in defence of my Country, surely no nobler sepulchre can be found than a battle field on which one had fallen in defence of his Country. Give my love to Ma and the boys. God bless you all. Farewell.

Your affectionate son,
CR Dahlgren

P.S. Direct your letters to care of G. W. Purcell & Co., Richmond.

CRD[10]

The spring and early summer of 1861 found Charles Dahlgren hustling to look after plantation affairs in Tensas Parish and business in Natchez in anticipation of his own service with the military in Mississippi. A strong believer in the necessity of local citizens to defend their home turf, Dahlgren was a philosophical proponent of states' rights and state-directed military operations. He was not alone, for many Southerners, when it came to a draw, put state interests above the Confederacy. As a young man, Dahlgren had been a member of the Adams County Hussars. Now, with misgivings, he saw Natchez and Adams County militia companies being siphoned off to Confederate service and sent to Virginia to support troops in the East. Who would defend the home turf?

Opposing Dahlgren's view of states' rights was Dr. A. C. Holt, who was set against pouring resources into a "Mississippi Army" because "it is running the State to a useless expense, and I think the Gov. [Pettus] has no authority to do as he is doing unless our State is likely to be invaded, which I do not think is likely to happen."[11] Dr. Holt's confidence, however, would be shattered the following year after the battle of Shiloh.

Recommended for service by a number of prominent Southerners, including Governor Isham Harris of Tennessee, Charles G. Dahlgren went to Jackson on 8 July 1861 and received the appointment of brigadier general, State of Mississippi, from Governor Pettus.[12] He was selected by Pettus and the Military Board on 23 July to command the 3d Mississippi Brigade (composed of two regiments of state troops). His orders were to make immediate plans for the defense of the Mississippi Gulf Coast against Union gunboats making preparations to take New Orleans. The enemy's reconnoitering craft in the Mississippi Sound were already evaluating Confederate defenses on Ship Island off the coast. The time had come for Dahlgren to muster the 3d Brigade at Pass Christian on the east side of Bay Saint Louis, at a site to be known as Camp Dahlgren, incorporate the local "seashore" companies, and effect a show of strength against hostile craft in the Gulf.

As a commander appointed by the governor of Mississippi and approved by the state's Military Board, Dahlgren acted in conformance with state regulations. They directed the governor to be certain that "no arms should be given to any companies until all the companies mustered into the *companies of the state were armed*."[13] Other Southern states, maintaining similar policies, also defied the central government by stubbornly holding up the transfer of supplies from their stockpiles. Historian Frank L. Owsley estimated that the state government of "Mississippi, already equipped with 2,127 rifles and other small arms, purchased . . . 5,000 stand of muskets."[14] The state, therefore, maintained proprietary control.

Having entrusted some of his personal business in Natchez to his friend G. Malin Davis, Dahlgren departed for the coast in a new uniform with the insignia of a brigadier general. Accompanying him as far as New Orleans was the beautiful Mary Edgar, age twenty-one, their son Van, not yet a year old, and two children from his first marriage, Austin Mortimer, age five, and John Adolph, age twelve.[15] The young mother was probably provided a suite at the St. Charles Hotel with appropriate amenities and protection. The general had left his son Bernard and a caretaker at Llangollen with six servants to look after the house and grounds. He kept his overseer, David Richardson, in charge of operations at Marydale and The Oaks.

After recruiting in Woodville and southern Mississippi, Dahlgren settled on the coast, where he received frequent reports on conditions at Natchez from Davis, who kept in touch by a series of letters about the city and its military supplies: "As to the Bowie Knives, Dufilho proposed to make not less than 500 of the dimensions, quality, etc. stated at $9.00 apiece. When I expressed surprise at the price he replied that he retailed a similar article, 11 in. blade, at $14.00 each. To show me the temper of the metal, he took one of the latter size, laid a bar of silver, about ⅛ in. thick, upon a block, and with a blow of the knife, cut the silver into two parts, without injury to the edge." Davis also reported on the cache of arms held by W. Cox and Company: "40 single barrel shot guns; 60 double barrel shot guns; 150 gun barrels of various descriptions; 180 muskets—with about 90 Bayonets; 130 rifles; 500 Total." Davis then wrote about intended distribution of the arms, encampment of troops, and his attention to Dahlgren's personal affairs. The letters of Davis to Dahlgren provide ample particulars about arms and supplies in Natchez during the early months of the war.[16]

In September, 1861, the 3d Mississippi State Regiment was reassigned to Dahlgren. The companies included the Sunflower Dispersers, Chunky Heroes, Biloxi Rifles, and Dahlgren Guards. The men took pride in their local associations.[17]

Few Southerners expected New Orleans to fall, the war to last for long, or the South to change very much during the autumn of 1861. Volunteers signed up for sixty days or twelve months. Numbers of breathless young men in their teens rushed to enlist and show their mettle before the fight was over. The Confederates under Beauregard and Johnston had already shown their strength at Bull Run in Virginia and driven the Yankees back in complete rout to the gates of Washington. It was time to arm the South to the teeth and invade the North. Loyalty to home and hearth, accompanied by a rousing Rebel yell and longer enlistments, would give the South control of its own destiny. The cause, the orators shouted, was not only just but righteous. With arms and prayers, they would establish in the South the will of a benevolent God.

◯◯

The New Orleans *Bee,* on 23 August 1861, noted the assembly of companies at Camp Dahlgren—four hundred men in one group and six hundred in another, together with seven companies from the coastal counties. The *Bee* introduced Dahlgren as "a soldier, a scholar, and a gentleman."[18] It called him a graduate of West Point in error, and remarked that his brother was the inventor of the Dahlgren gun. The *Bee* could not know that John Dahlgren, now a commander, was busy defending the Washington Navy Yard, keeping the Potomac River open, and increasing ordnance production around the clock. John also gave his son Ulric, age nineteen, a special assignment with the Navy after the youth left the law office of his uncle in Philadelphia and volunteered for service.[19] Patriotism was rising to a fevered pitch on both sides of the family as autumn approached and each side affirmed its loyalties.

The early recruits at Camp Dahlgren tried to sound cheerful when they wrote home, but with the arrival of new companies to outfit, arm, and feed, Charles Dahlgren was beset with numerous problems and frequent complaints. He wrote to Governor Pettus on 5 September that his men had only five wagons and no funds for supplies and commissary items. He needed requisitions for "such items as rafting of lumber down Wolf River to build a military hospital, mattresses for same, hiring of negro laborers, grinding of corn, barrels of flour, wharfage, drayage, and other freight charges."[20]

It would be difficult to say who was the most skittish about the situation along the coast—Dahlgren, his men, or his superiors in Jackson. Several recruits were so dissatisfied that they complained directly to Pettus with requests for transfer to other commands. Dahlgren pleaded his case with the governor on September 10: "We have no arms or ammunition . . . no artillery, or munitions . . . no horses . . . no cavalry . . . no gunboats sufficient to prevent our supplies being intercepted and cut off at any time." Adding to his anxieties was the notion that the encampment at Pass Christian was far too vulnerable to withstand an enemy attack of any force. Therefore, after the report of "heavy firing towards Ship Island," he petitioned Pettus to let him ferry his command across Bay Saint Louis to Shieldsboro on the opposite shore, where the men would not be easy targets for the enemy and risk being cut off from supplies. On 15 September, Dahlgren wired Pettus to acknowledge receipt of much-needed arms and munitions, then pleaded for cavalry.[21]

Two days later, against the recommendations of his officers, Dahlgren carried out his plans to transfer the brigade from Camp Dahlgren at Pass Christian to Shieldsboro. A local newspaper columnist, writing as "Patriarch Dismal," decried the move as "evincing, on the part of the General, great timidity and an entire ignorance of the geography of the country."[22] Residents of Pass Christian now felt abandoned; Dahlgren's troops, cheerless and sullen, marched to Henderson Point for embarkation to Shieldsboro.

Always obstinate about giving up his hard-won equipment and supplies to Confederate commanders, Dahlgren felt rebuffed when he received a telegram on 10 October from Governor Pettus in Jackson: "Turn over the mules to Confederate officers. Supplies can be sold to Confederate authorities."[23] Dahlgren had to obey, but he thought that Pettus was turning against him and weakening his ability to defend the coast.

The following day, Dahlgren received another telegram from Jackson, which was an even greater blow. It was a terse statement directed by Governor Pettus but signed by Adjutant and Inspector General W. H.

Brown: "Gov. decides that when all the troops under your command are transferred as per orders to Confederate Service, you are relieved from duty."[24] Pettus was pulling the rug out from under him as a state general. Dahlgren knew that it would be only a matter of weeks before his Mississippians would be swallowed up in the Confederate Army.

There was so much disapproval of Dahlgren on the coast and in Jackson that he felt obliged by 12 October to defend his action: "My removal from Pass Christian was on account not of my men, but of my supplies. . . . In my condition, with no country around me from which to draw supplies, with no means of securing any, and totally powerless to protect those I had, there was no alternative but to move. . . . I approached nearer to the source of my supplies, and in the event of their being cut off by water I had a reasonable hope of obtaining them by land. Not so at Pass Christian. . . ." Feeling that he had been wrongly judged, Dahlgren asked for understanding in "moving to a stronger point and a more desirable location" where he could protect the coast. Then, standing by his convictions, he said he would submit his decision "to the tribunal of time."[25]

Dahlgren closed the long address to his critics with a positive summary of his achievements: "I commenced the organization of the 3d Brigade in August last; I have succeeded in collecting, arming, and equipping nearly two thousand men, who, now transferred [from State] to Confederate service, wait only an opportunity to further illustrate the military annals of Mississippi."[26]

In spite of Dahlgren's gift of rhetoric, the critics did not let up. Lack of confidence in his leadership was common among his men, among his superiors in Jackson, and within the Confederate War Department in Richmond. As early as 29 September 1861, Governor Thomas O. Moore of Louisiana wrote from New Orleans to Secretary of War Judah Benjamin in Richmond expressing serious doubts about Dahlgren: "Cannot General Dahlgren take care of the lake coast? I fear he is not the man who should be there."[27] Once again, none of Dahlgren's detractors seemed fully to understand the odds stacked against Dahlgren or any other commander assigned to the coast.

By early October, the criticism was so pronounced that Dahlgren relented, divided his brigade in half, and transferred the 3d Mississippi back across Bay Saint Louis to Pass Christian. There, he established Camp Deason, named for popular Col. John B. Deason, a native of the coast.[28] The brigade continued to suffer, however, amid petty bickering and a further decline in morale. On an inspection visit from Shieldsboro to Pass Christian, Dahlgren tried to countermand the appointment of a new quartermaster by Colonel Deason and name his own man. He and Deason were at loggerheads when Deason confronted Dahlgren with regulations spelling out Deason's right to make the appointment. The case was referred to Governor Pettus, who acknowledged Deason's judgment over Dahlgren's, and the name of the Deason appointee was forwarded to Secretary of War Benjamin. Dahlgren, in the capacity of a state commander, had been overruled by the national command now that the 3d Regiment and Colonel Deason had become part of regular Confederate service.[29] His loss of the authority to protect the coast with local companies was a hard blow. He was a redundant state general and the 3d was now a national unit. Dahlgren blamed Jefferson Davis for failing to approve his promotion to brigadier general with national status.

The fact that the two Dahlgren brothers, Unionist John and Confederate Charles, had lined up on opposite sides offered an opportunity in early September for the rise of a rumor that they were in collusion. It came via a Mr. Ford of Memphis to Confederate Gen. David E. Twiggs on the Gulf Coast. Ford had met a Mr. Walworth in Louisville, son of Chancellor Walworth of Saratoga, New York, and the young Walworth told Ford that the Secretary of the Navy told him that ". . . a person near General Dahlgren, at Pass Christian, was in close communication with the powers at Washington, had given them all the information that they wished, and had told them of our want of ammunition in and near New Orleans. From the same source Mr. Walworth knew that extensive preparations were in the making to invade Louisiana early this fall. General Dahlgren is in command . . . at Pass Christian, and has a brother in Washington, an officer in the Black Republican Navy."[30] The Walworths, distant cousins of Mary Edgar Dahlgren and Unionists in New York, seemed intent upon retailing gossip that put both brothers under suspicion. The general's enemies in Mississippi had probably helped spread the rumors that were without foundation.

Another blow to Dahlgren's authority came when the aging General Twiggs, with only a few months to live, was replaced by Maj. Gen. Mansfield Lovell, who was assigned to the defense of New Orleans and the adjacent coast. The appointment of Lovell, a West Point graduate, was made by Jefferson Davis, and the notice went directly from him to Governor Moore of Louisiana. Dahlgren, his judgment questioned and his ego badly bruised again, bristled at being forced to take orders from Lovell.[31]

Nor were Dahlgren and Governor Moore on complimentary terms. Moore wrote Secretary of War Benjamin on 22 September 1861 that "General Dahlgren is over the lake with 1500 to 2000 men. Is that force not sufficient?" Then, in a cryptic paragraph at the end, Moore added, "I desire to write you relative to the gentleman above and may do so. If I do not another will." Moore's last sentence suggested that his lack of confidence in Dahlgren was also held by others.[32] Dahlgren would soon hear about the criticism and request a Court of Inquiry to defend himself against the complaints.

Indulging in a bit of speculation here, one could suggest that, if Dahlgren had been thirty-five years old instead of fifty, had been willing to leave Mississippi, and had accepted a commission in the Confederate Navy, his early years of experience at sea might have better served the South. Such a move, however, might have brought him into direct confrontation with his brother, Cdr. John Dahlgren, USN.

෬෧

In late 1861, another Dahlgren played a small part in a major confrontation on the Atlantic Ocean. Charles Bunker Dahlgren, Commander John's oldest son, had spent three years at West Point learning ordnance and steam engineering at the foundry there before joining the U.S. Navy Engineer Corps. Having graduated at the head of his class, he was transferred to the line and boarded the *San Jacinto* in Havana, Cuba, on 8 November 1861. The *San Jacinto* was ordered to pursue the *Trent*, an English mail packet, stop her, and forcefully remove two Confederate commissioners, John Slidell and J. M. Mason and their secretaries. The commissioners had boarded the *Trent* in Havana and were bound for Southampton to do Confederate business in England. Slidell was scheduled to proceed to France later as Jefferson Davis's ambassador.

Charles Bunker was a master's mate on the *San Jacinto* at the time and was asked to make his report to Capt. Charles Wilk, Commanding:

> . . . I hereby state that I was one of those who boarded the *Trent*, mail packet. Mr. Mason, Mr. Macfarland, and Mr. Eustis stepped quietly into the boats and were removed to the *San Jacinto*. Mr. Slidell, however, on a flat refusal to leave the ship in any manner, was, by a gentle application of force, placed in the boat and removed.
>
> Everything was conducted in an orderly, gentlemanly manner, as far as it came under my observation.
>
> Charles B. Dahlgren[33]

Twenty-two years old at the time, Charles Bunker little suspected he was beginning a career in which he would be party to a number of notable events in American history. At the time the *Trent* affair almost disrupted British-American relations. Following orders from Washington, the Americans had violated the sovereignty of a British craft on the high seas by removing four of her passengers, an offense vehemently denounced around the world.

❦

Meanwhile, Confederate attention was drawn to major developments in Kentucky and Missouri during the autumn of 1861. The two states, though not seceding from the Union, raised troops for the South and allowed the installation of Confederate garrisons. Gen. Leonidas Polk, Dahlgren's neighbor at Beersheba Springs before the war, had blundered by violating Kentucky's neutrality and establishing a force at Columbus, across the Mississippi River from Belmont, Missouri. Columbus and

Belmont had become the northernmost points of the river's defenses. Then, on 7 November, Union forces won a tactical victory over the Confederates at Belmont, and the call went out from General Polk for further reinforcements from the Deep South. In November, Dahlgren's 3d Mississippi Brigade now became a regiment led by Col. John B. Deason. It was combined with the 30th Louisiana Regiment under Col. R. L. Gibson. They were ordered by General Lovell to embark immediately for Columbus.[34] The decision had the official approval of Secretary Benjamin in Richmond and was not to be reversed, however much the coastal companies complained about being transferred out of Mississippi into the national forces.

General Dahlgren was fully aware that his equipment had been furnished by Mississippi, and he stubbornly refused to hand it over to the departing regiment. Colonel Deason then made an urgent appeal to Governor Pettus: "We are ordered to Ky. and have no blankets. Genl Dahlgren has sixteen hundred pairs. He will deliver half on your order. For God sake let us have them . . . he also has some clothing . . . give us an order for them . . . the men are in want. . . ."[35] As with other instances throughout the autumn of 1861, Dahlgren seemed reluctant to make decisions without the approval of Gov. Pettus and staff. He was also given to vacillation when under pressure. The telegraphic exchanges between Dahlgren and Pettus in September and October reflect the former's adherence to the chain of command at the state level until ordered to give over. He might have deferred several later decisions to Pettus because his earlier moves had been countermanded.

Dahlgren's dependence on Governor Pettus and the Military Board in Jackson is hardly consistent with the young Charles in Natchez—quick to act, alert to the demands of banking and business, prompt to respond with arms to an insult. In his personal life, he was regarded as a man of action. As a commander trying to organize his men and rally them to decisive acts of arms, however, Dahlgren was not able to win their confidence sufficiently to inspire them to carry out his orders.

With the transfer of his troops to Kentucky and the inevitable decline of morale in the regiment, General Dahlgren sent yet another telegram to Governor Pettus: "Have you any active employment for me? I have nearly completed my business here."[36] His second sentence is laden with irony because he had been able to accomplish little more than to assemble the 3d Brigade. On 5 December, he went to New Orleans for Mary Edgar and the children and set out for Natchez after warning Pettus that the coast from Bay Saint Louis to Pascagoula was open and vulnerable.[37] All of the local patriots and defenders had been shipped north and east. Apparently in disgust, Dahlgren retreated to Natchez for Christmas at Llangollen with his family. He turned his back on General Lovell and left him to guard the coast and look after the defense of New Orleans. A little later, Dahlgren set up new headquarters of the 3d Brigade at Jefferson College in Washington, Mississippi, a stone's throw from Natchez. He then began firing off proposals for acquiring warships for Confederate service and drawing lines of defense for the beleaguered South. He had now begun his new role as recruiter and advisor to the Confederacy, and he spoke with a confidence and a self-assurance that seemed pretentious to his superiors.

⊂ℓ℘

By November 1861, the Civil War in America served as a backdrop in Britain for "a diplomatic drama with a cast which included spies, diplomats, adventurers, *dramatis personae* more appropriate to a revolutionary conspiracy than to wartime diplomacy." So observed Capt. John B. Marchand of the U.S. Navy.[38] Each side in the American conflict courted British support. Involved at every turn for four years was Charles Francis Adams, Lincoln's ambassador to Britain, who was a son and a grandson of U.S. presidents. Adams and his legation tried to keep a steady eye on the Confederate agents in Britain and their negotiations for ships and arms. A particular vessel, the HMS *Gladiator*, an English propeller-driven ship, was suspected of violating Britain's neutrality by loading arms intended for the Confederacy and routed via Bermuda.

"I have good reasons for believing that the *Gladiator* is in reality Southern property, or will be on her arrival in some Southern port," wrote U.S. consul Morse to William Henry Seward in Washington to warn him on 6 November 1861 of Confederates sailing under the British flag.[39] It was the same ploy that William de Rohan had used in Italy when he raised the American flag over his three troop ships in the service of Garibaldi. As in Italy, the deception was common knowledge in England, especially along the Thames docks where the *Gladiator* was fitted out. Even the cargo of "1,120 cases of Enfield rifles, containing twenty rifles each (22, 240)" was known to the U.S. consuls.

As the commander of the *James Adger*, the only U.S. warship in British waters, Captain Marchand was brought into the intrigue by Ambassador Adams and personnel in the American legation. They proposed to Marchand that he put his crew to work at once to make necessary repairs to the *James Adger*, load on coal, and prepare to get under steam from Southampton at once in pursuit of the suspect *Gladiator*.[40] Marchand was obliged to be cautious because of the recent Trent affair off the Bahamas.

Late in 1861, George Francis Train, a wealthy American living in England who was sometimes described as "a half-lunatic, half-genius," had employed William de Rohan as his "detective" to report the movements of the *Gladiator*.[41] Train was an ardent Unionist; de Rohan was a master of intrigue, and he fit the bill exactly. Although Captain Marchand was aware of the currents of intrigue around him, he was not prepared for the visitor who called late one evening after he had already fallen asleep:

> . . . I was awakened by a rap at the door and a stranger was ushered in who announced himself as Captain de Rohan but whose real name is [William] Dahlgren, brother of Captain [John A.] Dahlgren. He frankly told me he was esteemed an [adventurer], that last year he aided Garibaldi by smuggling from England a large quantity of arms for Garibaldi and [by] hoisting American colors, took from Genoa and elsewhere a small fleet to Sicily and [he also] imparted [to me] an interesting interview he had with Commander [James G.] Palmer of the *Iroquois* in the Mediterranean.[42] [Palmer was part of the U.S. squadron in the Mediterranean until 14 May 1861.]

De Rohan's penchant for intrigue and his self-importance in international affairs struck Marchand forcibly:

He further added that beside myself and Mr. Train no human being in England knew who he was or to what nation he belonged. [This is a false claim because of de Rohan's publicized command of the *Emperor* the year before with the English volunteers for Italy.]

De Rohan was fully informed about the *Gladiator* and knew its Confederate destination from its owners, Traci Campbell and Company. He bragged:

> . . . that Mr. Campbell had offered him command to run the blockade of the southern ports knowing his filibustering character, [but] that he declined it (being Union in feeling) on the ground that his engagement with Garibaldi would not allow his acceptance.

Other details gave Marchand clues to de Rohan's double dealings among the arms suppliers in London who were already making profits from the American conflict:

> . . . [J]oint stock companies were forming upon the principle of sending three vessels [at a time, for] if only one was to enter a blockaded port and the remaining two captured, it would [still] be a profitable business. . . .

De Rohan went on to tell Marchand that Traci Campbell and Company, whose owners were pro-Confederacy businessmen, had consulted him "about charts and sailing directions for the coast of the United States." He advised them to assign their cargo to English ports, such as Nassau or Honduras, then transship by small vessels to the Southern ports.

What, then, was the purpose of de Rohan's midnight visit to Marchand? He came to assure the captain of the USS *James Adger* that he had every right to hunt down and capture the suspect *Gladiator* anywhere, but "more especially to dog her and make a seizure near our [American] coast. His suggestion was to steer a course so as to intercept her near the Bahamas."[43] The Old Salt liked nothing better than a sail-ripping chase at sea.

Thus began one of the great contests of the early days of the American Civil War—the USS *James Adger* chasing the HMS *Gladiator* with her British colors and Confederate cargo; Captain Marchand USN versus Capt. D. T. Bisbie, blockade runner. The latter, with his expert seamanship and favorable weather, moved from Tenerife in the Canary Islands across the Atlantic to Nassau in the Bahamas, her listed and legal destination, on 9 December. From there, the Confederate cargo "was transferred to several smaller and faster steamers for the short run into a southern port."[44] The Confederates had won, but each captain had heeded the counsel of de Rohan, apparently to the letter. The loser, Captain Marchand, in listening to the crafty old seaman, might well have won and his adversary Bisbie lost. The counsel, to both men, had been sage. It mattered little that the counselor himself was a man both duplicitous and cunning.

The *Gladiator* had been identified earlier in a "List of Suspected Vessels" by Admiral S. F. DuPont, Flag Officer Commanding, South Atlantic Blockading Squadron, U.S. Navy. The details, probably provided by de Rohan, had reached Washington and were published in the Navy bulletin on 15 November 1861:

The Confederate Steamer "Gladiator," carried out a variety of rockets and other fire signals which are to be used as she approaches different points on the coast. An arrangement has been effected with the Rebels along the Atlantic and Gulf coasts to give her warning if in danger, and to notify her if the chances are good for her getting into port. The signal system is said to be well understood by those on the coast and on board the approaching ships, it having been arranged especially to overcome the difficulties interposed by our Blockading Squadrons and Cruisers. She entered outward for Lisbon, Magador and the Canaries. A day or two afterwards she re-entered for Teneriffe [sic], Nassau and Honduras, soon after the latter ports were obliterated without the knowledge of any one in, or belonging to, the Custom House. She will coal at the Western Islands, and go to Vera Cruz and Nassau, and wait and watch her chance to get in, perhaps after re-shipping part of her cargo. But no confidence is to be placed in any reported movements of these vessels, only that those who control them are determined to get them with their cargoes into rebel ports.[45]

The *Gladiator* ran the blockade to her Southern destination, discharged the cargo of guns and powder, and proved to be a triumph for Captain Bisbie. With that news, William de Rohan might have strolled along the Thames embankment, visited the docks again, and sized up a number of other vessels and their cargoes. He might have sat on a convenient park bench facing the river, pensive, plotting, paring his fingernails.

∝∾

On 23 December 1861, Charles Dahlgren addressed Jefferson Davis from "Headquarters of the Third Brigade, Army of Mississippi," in Natchez. It was not his first letter to Davis because he mentioned earlier ones that had been ignored, but ". . . conceiving it my duty as a soldier and citizen to do all in my power for our common cause and having no pride, merely of opinion to be wounded by the non-acceptance of my views, I respectfully request your attention. . . ." Then he admitted to Davis that his earlier proposals to procure arms from Europe via Matamoros, Mexico, and Texas, "although proper and feasible months ago, would now be too slow."

With the Gulf Coast and New Orleans imminently threatened, Dahlgren proposed "more prompt and rapid measures." These included ". . . fifty vessels of war . . . armed and equipped in Europe for our Navy . . . a sufficiency of arms, powder, woolens and munitions . . . placed . . . in merchant ships, the latter to be convoyed by the former, to some of our ports, and if necessary to fight their way to a safe landing. . . . Seamen could be hired abroad to serve as far as Madeira, where our men could be in residence to assume their places. . . ." Then he suggested payment in specie from the banks of the South in a complicated system of exchange through French and English consuls. Thus, "the vessels bringing in arms, etc. could and would load with cargoes of cotton for foreign consumption, as of greater value. . . ."[46] Davis and his cabinet in Richmond must have received the proposals with incredulity because Dahlgren had failed to take into account the effectiveness of the Atlantic blockade.

The silence from Richmond and the loss of favor with Governor Pettus in Jackson prompted General Dahlgren to write to Pettus and resign his appointment in January, the reason given his poor health. Pettus replied politely on 15 January 1862, regretted the loss of Dahlgren's services, and asked him to accept the appointment of commissioner to direct the proposed construction of gunboats for seashore defense. The letter from Pettus was tactful and guarded. It recognized some of Dahlgren's earlier suggestions and agreed to make use of his proposals, as far as practicable, and promised "to give you such Colleagues on this Commission as will make a harmonious and energetic board."[47]

Dahlgren's reasons for resigning can be traced to deteriorating morale on the Gulf Coast. His health might have suffered a temporary decline, but it was hardly the real reason, and his appointment as commissioner was an appeasement that would salve Pettus's conscience. A few months later, Dahlgren's good friend, aide, and confidant in Natchez, Capt. G. Malin Davis, also asked to retire from service because of a severe "disease of the eyes." He offered medical certification from two physicians in Natchez and was duly relieved of duty.[48] What Dahlgren's new status might have had to do with the decision of Captain Davis is a matter of conjecture. It seems possible that both were growing more and more disenchanted with the Confederate leaders.

Having once again had his proposals ignored by Jefferson Davis, Dahlgren went public with his ideas for the defense of the South. On 23 March 1862, he sent a long, detailed plan to the *Daily True Delta*. His strategy was calculated to protect the South from Union forces and to repel all military advances. The scheme, worked out geographically, called for three lines of defense:

The first lines should consist of entrenchments or fortifications [on the North-South borders] with sufficient numbers to prevent sudden inroad and to maintain their ground until the arrival of reinforcements from the second lines.

The second lines should be composed of larger bodies, at short strategic distances, to render prompt succor, until the arrival of troops from the third lines. The third line should be the reserves, to throw aid to any point needed; here should be the magazines, depots, foundries, arsenals, store-houses of every description.[49]

He then added in support of the arrangement: "The entire communication being by railroad, affording easy connection, requires no explanation to a military man."[50] The plan, "drawn up some time ago," was meant as a rebuttal to the neglect shown him by Jefferson Davis.

Dahlgren's plan followed Napoleon's Skeleton Regiment. According to that rubric, however, Confederate forces would be defending an impossibly long geographic line stretching over hundreds of miles, a line too weak anywhere to offer a real defense. The Skeleton Regiment was a kind of defense cordon, weak everywhere, strong nowhere. Napoleon himself was said to have repudiated it. Already the first and second lines of defense in Dahlgren's plan had been shattered by the enemy. The Union commander, Brig. Gen. Ulysses S. Grant, was poised to penetrate the heart of the Confederacy. On the coast, Flag Officer David Glasgow Farragut began moving toward New Orleans. He would occupy the city on 28 April.

As if there were still viable ways to win the war without English or French intervention, Dahlgren furnished a list of "ways and means":

1. I would make every State a military district, with a camp in every county, where three-fourths of all the men should do military duty.

2. Divide the old troops in two parts and fill them up with recruits, upon the plan of Napoleon's Skeleton Regiment.

3. Build all gunboats, rams, etc. as rapidly as possible, and wherever they could be constructed.

4. Start every rolling mill, foundry, workshop to making mortars, cannon, artillery, etc.

5. Put every blacksmith and other mechanic to making gun barrels, small arms, Bowie knives, etc.

6. Call upon the women and the weakly men to making clothing, etc.

7. Let our slaves raise meat, bread and supplies of every kind.[51]

These are best judged as theoretical proposals in preparation for a war; they were clearly not feasible a year after the conflict had begun and the South was already invaded. But Dahlgren ended his "defense" that March with full confidence in his authority and added, "I boldly challenge criticism and investigation, believing that alone necessary to insure conviction."[52] Readers of the *Daily True Delta* would not have been convinced of Dahlgren's projections nor would they have shared the author's enthusiasm.

CℓℬO

The military losses in the Mid-South caused the Deep South to look for quick measures of defense. Bad news was telegraphed from Tennessee after Confederate forces were outnumbered and defeated by Federal infantry and gunboats under General Grant at Fort Henry and Fort Donelson. Nashville, the most important city south of the Ohio with the exception of New Orleans, was the next target. Ten days after the loss of Fort Donelson, undefended Nashville was handed over to Brig. Gen. Don Carlos Buell by the city's mayor R. B. Cheatham.

Under the terms of surrender at Fort Donelson, Grant took control of twelve thousand Confederate troops, whom he soon dispatched to Union prisons. Among them was Col. Randal W. McGavock, age thirty-six, a Harvard Law School graduate, European traveler, newspaper correspondent, youngest mayor of Nashville, and grandson of the renowned lawyer Felix Grundy. A commanding presence at 6 feet, 2½ inches in height, McGavock was a bon vivant who had made the rounds of parties in Nashville and nearby counties where he enjoyed extensive family connections. When he was shipped off to prison on George's Island in Boston Harbor, he made the most of his incarceration by writing a detailed report of the bungling of Confederate generals responsible for the fall of Fort Donelson: "I did not surrender. I was surrendered." From the island, he wrote long letters to his old law professors at Harvard and argued the case of the South and defended secession. He also contacted his Boston tailor, who had his measurements on file, and ordered a new Confederate uniform to wear when he was exchanged for three Yankee lieutenants in August 1862.

Southern loyalists quickly criticized the weak leadership of Brig. Gen. Pillow, Brig. Gen. Floyd, and Lt. Gen. Simon Bolivar Buckner at Fort Donelson. Nashvillians felt compromised because their city was the first capital in the South to be occupied by the enemy. The only cheerful news concerned Col. Nathan Bedford Forrest. He had quickly outwitted the Yankees at Fort Donelson and escaped with eight hundred cavalry and infantry troops.[53]

∂℘

Two months later, Union and Confederate forces clashed again at Shiloh in southern Tennessee. Partial success and anticipation of victory were felt by the Confederates at the end of the first day. On the second day, Brig. Gen. Albert Sidney Johnston was wounded by a minié ball that opened an artery in his leg, and he died a short time later. Johnston's death was a heavy blow to Confederate morale. Another blow was General Beauregard's premature orders to fall back. At best, Shiloh was a draw and another disappointment to the South.

Among the leading citizens determined to escape the Federal occupation of Nashville in 1862 were Mr. and Mrs. Irby Morgan. They fled with their children and two servants to Lookout Mountain, Chattanooga, to wait for the end of the war. Expecting hostilities to end within months or last no longer than a year, Mrs. Morgan took a group of mountain women with her to tag the native flora that she intended to transplant in Nashville when she returned in the spring. She designated her choices with white, red, and black strings "so I would know them when I got ready to take them up." But, she wrote later, by 1863, "stern reality occurred to fill the heart" as the family retreated further south, and she abandoned her selection of wild flowers forever.

At Chattanooga, Mrs. Morgan called on Mrs. E. W. Cole and other ladies who were responding in various ways to show their support of the Confederate cause. The former Louise McGavock Lytle of Williamson County, Mrs. Cole was described as "a big-hearted thoroughgoing woman and loyal to her country." Mrs. Morgan reported: "On entering the room I heard a peculiar noise, and I asked what it was. She told me it was silk worms feeding; and sure enough there they were, feasting on leaves. She said: 'The soldiers, many of them my friends, need silk handkerchiefs, and I have already woven quite a number.' And when she showed me the results of her labor, I was astonished."[54]

With the two losses in Tennessee, foreboding swept throughout Mississippi. It was feared the state would become a battleground as bloody as Virginia. Already the Confederates had fallen back to Corinth to regroup. Now eyes turned toward Vicksburg with its guns defending the high, commanding bluffs. For good reason, Vicksburg was christened "the Gibraltar of Mississippi," the key position to Confederate command of the river and survival in the West. The hopeful could find at Vicksburg a reason to go on dreaming a little longer.

∽ Five ∾

Defeat at Vicksburg and Gettysburg

In May 1862, after New Orleans and Baton Rouge had fallen to Union forces, the rumors of gunboat activity upriver toward Natchez were verified. On 13 May, Mayor John Hunter called a hurried meeting of the Natchez selectmen at 8:00 A.M. to read a communication that he had received the previous day from Commander Palmer of the USS *Iroquois*, then at anchor off Natchez:

> In advance of the squadron now coming up the Mississippi, I am instructed by the flag officer to demand the surrender of the city of Natchez to the Naval forces of the United States.
>
> The same terms will be accorded as those granted to New Orleans and Baton Rouge. The rights and property of all peaceable citizens shall be respected; but all property in this city belonging to the so-called Confederate States must be delivered up, and the flag of the United States must wave unmolested and respected over your town.

Mayor Hunter, with the approval of the alderman, replied to Palmer that the city was unfortified and defenseless and would meet the conditions that he had outlined. "Formalities are absurd in the face of such realities," Hunter added.[1]

Later that same day, however, Hunter received an urgent communication from the Commandant's Office, Confederate Post, signed by C. G. Dahlgren. It pointed out that Commander Palmer had violated the "courtesies of war" in his ultimatum and that Mayor Hunter erred in accepting the terms forced upon the city. Both Porter and Hunter, Dahlgren charged, had failed to observe protocol and were guilty "in the highest degree" of not abiding by the formalities. (Minute Book No. 15, 1860–1872. Municipal Records Office, Natchez, Mississippi. Abbreviated M B in Primary Sources.)

Dahlgren's communication took the trouble to explain to Hunter the steps that he and Palmer should have taken:

> Where two parties are at war, each are liable to be shot down on meeting; either party desiring a momentary cessation of hostilities, for a peaceful object, expresses that desire by a flag of truce; when this is not done, it is impossible that any act of a peaceful character can occur, the strength or weakness of either party does not effect the question; for neither can be ascertained until after a peaceful interchange or acknowledgment.

Dahlgren reminded the mayor and aldermen that, as the Confederate commandant, he had reluctantly turned the city over to them, as the civil authority, and expected them to press the enemy for a flag of truce:

> I supposed they would have done. Had the enemy landed his force he could have marched through the streets, which is more than he can do yet, if everything is not yielded to his exactions, as the surrender of the city, which I presume will not be dreamed of—

Dahlgren's argument was the response of a man unwilling to face the reality of the situation. His final word advised Hunter and the aldermen, in the event of actual enemy occupation, to announce to the citizens of Adams County that they should "retire to their houses, with their servants, and afford no notice of the existence of such an unscrupulous enemy as we are warring with."

After the reading of Dahlgren's communication, Mayor Hunter and his council made no comment but unanimously passed a motion to adjourn. They promptly ignored Dahlgren's remarks because they had already bowed to the circumstances.

The argument that Dahlgren made to the Natchez mayor and aldermen echoes Cervantes's comic knight, Don Quixote, when he addressed his faithful squire Sancho Panza. The two of them had been badly outnumbered and drubbed by a group of low-class rascals after a dispute over Quixote's horse Rozinante: "You must know, friend Sancho, that the life of a knight-errant is subject to a thousand perils and mischances, yet equally they may become kings and emperors. . . ." Quixote then pointed out that his recent error was in demeaning himself by brandishing his sword against a socially inferior group of brigands armed with staves: "When you see such rascally rabble do us harm [in future], do not wait for me to draw my sword against them for I will not do it on any account . . . [only] if knights come to their assistance."[2]

Quixote had resolved to observe the code of chivalry. Dahlgren had urged the mayor of Natchez to "afford no notice . . . of an unscrupulous enemy" who had violated the rules of warfare in not following the military manuals. The humor in Quixote's and Dahlgren's decisions would have escaped each of them, but it would not have been lost on their contemporaries.

When Dahlgren reported later to Gen. Thomas Jordan on the Union craft anchored at Natchez in May 1862, there is a marked shift in his tone. His account is a painful statement of the city's embarrassment that only fourteen men rose to defend it against an enemy force of 130. With his conscripts "positively refusing to do duty," Dahlgren had transferred control of the city to its civil authorities. But the Federals chose not to come ashore and occupy Natchez at that time. Dahlgren retreated to his headquarters at nearby Washington, Mississippi, where he filed his report to Jordan in Corinth, on May 17.[3] He noted that he had ordered all the cotton burned within 10 miles of Natchez to prevent its falling into Union hands. This precaution was taken elsewhere along the Mississippi, but Dahlgren's orders drew skeptical responses from the owners around Natchez, even though most of them obeyed to keep the cotton from the hands of greedy Yankee speculators.

One such planter was the wealthy James Surget, who dutifully followed the edict and was quoted by Matilda Gresham. "When the order came May 5, 1862 . . . I burned 1200 bales of my own cotton on the Ashley plantation and 500 bales on the Waterloo plantation in Concordia Parish. I also, under the same order, burned 500 bales of cotton eight miles below Natchez on the Mississippi side that belonged to Washington Ford." Surget's compliance in following orders to destroy Ford's cotton landed him in court when the war was over. Ford sued him for $200,000 for compensation in the Circuit Court of Adams County, where a jury absolved Surget. An angry Ford then took the case to the U.S. Supreme Court, where Surget won again. "The Court held that while the acts of the Confederate Congress were void, the military duress I was under was a reality, and Ford had no recourse on me."[4] Other cotton producers targeted Dahlgren as the culprit, however, and caused him to defend himself later in letters to Brig. Gen. Thomas Jordan and to President Jefferson Davis.

A vivid account of the destruction of cotton on the Gordon Shields plantation south of Natchez was given in the 1930s during an oral presentation by a former slave, Charlie Davenport, who was then past one hundred years old:

> I was on the plantation closer to town, called "Fish Pond Planta-
> tion." De white folks come and told us we must burn all de cotton
> so de enemy couldn't get it. Us piled it high in de field like
> great mountains. It made my innards hurt to see fire attached to
> somethin' dat had cost us niggers so much labor and honest sweat.
> If I coulda hid some o' it in de barn I'd a-done it, but de boss
> searched everywhere. De little niggers thought it was fun. Dey
> laughed and brung out big armfuls from de cotton house. One
> little black gal clapped her hands and jumped in a big heap. She
> sunk down and down till she was buried deep. Den de wind picked
> up de flame and spread it like lightenin'. It spread so fast dat before
> us could bat de eye, she was in a mountain o' fire. She struggled
> up all covered with flames, a-screamin', "Lordy, help me!" Us

snatched her out and rolled her on de ground, but 'tweren't no use. She died in a few minutes.[5]

Thus Charlie Davenport's experience of cotton burning and his recollection of this sorrowful incident remained in oral circulation well into the twentieth century.

Dahlgren's final remarks to General Jordan in 1862 also sound a poignant note: "Our condition here is a matter of deep regret and solicitude to me. Without any organized military power, with conscripts who refuse to serve . . . without arms, without supplies, equipage, munitions, or commissary stores . . . with a population the strength of which has already joined the army . . . the residue . . . wavering in trepidation of their property or personal security. . . . All these are matters that I desire to lay before you. . . . "[6] The irony inherent in this official report reveals a man who in March had urged, like the advocates of states' rights "every State a military district, with a camp in every county, where three-fourths of all men should do military duty." His idealism was shattered when Natchez, the city of rich men and great houses, failed to muster enough troops to defend itself and proclaim its superiority in the eyes of the world.

Just before Natchez officially capitulated, Dahlgren had seen one hundred local recruits, unarmed though they were, hurried off to Virginia. By then, his son Charlie Routh had been there for nearly a year. Because of the persistent threat of Yankee occupation in Natchez, Dahlgren instructed Mary Edgar to hide her valuables or bury some of them in a large tin box in the garden. With the help of her stepson Bernard and the caretaker Mr. Dolan handling pick and shovel, she followed her husband's orders.[7] Then, on 27 May, while the general was at his new headquarters in Fayette, Mississippi, Mary Edgar gave birth to her second son. They named him Rowan Foote, which used his grandmother's maiden name and honored Judge Edwin Foote of Philadelphia, a friend of Bernard Dahlgren.[8] The little boy arrived in an atmosphere of concern over enemy gunboats on the river and the spectre of Yankee troops invading the sovereign state of Mississippi.

ལ ༡

From Fayette, a village "healthy, convenient, and central," and only 26 miles from Natchez, General Dahlgren wrote to General Jordan again and asked for "stores, supplies, arms, ammunition, hospitals, depots, provender, forage, repairing arms, perhaps foundries . . . in short all the wants and necessities of an army." He also asked Jordan for "instructions in full," to state the extent of his authority, and to approve his recent orders to burn the cotton. He deplored the lack of volunteers to the cause and reported "but seven conscripts appeared for duty until yesterday, when perhaps twenty came, undisciplined and unavailable."[9]

Dahlgren warned Jordan that the enemy could establish and support strong pickets and "isolate a large extent of country and secure the cotton . . . [so] I have issued a proclamation calling upon planters to prevent the enemy obtaining supplies of any kind, allowing which to the enemy constitutes in my opinion treason against the Confederate States." He probably had in mind several prominent planters in Natchez who preferred to remain "neutral" in the course of the war and who might therefore give comfort to the invaders. Among them were such avowed Unionists as Stephen Duncan of Auburn, Levin R. Marshall of Richmond, Ayres P. Merrill of Elmscourt, William J. Minor, William Newton Mercer, and Judge Josiah Winchester. All of them had strongly opposed secession in 1861. Closer to Dahlgren were Julia and Haller Nutt, who were his in-laws by marriage because Julia Nutt was a niece of Mary Routh, Dahlgren's first wife. In 1861, Julia was busy urging the skilled workmen, a number of them from the North, to complete her octagonal palace outside Natchez, but she could not persuade them to stay and finish the house. Longwood stands today as the artisans left it. Union troops arrived in 1863, occupied the shell, and staged gambling and drinking parties in the deserted halls.[10]

Jordan forwarded Dahlgren's plea for men and supplies on to General Beauregard in Corinth on 17 May, and Beauregard replied on 25 May. He answered Dahlgren's questions and extended his approval of Dahlgren's handling of affairs within his command, including the destruction of the cotton. He also approved of "arresting disloyal citizens" but suggested:

"As to the minister of the Gospel [who refused to pray for Jefferson Davis on the Sunday set aside] I would not interfere with him so long as he does not preach obedience to Northern rule and does nothing contrary to Confederate laws." Beauregard went on to state his approval of the camp at Fayette, but regretted "I have no troops of any description to send there, for all you refer to are required here and at Vicksburg."

General Beauregard, who was aware of Dahlgren's impetuous nature and determination to punish civil offenders, ended the letter with some tactful advice: "I commend your zeal and patriotism and the course pursued in all your late duties and actions . . . but whilst strictly performing your duty I must counsel you to endeavor to persuade and conciliate our people in preference to adopting harsh measures, which at present we have not the means of carrying into effect."[11]

Beauregard was trying to prevent Dahlgren from further antagonizing the local populace; at the same time, he was trying to stall long enough to establish Maj. Gen. Earl Van Dorn over Dahlgren's domain. He achieved that move in June, and Dahlgren severed his relationship with Beauregard.

Charles Dahlgren, however, did not move from one phase of his career to another without setting down the events that prompted his decisions. His letters to his superiors in the Confederate chain of command and his explanations of the rationale that brought him to his conclusions demonstrate his rhetorical force. He wrote to General Jordan on 8 June 1862 and summarized his difficulties with recruitment. "Some objected to going into Confederate service, some objected to leaving Adams County, others refused to enter into any organization to attack the enemy." Discouraged with the lack of patriotism in Natchez, Dahlgren had moved his headquarters to Fayette to recruit, "at one time sleeping all of three nights in my travelling wagon," but "could not procure a sufficient number of conscripts, nor the officers to properly organize them." He could not account for the indifference and refusal to bear arms when "the enemy were occupying Natchez or landing marauding parties on the river, where they shot cattle, took over other stock, robbed gardens, houses, and stores with wantonness and insult."[12] Mississippi needed defenders as never before, but no amount of appeals to honor would bring them forward. The stalwarts had been siphoned off and were laying their honor on the line in Virginia.

Dahlgren wrote with the grammatical balance of a rhetorician as he concluded his final letter to General Jordan: "In all my actions I have endeavored to carry out what I conceived were your views. I had no friendships to please; no animosities to indulge in; no love of power to gratify, but singly and only what was the good of my country, which I know was your desire. I endeavored to be rapid without haste; energetic, but systematic; firm without severity, and if I appeared to have been too pressing, it was from the necessities of the case; if too stringent, from zeal for the welfare of those entrusted to my care; and if too urgent from a desire to shield our cause from insult and contumely."[13] If these remarks seemed to his military superiors like oratorical excuses on Dahlgren's part, his patriotic intentions and troubled conscience are also apparent.

Finally, Dahlgren asked for compensation for some lawful expenses incurred in the line of duty. "For myself, as I did not accept the command with the view of any pecuniary gain, so I desire not to accept remuneration for any services I may have rendered." And again, as he had on the coast, he asked his superiors to "criticize my military views and operations, as to correct my errors . . . a benefit to me in future undertakings."[14] He was nearly fifty-two at the time and wondering what further efforts he could make to aid the Confederacy.

In a postscript to Jordan, Dahlgren reported his final official act for the benefit of landowners in the areas of his command: "I issued a Proclamation postponing collection of all taxes until 1st July next [1863] upon condition that no lien nor security was lost or waived, which I hope will meet with your approbation; and if the present state of affairs continues, still further postponement is imperatively called for."[15] He wanted to prevent the banks and the sheriff from selling off the properties of his peers at the courthouse door while areas of the state were under Federal occupation. While the edict protected the interests of many landowners with major debts, it also bore on Dahlgren's own situation. He had several outstanding obligations, including a mechanics lien on Llangollen and loans from Stephen Duncan.

In replying to Dahlgren's letter of June 8 and the futility that it expressed, General Jordan offered the sincere hope that "the panic will pass by speedily, and the inspirations of patriotism, loyalty, and the manhood of our fathers will resume full sway, sweeping aside the despicable and cheating promptings of selfishness."[16] Jordan's words could not have provided a great deal of comfort for a man floundering like Dahlgren, an officer without command, a leader without followers, a patriot without zealots.

◌ॐ◌

On 2 September 1862, the USS *Essex* drew up opposite Natchez and began a brief shelling of the city as a show of strength to bring the populace to its knees. Although Mayor Hunter had quietly surrendered the city to the Yankees on 13 May with no casualties, shells from the *Essex* injured five men and killed seven-year-old Rosalie Beekman, who was fleeing with her family from Natchez-under-the-hill. With Union gunboats and converted steamers now making passage in the channels of the Mississippi and with Grant getting poised to move south from Memphis, all Confederate efforts were concentrated on fortifying Vicksburg. Federal control already stretched from just north of the Yazoo River and south from Port Hudson to Baton Rouge. If Vicksburg fell and the Mississippi was open to Union craft the demise of the Confederacy in the West was at hand.

After returning to Fayette, General Dahlgren addressed Confederate Gen. John C. Pemberton in Jackson with some good advice about the Louisiana side of the Mississippi, an area that he knew well. His dispatch of 6 December 1862 warned Pemberton that Union gunboats from New Orleans could reach Vicksburg and do untold damage by taking a circuitous route: "I allude to the Atchafalaya River. Gunboats and transports of the enemy can pass through to Red River . . . (ascending the Atchafalaya) and masking [avoiding] your batteries at Port Hudson [then] reach Vicksburg without opposition. . . . I would suggest, therefore, that additional batteries be erected [to prevent such a maneuver]."[17] In forwarding the letter to Richmond, Pemberton cited it as being "of great importance" and referred to the author as *Mr.* C. G. Dahlgren, a brother of Commander Dahlgren.

Finally Dahlgren closed his letter to Pemberton with this reminder: "I believe that I first urged the value of Vicksburg as a military point [a year and three months ago], which has been fully verified, though my plan contemplated entire intrenchment, and victualizing and garrisoning for twelve months' siege, which done would render it impregnable." By calculation, Dahlgren's warning would have been made in September 1861. When Grant sent additional troops for the invasion of Mississippi in 1862, the ultimate target being Vicksburg, Jefferson Davis moved General Pemberton from South Carolina to block Grant and defend the town on the bluff at all costs.

There are certain parallels during the early years of Charles G. Dahlgren and John C. Pemberton. Both were Philadelphians, the first born in 1811 and the second in 1814. Both had good educations, were adventurers by nature, and both had married Southern women. Dahlgren, in 1861, seems not to have vacillated about accepting a role in the Confederate military. Pemberton, a graduate of West Point, a veteran of the Mexican War, and a captain in the U.S. Army in 1861, had difficulty at first in declaring a choice between North and South. Finally, following his conscience, he resigned his commission in the U.S. Army on 24 April 1861 and headed south to Richmond to cast his lot with the Confederacy. He took the stand of such West Point classmates as Braxton Bragg and Jubal Early.[18]

Pemberton's move south was welcomed by his wife in Norfolk, and numerous friends in Richmond. The Southerners saw the Yankee from Philadelphia as a subscriber to their cause and a patriot ready to put his life on the line to uphold Southern sovereignty. Mississippians initially responded as favorably to the stand that Charles Dahlgren took in July 1861. Both men had family members in Philadelphia who strongly opposed secession. The fact that Dahlgren's brother John Adolphus was a commander in the U.S. Navy caused their contemporaries to be struck by all the ironies of their circumstances.

Besides his espousal of the philosophy of states' rights, Dahlgren was obliged to protect his plantations and two hundred slaves across the river in Louisiana. As an ambitious professional soldier, Pemberton was set to play his cards for the approval of his superiors and swift promotions. Both men wanted to advance as leaders and looked for opportunities to express their patriotism and to satisfy their conceits.

There is no record that Pemberton and Dahlgren ever met, but each knew who the other was and they corresponded when Pemberton assumed his command in Mississippi in October 1862. Dahlgren, however, at that time was acting in the capacity of advisor to Governor Pettus and was growing increasingly disenchanted with Jefferson Davis and his advisors in Richmond. Further, Pemberton's problems in administration in South Carolina had been generally broadcast before he was sent to Mississippi. Although Davis stood by him and believed him capable of carrying out the new command, including the defense of Vicksburg, Pemberton arrived there at a low ebb in his career. Dahlgren, already out of uniform, looked at Pemberton with little or no confidence and resented his presence at Vicksburg, especially because he was accompanied by Jefferson Davis on his arrival in December.[19]

Although Vicksburg had been a prime target as early as 1862 when Union Gen. Thomas Williams and Flag Officer Farragut had shelled it, General Grant devised and carried out a successful offensive the following year from both sides of the river. Knowing that a frontal assault would be futile, as Williams and Farragut had discovered, Grant decided (1) to march his men overland through Louisiana on the Mississippi's west bank; (2) to ferry them across on steamers, which would run the Vicksburg batteries; and (3) to move troops overland again, through Mississippi, to Vicksburg's defenseless backside. This maneuver brought men and craft downriver from Milliken's Bend, Louisiana, to Lake Saint Joseph and involved Generals John A. McClernand, William Tecumseh Sherman, James B. McPherson, and Frank Blair. The flotilla was commanded by Adm. David Dixon Porter, who is said to have directed eighty-one steamers and gunboats.[20]

As part of the Confederate forces defending Jackson, Mississippi's capital, on Monday, 11 May, Col. Randal W. McGavock was in command of the 10th Tennessee Regiment, a wing of Gen. John Gregg's brigade. McGavock was ordered to Raymond, a small town between Vicksburg and Jackson, to defend the capital from the Union forces commanded by Maj. Gen. John A. Logan. The Battle of Raymond was fought on 12 May with Colonel McGavock leading his regiment as they approached the crest of a small hill. As he directed the charge, the men followed the tall figure, the sun highlighting his red hair and beard. Within a few seconds, he fell, mortally wounded, his coat riddled by eight bullets. The scion and favorite son of the McGavock and Grundy families of Nashville had now paid his dues to the Confederacy in a last fatal gesture.[21]

Mary Edgar Dahlgren would hear the news and think of the charm that McGavock had had for her back home when she was a little girl at the Presbyterian church on Sundays.

Then, after a long siege and forty-three bitter days of deprivation by the military and civilians alike, Vicksburg fell when Pemberton surrendered to Grant on 4 July 1863. Now the Confederacy was agape, seriously cleft. The worst had come to pass.

Shortly after the defeat, General Dahlgren gathered up his family and a number of his servants and made arrangements to transport them to Atlanta. He would not suffer the indignity of enemy troops bivouacking on his lawn at Llangollen. The move was a desperate measure and the risks were great, but many Southerners retreated behind the lines to hold on to the old ways a little longer and to offer more prayers for victory.

◌◌

Early in 1863, Admiral John Dahlgren's oldest son, Charles Bunker, who had witnessed the incident between the *Trent* and the *San Jacinto* in 1861, was made an acting ensign and assigned to the gunboat *Glide* at Cairo, Illinois. Young Dahlgren and the *Glide* were part of the Mississippi Squadron under Admiral Porter, who was preparing for the combined assault on Vicksburg by both land and river. But the *Glide* caught fire about 5 A.M. on the morning of 7 February. According to the report of Ensign Dahlgren, all attempts to save her failed:

> Every exertion was made to extinguish the fire by officers and men
> of both ship and station, but the intense cold, high wind, and

light, dry material of the ship set at defiance every exertion. Nothing was saved except that which we all stood in.[22]

Charles Bunker Dahlgren was then assigned as executive officer on the *General Sterling Price*, a Confederate gunboat captured by the Union. With other gunboats Charles Bunker moved south against Vicksburg and later recalled this incident when he was serving under Porter:

The Fleet was at anchor one early morning about 500 yards from a sand spit on which a flock of geese had slept that night. Lieut. D. trained a 12 lb. Dahlgren Howitzer on the flock, which was already preparing to take flight. He made allowance for distance, wind & their rapid walk just before taking wing & pulled the lanyard. The schrapnel burst just as they had risen & over 40 were picked up by the boats. The shot, unauthorized, had alarmed the Fleet, & the Flag Ship at once made Signal to "repair on board." But the present of 3 brace of fine fat geese appeased the irate Admiral, who was short of meat. Otherwise it would have gone hard with the offender.

This & my excellent practice in my IX inch siege battery at Vicksburg gave me the reputation of being a crack shot with "heavy guns," which I was in fact.[23]

Charles Bunker, as the daredevil son of an admiral, was ready to concoct some horseplay before the guns invented by his father were to be discharged in earnest. He was later awarded a commendation for his "management of two IX-inch guns, which were admirably served."[24] After Vicksburg fell on 4 July 1863 Charles Bunker learned that his first cousin, Pudge Dahlgren, had surrendered with the Confederates. Like many of his comrades, Pudge found no time at fourteen to comprehend Lee's debacle that same day at a little town in Pennsylvania named Gettysburg.

☙

Bishop William Henry Elder of Natchez recorded in his diary the turmoil in the Vicksburg area from 1862 to 1865. The peripatetic clergyman, in performing the offices of the Roman Catholic Church, traveled to congregations in Jackson, Port Gibson, Brookhaven, and Vicksburg. He said Mass, baptized families, and heard confessions. On 15 July, eleven days after Vicksburg fell, Bishop Elder recorded:

> Started about 6 AM—rough saddle. Folded my overcoat and sat on it. Crossed Pearl River at Deer's Ferry about 9 1/2 AM. About twelve overtook a large body of paroled prisoners from Vicksburg going toward the camp at Enterprise or other points eastward. Walked for some distance & let a sick man ride. They [soldiers] give a sad acct. of their sufferings in Vicksbg—47 days in the trenches without relief—quarter rations. Mule meat was eaten by some. They found no objection to it but the name.[25]

Accounts of the privations at Vicksburg were later recalled by many other civilians and military men. One such account is a little-known recollection by a former slave who accompanied his master during the final days of the siege. Isaac Stier, the body servant of Jeems Stowers of Jefferson County, related his recollections in Natchez when he was more than ninety years old:

> De hongriest I ever been was at de Siege o' Vicksburg. Dat was a time I'd lak to forgit. Da folks et up all de cats an' dogs an' den went to devourin' de mules an' hosses. Even de wimmin an' little chillun was a-starvin'. Dey stummicks was stickin' to dey backbones. Us Niggers was suffein' so us took de sweaty hoss blankets an' soaked 'em in mudholes where de hosses tromped. Den us wrung 'em out in buckets an' drunk dat dirty water for pot-likker. It tasted kinda salty an' was strength'nin', lak weak soup.
>
> I tell you, dem Yankees took us by starvation. Twant a fair fight. Dey called it a vict'ry an' bragged 'bout Vicksburg a-fallin', but hungry foks aint got no fight lef' in 'em. Us folks was starved into surrenderin'.[26]

Stier's account continued after the surrender of Vicksburg on 4 July. He recalled how he was treated by the Yankee victors:

De war was over in May 1865, but I was captured at Vicksburg an' hel' in jail 'til I 'greed to take up arms wid de Nawth. I figgered dat was 'bout all I could do, 'cause dey warnt but one war at Vicksburg an' dat was over. I was all de time hopin' I could slip off an' work my way back home, but de Yankees didn' turn me loose 'til 1866.[27]

At least, with the Yankees, Isaac had better rations than those his own folks could give him.

Young John Adolph Dahlgren, half-starved after three months with the 31st Louisiana Infantry, was paroled on 9 July 1863 at Vicksburg and allowed to go home to Natchez. His military career was over at age fourteen, when he swore no longer to bear arms for the Confederacy. He was followed on 13 July by a detachment of Federal troops who would occupy Natchez and set up military rule. Along with the Yankees, John Adolph encountered hoards of riffraff, scavengers, and lawless men from the country who were looking for booty and preying on the defenseless. They had never been Rebels, they told the Union command; the average Yankee recruits believed them and winked at their behavior. Together, the two groups would show their scorn for the high and mighty aristocrats who started the war in order to keep their slaves.

A contemporary remembered the chaos:

. . . [T]he Bushwackers and their families WORMED in and were given possession, BY THE YANKEES, of the homes whose owners had left on the approach of the Yankees. [They] were for the most part the lowest, vilest folk one can imagine; ignorant, with no sense of either common decency or truth, a number were deserters from both armies. . . . All of the Bushwackers were paid spies of the Yankees.[28]

Natchez was now overrun by the military, by homeless blacks, by hordes of marauding civilians without allegiances. Although the Western

Confederacy had fallen and the Mississippi was open from source to delta, the war was still raging in the East. Neither Louisiana nor Arkansas offered protection. The safest bastion of any size in the South in 1863 was Atlanta, which was receiving affluent refugees from Natchez and other parts of the Confederacy. Alabama received them as well. Mrs. Frisby Freeland, with her two children and servants, left Warren County for Demopolis, Alabama, well behind the lines, as did others who traveled by the Alabama and Mississippi Railroad eastward to look for temporary homes.[29]

As General Dahlgren had taken Mary Edgar with him to the Gulf Coast in 1861, Union generals sometimes brought their wives to occupied Natchez. Matilda Gresham, wife of Gen. Walter Q. Gresham, joined her husband there after he was assigned to the command of the 3d Brigade. They were provided quarters at Rosalie, the Natchez home of A. L. Wilson, who had gone to Texas. Mrs. Gresham gave a favorable report on the treatment that she and her husband received among the Natchez gentry of Unionist persuasion: "Hospitable by nature, these men were almost universally cordial to my husband." Her friendly relations with several ladies of Natchez continued many years after the army had withdrawn.

General Gresham was commended in Natchez for providing as much protection as possible for the residents whose homes were targets for looters. Living at The Elms, at the head of Washington Street on the outskirts of the city, were Nancy W. Winston, Anne Stanton, and Mrs. Winston's granddaughter, Nanny W. Thornhill, a girl of fifteen. Having had the protection of a young soldier and an older one, both of whom were sent by General Gresham, the ladies were greatly disturbed when they received the news that their protectors were being transferred to Vicksburg.

Mrs. Winston appealed to General Gresham in person. The general honored her entreaties and agreed to leave the older man to guard the ladies. "But we don't want the old man. We want the young man. The old man is stupid," Mrs. Winston replied in her blunt, forceful manner.

Backed into a corner, the general agreed to settle the issue by having the men draw straws as to which should go and which should stay. "I was to superintend the drawing," Mrs. Winston stated later. "I did so, and we got the younger soldier."[30]

Wars, civil strife, and armies of occupation are not always a match for strong-willed women. Nor can such obstacles put an end to the amorous intentions of the young. The younger soldier, Lt. William P. Callon, and Nanny Thornhill were married in 1868 at her family's home, Traveller's Rest, in Adams County. Callon took his bride to Illinois, where he practiced law and served in both houses of the legislature. He returned to Natchez with his wife and family during his final years.[31]

Although Natchez was spared major destruction by the military, many "citizens had abandoned their town property *en masse*" and refused to live under military rule. As one historian notes, "The 'day of jubilee' had arrived for many freedmen who wanted to see the fabled glories of Vicksburg, Natchez, and Columbus. . . . As a result, hundreds of Negroes gathered in black belt towns . . ." and Natchez became a center for an unemployed, unruly black population.[32] Bushwackers had trickled in from the piney woods, adding to the confusion and disorder. The Yankee generals found that establishing the rule of law was not only difficult but hazardous because the flood of seething humanity in Adams County in 1863 was matched only by the spring rampages of the Mississippi.

⊘ Six ⊘

The Flight to Georgia

I f General Dahlgren had commanded the first successful repulse at Vicksburg in 1862, as he later reported,[1] he was not part of the action when the city fell in 1863. After that, with Federal troops occupying both sides of the river, Dahlgren was virtually cut off from Marydale and The Oaks. The Federals moved quickly to occupy buildings suitable for quartering troops and began to bargain for commissary supplies. The invaders classified local householders according to their political stance. Those of unquestioned loyalty to the Union were allowed to retain control of their property and were expected to cooperate with the occupying forces. Secessionists risked having their premises and possessions taken for government use; the decisions were left to each commanding officer.

The plantations were under similar edicts. If an owner were a declared Union sympathizer, he or she could usually continue on the land and take other plantation owners of like persuasion as partners. Planters who had defected from the Union and supported the Confederate cause were liable to have their land and their crops taken from their control. The land was leased to Unionists or entrepreneurs who followed on the heels of the troops moving south.[2]

Most of the Tensas landowners had fled. They carried whatever they could in wagons loaded with trunks, crates, and barrels of flour, bacon, and corn. The Emancipation Proclamation applied only to rebelling states, and there were no means of enforcing it until Federal troops arrived. Therefore, some owners made arrangements to transport their slaves to leased land in Texas. Dahlgren's stepdaughter, Sarah Ann Ellis Dorsey, and her husband led their slaves west to Crockett, Houston County, where most slave-owning Texans stood adamant against Lincoln's proclamation and offered refuge for fleeing Southerners and their retinues. Brief glimpses of the Dorseys' journey with more than one hundred slaves have been recorded. There were two overseers to conduct the exodus, but measles broke out, and many slaves died. Others perished from malaria when quinine ran out. The preparation of meals was a chore, even when supplies were adequate. To add to the hardships, Sarah Ann's tent, made of carpet, leaked in the rain.[3]

Once they were settled in Crockett and her charges taken care of, Sarah Ann nursed ailing Confederate soldiers in a local hospital.[4] She also added her energies to the building of All Saints Episcopal Church in Crockett. She and her husband appear in the manuscript, "Journal of Official Acts," kept by Bishop Alexander Gregg during 1863 and 1864. Gregg recorded that, among the lay leaders, was "Mr. Dorsey, planter refugee from Louisiana." When the four children of German emigrant Johaner Zimmerman were baptized on 9 November 1864, both Dorseys were listed as sponsors.

Sarah Ann was also a leader in the conversion of the slaves in the community: "Vachel, Samuel, Hackett, Rosella, and Fanny Cromwell—colored children belonging to Mrs. S. W. Dorsey. Witness: Mrs. S. A. Dorsey on plantation, and at night, 9 Nov. 1864." The next day twenty-three "of the personal servants" were confirmed "largely through the zeal of Mrs. Dorsey."[5] In spite of makeshift conditions in Texas and all of the uncertainties attendant to the move from home, Sarah Ann was committed to her role as guardian of the people whom she had led away. If they labored by day for their bread and for her, she ministered to them and their spiritual needs with services at night. Later, after they returned to Louisiana, she built and supervised a school for the faithful on the plantation.

Before leaving Elk Ridge in 1863, Sarah Ann, "always practical, had tossed a portfolio of rare Dusseldorf engravings and her mother's silver goblets into a trunk" to accompany the move to Texas.[6] She later presented one of the goblets to Governor Henry W. Allen of Louisiana upon his retreat to Mexico in 1865. She presented two identical goblets to All Saints Church for the Communion of the Blessed Sacrament— one for the white and one for the black communicants.[7]

Other families from Natchez and Tensas Parish took their slaves to locations in Texas. A. L. Wilson, master of Rosalie, took his people west to save them, as he pronounced, from "the degrading effects of Emancipation." Others who went west were Kate Stone and her family of Brockenburn in Louisiana. Kate had been a classmate of Mary Edgar Dahlgren at Dr. Elliot's school for young ladies in Nashville during the late 1850s. Led by her widowed, very capable mother, Amanda Regan Stone, Kate, her little sister, and other relatives made their way first by train to Monroe, Louisiana, where they boarded for several weeks. Some weeks earlier, Mrs. Stone had dispatched 130 slaves to Lamar County, Texas, in the care of her overseer. The mother and daughters followed later in a Jersey wagon and all but perished before reaching the farm that Mrs. Stone had leased in North Texas. Kate deplored the primitive life and wrote in her diary that Lamar County was "the dark corner of the Confederacy."[8] Brought up at Brockenburn, she was ill at ease living in a log cabin near rough countrymen and their barefoot women and children. To her diary she confided: "There must be something in the air of Texas fatal to beauty."

Later, the Stones found the society in Tyler more to their taste. Kate named their second Texas home Bonnie Castle, enjoyed the companionship of other refugees from Mississippi and Louisiana, and practiced her social skills in games and masquerades. Young officers from nearby cavalry units came calling in uniform. They flirted with the girls and teased them with playful innuendoes. In Tyler, Kate first entertained Lt. Henry Bry Holmes, who in 1869 became her husband.[9]

◌◌

Precisely on what date General Dahlgren took his family to Atlanta is difficult to ascertain. They probably traveled part of the way by the Alabama and Mississippi Railroad, but how many servants they took and how finances were arranged are details now obscured. According to an entry in his diary on 24 May 1865, Dahlgren sold his cattle to a Mr. Thompson of Bladen Springs, Alabama. Also, a single surviving letter from sixteen-year-old Bernard, Dahlgren's second son by Mary Routh, indicates that he and Mr. Dolan remained in Natchez and shared Llangollen with a detail of Yankees and the older house servants.[10] Son Charlie Routh, twenty-two in 1863, was still fighting in Virginia with the Adams Troop, Jeff Davis Legion.

In the retreat to Atlanta were General Dahlgren, then fifty-two years old; Mary Edgar, twenty-three; her stepson John Adolph ("Pudge"), fourteen; and her own sons Van, three, and Rowan, one. They took female servants to cook, wash, iron, and look after the children and men to attend to the garden, stable, wagons, and carriages on the acreage that Dahlgren had bought in South Georgia. Other Mississippians were making their way to Atlanta, among them Ann Eliza Bowman Wilson of the Natchez estate Rosalie. A vehement defender of the South, Mrs. Wilson saw her home taken over by Federal commanders and occupied successively by Generals Thomas E. G. Ransom, Walter Q. Gresham, U. S. Grant, and Marcellus Monroe Crocker. Mrs. Wilson was so outspoken against the enemy that General James Madison Tuttle had her locked up for ten days and then banished. In Atlanta, she joined the Dahlgrens for several weeks before going into nursing in makeshift hospitals behind the lines.[11]

Many Nashvillians had first retreated to "safe" areas in North Georgia, such as Tunnel Hill and Catoosa Springs. Still others went to the mountains and remote watering places that they had enjoyed during the 1850s. Among them were Lucy Virginia French of McMinnville, Tennessee, who fled with her three young children to Beersheba Springs to escape the humiliation of Federal soldiers camping on her estate. The French diaries reveal that this sensitive lady was nevertheless troubled at Beersheba by gangs of mountain men and women who plundered the cottages and carried away furniture and books belonging to the resort's absent owners. Confederate lawmakers, politicians, and military advisors found food and lodging with Colonel and Mrs. John Armfield when they passed through Beersheba on the mountain road to Chattanooga.

Atlanta finally became the refuge for migrant families, such as the

Dahlgrens, because it "boasted all the attractions the homeless looked for in an urban area . . . and was so valuable to the Confederacy that the city would be held at all costs."[12] Thus, by early 1864, every boarding house was crammed with families. Matters rapidly grew worse when food prices soared with the short supply. The late arrivals, sometimes only a few weeks ahead of the Federals, resorted to makeshift shelter in barns, tents, and converted wood houses. They endured the fight for survival because they found good company among their equally pressed peers.

Fulton County deed books record that Charles Dahlgren bought a house and lot on Garnett Street, Atlanta, on 8 August 1863 from a Mrs. Griffin. The price was $12,000.[13] Garnett Street is the address where the Dahlgrens were living when they attended the Central Presbyterian Church nearby and were welcomed by the Rev. Robert Q. Mallard and his wife, Mary Jones Mallard, who wrote to her mother in Savannah: "A General Dahlgren, said to be brother of the commodore, has been attending our church regularly for some Sabbaths past with his family. They are very genteel, attractive persons in their appearance. Mr. Mallard and I intend calling on them, as we hear they are going to remain here. It is said this brother gave our government the pattern of the Dahlgren guns invented by his Yankee brother."[14] A sentence that begins with "it is said" immediately evokes a question of its veracity. In fact, Dahlgren guns were used by the South, but were "inherited" at military sites, such as Norfolk, that had been established in the South before 1860. In Richmond, the Tredegar Iron Works was one of four foundries that had produced heavy Dahlgren guns before the war. There is no record, however, that John Dahlgren ever acknowledged help from his brother Charles.

Mrs. Mallard wrote in another letter to her mother: "We have formed General Dahlgren's acquaintance. . . . He has a son in Virginia [Charlie Routh] who has passed through twenty-three pitched battles and has never received a wound. Is not this a wonderful providence? On several occasions comrades on either side have been killed, and still he was preserved unhurt."[15] Only two letters from Charlie Routh to his family have survived, and his Confederate service record is too brief for details of these encounters. His service record does record two periods of sick leave and hospitalization, neither of which seems to have been the result of combat.[16]

In contrast, Charlie Routh's cousin Ulric was receiving a great deal of notice for his military feats in Maryland. As the second and favorite son of Commander Dahlgren, Ulric drew the attention of his superiors and the Northern press when he was commissioned a captain by President Lincoln in May 1862 at a mere twenty years of age. He commanded a company of Brig. Gen. Franz Sigel's bodyguard, the 3d Indiana Cavalry, and saw action at Fredericksburg in December and also at Chancellorsville and second Bull Run. A tall, dashing figure with light brown hair and soft chin whiskers, Ulric asked his commanders to send him wherever the cavalry would be likely to see action. Between engagements, they saw to it that he was photographed with visiting dignitaries, including Count Ferdinand von Zeppelin, an observer from the Prussian Army, and several high-ranking Union officers.[17]

Ulric received even more attention in July after a skirmish at Hagerstown when Robert E. Lee retreated south from Gettysburg. On horseback, Ulric was shot in the right foot as his troops marched out of town. Accompanying them was E. A. Paul, a war correspondent for *The New York Times*, who was assigned to the campaign. Dahlgren spurred his horse into a gallop, finally shouting to his companion, "Paul, I have got it at last."[18] The bleeding was so severe that he was soon out of action. Three days later, he was carried on a litter to his father's home in Washington, where the leg was amputated below the knee. During a slow recovery, Ulric walked on crutches and wrote to his Aunt Patty Dahlgren: "I think over what I have seen and what has taken place [and] it seems like a dream . . . how little we know who will go next."[19]

With the loss of his foot and months of inaction, the young captain had won the admiration of the Northern press and his Union comrades. He also remained a favorite of his Uncle Charles in Atlanta and his cousins in the South. They addressed Ully with letters repeating their family bonds and expressing their concerns about his wound. They hoped the authorities would allow delivery of their messages at the Navy Yard, where he was convalescing.

Many Southerners, on the other hand, thought the arrogant young man deserved a measure of what he got. Lucy Virginia French of Tennessee, who had criticized him for his posturing in 1860 at Beersheba Springs, wrote, ". . . That young tiger-cat whose claws were once [1860] all sheathed in velvet—Ulric Dahlgren. He is now a colonel in the Union Army, and I presume will have a chance to show his talons—and talents."[20] She further denounced Ulric after the news traveled south that Abraham Lincoln had visited the young man's bedside when he was brought home. Then, in a few months Secretary of War Edwin M. Stanton approved Ulric's promotion to colonel, skipping the intermediate rank of major. When he was well enough, Ulric was fitted with a wooden leg and vowed he would ride again in combat. Although maimed, he was headstrong about proving his commitment to his country. From what we know of his cousin Charlie Routh and Charlie's four years of service in northern Virginia, the same code of honor and the same recklessness drove Charlie as well.

ॐ

In July 1863, Charles G. Dahlgren bought more than 101 acres in DeKalb County, Georgia, east of Atlanta, from Daniel Melton for $8,000.[21] Part of this property, near Decatur, was bounded by Sugar Creek and included a spring. It was good farmland that would eventually become choice building sites. Years later, one of Dahlgren's younger sons, John Armfield, noted in the family papers that his father bought the property for two hundred bales of cotton, "so stated by Father to a Mr. Lyle of Atlanta, July 18, 1863."[22] Whatever the terms of the transaction, the records indicate that the vendor was illiterate and agreed to the sale by making his mark. With Dahlgren at the time was son John Adolph, who witnessed Melton's "sign" on the deed. The following April, John Adolph was called back to validate Melton's mark. For some reason, that formality was repeated in July 1864, and the transaction was finally recorded in 1869 in Fulton County. The registrar's records fail to indicate any additional details.

After buying the town lot in Atlanta and the farm near Decatur, Charles Dahlgren went by rail to South Georgia to look for more land.

Albany, in Dougherty County, appealed to him for a variety of reasons. The area had soil proven ideal for cotton; the Flint River was a means of sending crops to market; there was access to Atlanta by rail; the farms in Dougherty County were comparatively large, with twenty-eight containing more than 1,000 acres; and the county boasted that it was "the wealthiest in the United States, with an average capital of $22,747 for each voter."[23] It was also a conservative, strongly secessionist community that had supported Breckinridge in 1860. When Lincoln was elected, the editor of the Albany *Patriot* declared that anyone circulating Northern newspapers in Albany should be "ferreted out and hanged to the highest limb on the first tree."[24]

General Dahlgren liked what he found in Dougherty County and purchased 750 acres, 8 miles south of Albany, on 19 October 1863. He paid William E. Collins $30,000 for the tract and made arrangements for his hands to prepare the ground for spring planting.[25] In the 1860 census, Collins is listed with twenty-seven slaves, fifteen males and twelve females. They were not mentioned in the sale. Dahlgren left Mary Edgar and the children in Atlanta with the house servants, and the railroad between the two cities was the link that kept them in touch. In spite of Lee's defeat in the three-day battle of Gettysburg and the surrender of Vicksburg on 4 July, the Dahlgrens were determined to maintain a hopeful stand in Georgia.

During the autumn of 1863, Mary Edgar wrote to her stepson Bernard ("Berney") in Natchez and gave him the family's news.[26] She reported on a number of refugees from Nashville and Natchez who had managed to cross the Union lines. "It was an unexpected pleasure seeing Mr. [William] Cannon [of Glencannon near Llangollen]. Am sorry he cannot remain longer. He will give you a better account than I can be permitted to write." She told him about a visit from Charlie Routh, who had come to Atlanta on furlough: "He was well. . . . I disliked to see Charlie leave. He is such a good & noble boy." She told Bernard of looking ahead to Christmas and the pleasures of the season. "Eggnog & turkey are both the order of the holiday." It is a cheerful letter designed to raise Bernard's spirits and to assure him "all will come right in the end. . . . These are some of the shadows of life & are given to try us & make men & women of us."

In quite a different vein, however, she lamented the impressment of Llangollen by Federal troops and worried about the furniture and household items left there. Llangollen was a prime target for the Yankees because of General Dahlgren's rank and absence and his determination to continue his support of the Confederacy. Nevertheless, Mary Edgar asked Bernard to salvage what he could and to send several articles to her in Atlanta: "I wrote [you] by Lieut. [Aaron] S[tanton, son of David Stanton of The Elms, Natchez] for you to look in the linen chest [at Llangollen] & send me a bolt of table linen & napkins. The handsomest piece . . . send shirting . . . my colored table cloth . . . some shoes for me & the children—Morty, Van, & Rowan—by Lieut. Stanton." Natchez, in spite of the Yankee occupation, was apparently a better place for "articles you think I would most need" than Atlanta in 1863. If the eggnog and turkey materialized that Christmas, they would be rare indeed and the envy of the other refugees.

Mary Edgar closed her letter with instructions to Mr. Dolan "to take my chest & carpets out to Dr. [Barlow] Baldwin's [where] they would be safe" outside Union lines. She advised Bernard to dispose of "wines & such things . . . as they may be disturbed & no telling what the Yankees won't do." Finally, she inquired about the servants—Julius & Pheby & "old Aunt Dinah." The letter reflects a great many concerns but ends on a note of optimism.

Mary Edgar Dahlgren had just turned twenty-three that September.

◌໐

The Dahlgrens spent Christmas and the winter months of 1863–64 safe behind the lines in South Georgia. Peace and a resemblance of tranquility were perhaps more possible there than anywhere else in the Confederacy except Texas. They found a number of other families of their rank and station with whom they could share social affairs, dinners, and excursions. Basic provisions for the table and provender for the horses and mules were ample, as South Georgia was also one of the major supply areas for the Confederate military. Prices were more reasonable than those in Atlanta, and neighbors vied with each other to provide delicacies, as well as the necessities. General Dahlgren had a carriage drawn by fine horses, and he entertained the children and their friends in a large pleasure boat on the Flint River. The horses, carriage, and boat were probably part of the purchase from Collins. The general and Mary Edgar were often seen on the main roads making calls on local families, including the Callaways, Mallarys, and Andrews.[27]

In March 1864, the Dahlgrens were stricken by the news of Ulric Dahlgren's death while the young nephew was leading a cavalry raid on Richmond under the command of Gen. Judson Kilpatrick. Dahlgren and Kilpatrick first joined forces in Virginia at Culpeper Courthouse, rode together as far as Mount Pleasant, and separated there. They expected to surprise Richmond with two points of attack, Kilpatrick from the north and Dahlgren, after crossing the James, from the south. Plans went awry, however, when Dahlgren and his 460 troopers were unable to ford the swollen James River. They were forced to move north and east away from the city, eventually to be chased and ambushed by a Richmond patrol near King and Queen Courthouse.

The word was quickly broadcast throughout North and South—newspapers noted that Ulric was the admiral's second son and a colonel at age twenty—and there was damaging evidence in the orders found on his body that, in addition to freeing the starving Union inmates in Libby Prison, his mission was to assassinate Jefferson Davis and his cabinet. "What a diabolical attempt on the part of Colonel Dahlgren," wrote the same Mrs. Mallard of Atlanta to her mother, "to liberate the [Union prisoners in Libby Prison], kill our President, and burn Richmond."[28] Southerners shared her outrage when the Richmond papers printed verbatim the "diabolical" document from Ulric's coat pocket: "[W]e will cross the James River into Richmond, destroying the bridges after us and exhorting the released prisoners to destroy and burn the hateful city; and do not allow the Rebel leader Davis and his traitorous crew to escape . . . Jeff Davis and Cabinet must be killed on the spot."[29] After the discovery of this document, the Southern press referred to Dahlgren as Ulric the Hun.

Ulric's body was found lying face down in a trough of mud. It had been riddled by buckshot in his back and also mutilated by the local brigands bent on vengeance. They had cut off a finger to take the ring that his little sister Elizabeth had given him and carried the body to Richmond to exhibit it in the railroad station. There, it was jeered and spat upon. His wooden leg was displayed in a Richmond shop window. Finally, responsible authorities stole the corpse away and buried it secretly in an unmarked grave outside Richmond.[30]

This was Ully, the son and brother and nephew and cousin, surveyor of Marydale and Beersheba Springs, a fallen hero and Union martyr. The admiral grieved openly. President Lincoln came to the Navy Yard to offer his consolation. The general and his family in Georgia spoke in somber tones about Ully's visits to Natchez and Marydale. The servants remembered his galloping the colts and his ease with the rifle.

While preparing for the Kilpatrick raid, Ulric had written to his father to express his enthusiasm for and solemn commitment to the action. With the loss of one leg, limping on a wooden substitute and awkwardly assisted by a crutch, Ulric felt that he still had not fulfilled his promises to his father and his country. He vowed again to uphold the tradition of honor expected of him. "[T]here is a grand raid to be made, and I am to have a very important command. If successful it will be the grandest thing on record; and if it fails, many of us will 'go up' . . . but it is an undertaking that if I were not in, I should be ashamed to show my face again."[31] With the failed raid on Richmond and his death by ambush on 2 March, Ulric's valor had been tested for the last time.

In a sentence recalling the reaction to young Dahlgren's death and the violation of his corpse in Virginia, historian Bruce Catton later wrote: "So in both North and South there was fury, and the propagandists righteously sowed the wind, and the war between the sections, which once seemed almost like a tournament, had at last hardened into the pattern of total war."[32] The two Dahlgren families—North and South—

did not feel the exact fury of the aroused abstractionists on both sides, but shared a deeper grief over the loss of their own flesh and blood.

A few months after Ulric's death, the same degree of family mourning cast a gloom over Lincoln's White House. At the battle of Chickamauga on 20 September, Confederate Gen. Benjamin H. Helm fell mortally wounded. News of his death was speedily relayed to the President and Mary Todd Lincoln. Helm was the husband of Mary's half sister, Emilie Todd, who was living in Selma, Alabama, and affirming her support of her husband. After Helm's funeral in Atlanta, Emilie made her way to Washington and stayed quietly at the White House. She was grateful for Lincoln's intervention in getting across the lines. The loss that the sisters shared, like that of thousands of families, had become, after three years of internecine war, the nation's incomparable tragedy, its compelling and inescapable grief.

$$\alpha \wp$$

Bernard Dahlgren wrote to his father from Llangollen on 13 April 1864, six weeks after Ulric's death: "I am glad you are going to try and I hope will succeed in recovering the body of Ully. I shall write to Uncle John and let him know."[33] Perhaps the general would have some influence with Confederate leaders in Richmond if he implored them to locate his nephew's body and send it through the lines to Washington. Although he diligently tried, the Rebel brother was not successful. To exhume Ulric and openly convey the body out of Richmond was to invite further acts of desecration. Emotions ran too high. Only two men, one a black gravedigger, knew the whereabouts of Ulric's body after it was interred under cover of night. They were under oath and at risk of their lives if they revealed the secret.[34]

On 24 April, Admiral Dahlgren arranged a memorial service at the First Presbyterian Church in Washington to honor the young colonel and his attempt to free the suffering Federal prisoners in Richmond. The Reverend Dr. Byron Sunderland chose II Samuel, 3:34, as his text: "Thy hands were not bound, nor Thy feet put into fetters: as a man falleth before wicked men, so fellest thou. And all the people wept again over him!" The eulogy was printed by Admiral Dahlgren in a monograph of forty-eight pages. It reviewed Ulric's life: his family, siblings, schooling, horsemanship, military assignments, and the amputation of his leg after the wound received at Hagerstown had failed to heal. The minister mentioned both his brothers—Charles Bunker "in the trenches at Vicksburg" and Paul at the Naval Academy at Newport. There was no reference to a Confederate uncle and cousins fighting for the South; no mention of Charlie Routh on horse furlough and ill in a Richmond boarding house at the time of the raid. The Reverend Mr. Sunderland closed his remarks by asking the mourners to share with him "a pious and reverential awe" at the life and deeds of the fallen hero.[35]

The *Richmond Daily Examiner,* as expected, praised Lt. James Pollard on 5 March for "the brilliant affair of a small body of Confederate cavalry" that attacked the Dahlgren raiders, ambushed them at 11 P.M., and killed "the wretch who commanded them. . . . It would have been well if the body of the land pirate had been gibbeted in chains on the spot where he fell." The instructions found on Dahlgren's body were of a "diabolical character," reported James A. Seddon, Confederate Secretary of War, and he straightway published them in full. With evidence of this kind, the hatred and bitterness raged anew and swiftly obliterated all prayers for peace.[36]

ᘉᘏ

Meanwhile, in the world of politics, the calendar for 1864 called for national elections. The country had become more deeply and bitterly divided than ever, and there was failing confidence by many Northerners in Lincoln's military appointees. The Union party mustered delegates in Baltimore, however, and nominated Lincoln again as its candidate for president and Democrat Andrew Johnson of Tennessee for vice president. Northerners complained about the way the war had dragged on for three years without bringing the weakened South to its knees. Although there were overtures from Richmond to discuss terms for ending the war, a peace mission to Canada headed by Horace Greeley came to naught. In order to satisfy his critics and to be reelected in November, Lincoln vowed "to prosecute the war," a major plank in his platform.

Part of Lincoln's promise was made good on 2 September when General Sherman burned Atlanta and again divided the Confederate forces. With the news from Atlanta, the North began to renew its confidence, and Lincoln was reelected on 8 November by a margin of about half a million votes. Soon after the election, Sherman mustered his troops outside Atlanta and led them, pillaging and burning, on a scorched-earth foray 300 miles long and 40 miles wide to Savannah. The Deep South shook now under the onslaught of total war as the tidal wave made its way summarily to the sea.

General Dahlgren and his family fled Atlanta when Sherman approached. There was skirmishing at Sugar Creek and on part of the Dahlgren property.[37] The Dahlgrens retreated to Albany and the acres they called Soldier's Home as Sherman marched on.

Inflation was growing to disastrous proportions as prices for food and the bare necessities skyrocketed in Georgia during the fall of 1864. Civilians and the military alike found cause to shudder. On 17 November, a young Sergeant Barber of the 15th Illinois Volunteer Infantry, a prisoner near Millen, Georgia, wrote in his diary, "[M]eal sells at ten cents a pint, rice sixty cents a quart, salt five cents a teaspoon, sweet potatoes twenty dollars a bushel."[38] A civilian in Albany had noted that lard was selling for $3 a pound, turpentine for $12 a gallon, brandy at $50 a bottle, and shoes for $80 a pair.[39]

Dahlgren had patriotically invested in Confederate Treasury Notes. There is one in his Confederate service record in the National Archives. It was issued by the Depository Office, Macon, Georgia, and reflects a deposit of $1,100 on 17 November 1864, Old Issue, for which he would be paid $733.34 in "Notes of the New Issue . . . when the Notes of the New Issue are received." It is likely that such exchanges were never made. By 7 May 1865, when Dahlgren left Georgia, the Confederate notes were generally refused.

On 4 December 1864, in time for Christmas, Charlie Routh wrote his family from the headquarters of the Cavalry Corps in Northern Virginia. He was glad to have their earlier letter and to know they were still "comfortably situated" in South Georgia, "not disturbed by Yankees," and able to make a good crop. "How are all the Negroes?" he asked. "Well, I hope." He was assuming they had not forsaken the general and his family.

Charlie reported some news brought him from Natchez. His brother Bernard was "acting in the capacity of a Scout and his actions have been a little remarkable." Then he made a request: "I would like very much to have Ully's likeness. His Father's letter I saw but did not admire much . . . he allows himself to become too violent, which is bad taste." Charlie's comments clearly represent a combination of loyalty to his cousin and a stoic attitude toward the casualties of war. Charlie felt that his Uncle John's public mourning for Ully was excessive, lugubrious, not becoming a military leader.[40] He also expressed a wish for a furlough to Marydale for a few weeks "but fear it is an impossibility. On entering the army one finds a realization of the sentence that Dante found written on the gates of Hell: He who enters here must leave all hope behind."[41] This familiar quotation was painted on a wooden shingle tacked over the door of the bachelor cabin at the rear of the Dahlgren cottage at Beersheba Springs. It survived intact and kept Charlie Routh and Dante posted in memory well into the twentieth century.

⊘⊘

Through the eyes of a teenage girl, Eliza Andrews, who kept a diary at the end of the war, one can see occasional glimpses of the Dahlgrens in early spring 1865. Because of heavy March rains and flooded streams in Dougherty County, it was difficult to travel from one plantation to another. Eliza Andrews wrote on March 21: "Sister and I thought at first of getting Gen. Dahlgren to send us across in his pleasure boat, but soon gave up the idea and concluded to stay at the Mallarys' till the creek became fordable. . . . Gen. and Mrs. Dahlgren called after dinner and said we ought to have stopped with them." Eliza then recorded some candid impressions: "Mrs. Dahlgren is a beautiful woman, and only twenty-two years old [actually twenty-four], while her husband is over sixty [actually almost fifty-four]. He is a pompous old fellow and entertained us by telling how his influence made Gen. Joseph E. Johnston commander-in-chief of the Army of Tennessee; how Hood lost Atlanta by not following his [Dahlgren's] advice; how he was the real inventor of the Dahlgren gun, which is generally attributed to his brother—the Yankee admiral—and so on."[42] By recording these notes in her diary and publishing them several years later, Eliza Andrews made clear that she thought the General was inclined to indulge in exaggeration.

It is a matter of record, however, that Dahlgren did send his advice to Confederate leaders during his time in Atlanta, notably to General Johnston and Jefferson Davis. One letter to Johnston, then at Meridian, Mississippi, dated 2 December 1863, outlined Dahlgren's reasons for having the cotton burned in the vicinity of Natchez as the gunboats of the enemy advanced: "The cotton nor any other property of our citizens should be destroyed, if possible to be avoided, but cotton at least should be unhesitantly destroyed before it should be suffered to strengthen our enemy or invigorate the prosecution of the war."[43] Thus, Dahlgren continued to rationalize and defend his earlier orders; however, any claim of his that shows he was influential in General Johnston's selection as commander of the Army of Tennessee has not come to light.

On 3 December 1863, Dahlgren also sent a letter to Jefferson Davis in Richmond. Again, the subject was the value of any cotton that would fall into Union hands. As a cotton grower and broker, Dahlgren showed how cotton bought in Mississippi for $250 a bale was sold in Liverpool for $500, "which at the present rate of exchange in New York would bring $750." He knew that profiteering was running amok. Then, he repeated his argument for keeping the cotton from the Yankees: "I think, therefore, that I have clearly shown that our enemy can only be saved from bankruptcy by spoilation from us without cost to himself and with numerous profits. So long as this is suffered so long will our enemy strive and labor to continue to war, urged on by all the passions of native fanaticism, envy, and cupidity."[44] Regarded in one light, this letter is a defense of his May 1862 orders that angered his neighbors up and down the river. In another light, it argues that Southern cotton could be the chief factor in financing the North and prolonging the war indefinitely. This is the final communication from Dahlgren to find a place in the

Official Records, although there might have been other such letters from the armchair general, for he never seemed reluctant to give advice and suggest strategies that he believed workable. His devotion to the South and its independence was beyond question, but his confidence in its leaders was another matter.

Eliza Andrews, earnest about her diary and her social life, reported another meeting with the Dahlgrens on 27 March 1865: ". . . [W]ent to call on the Callaways, Mallarys, and Dahlgrens. The general and his wife were just starting out to make calls when we drove up, so we all went along together."[45] The same day that Eliza and the Dahlgrens went calling in the neighborhood, Union Rear Adm. Henry Knox Thatcher began his assault on the city of Mobile, Alabama. While the Dahlgrens were keeping the social conventions of the fading South, they were also making plans to return to Mississippi. The dream for Southern independence was finally at an end. The enemy was as close as Mobile and attempting to remove Confederate torpedoes at the mouth of the Blakely River. Three Union ships already had been sunk, but Mobile's capture was only a matter of days. Meanwhile, the planters still looked for comfort in the company of their neighbors as reports of the surrender of Robert E. Lee and the Confederate forces at Appomattox reached Georgia. Many Southerners felt that they were being forced to accept the bitter judgment of a punitive God.

Cornelia Peak McDonald, a gentlewoman of Richmond, was "seized with utter despair. I felt that God had forsaken us, and I wished, Oh! I wished that He would at one blow sweep me and mine from the earth."[46] A Methodist minister and Confederate chaplain, Richard Polis Ransom, reminded a hospital ward of sick and dying soldiers in Georgia of the iron rod and vengeful ways promised by the God of the Old Testament. Ransom preached that the Almighty was dealing with them and the South as a surgeon would deal with spiritually sick and troubled men; that they were morally ill; that God was giving them bitter medicines to cleanse their souls.[47]

The ragged, starved soldiers that Eliza Andrews saw returning on foot to their homes in Georgia were pathetic signs of the South's defeat: "These are unceremonious times, when social distinctions are forgotten and the raggedest rebel that tramps the road in his country's service is entitled to more honor than a king. We stood on the bank a long time, talking to the poor fellows and listening to their adventures." But Eliza was confident that there soon would be a supply of young men at the picnics, balls, masquerade parties, and April Fool frolics. New dresses would soon replace those pieced together from faded taffeta and decaying silk. Then she wrote her solution to the problems of the Negroes: "I think the best thing to do, if the Confederacy were [ever] to gain its independence, would be to make a law confiscating the negroes of any man who was cruel to them, and allowing them to choose their own master. Of course they would choose the good men, and this would make it to everybody's interest to treat them properly."[48] But the Confederacy had already lost its fight for independence and the slaves were already free and the times that followed would give Eliza Andrews a stinging slap on the side of her pretty little cheek.

❧

While Eliza Andrews and the Dahlgrens were making calls, Mary Edgar was still nursing Edgar McWhorter, born on 14 May 1864, her third son in four years. She left him, Van, and Rowan in the care of servants when she and the general went visiting. General Dahlgren also made frequent trips into Albany to find supplies and gather news. He was friendly with a prosperous South Carolinian, Thomas H. Willingham of the Barnwell District, and the two struck up a deal. Willingham owned a large plantation near Dahlgren's and seventy-seven slaves. His relatives, W. A. and E. G. Willingham, also held tracts of land in Dougherty County and fifty-four slaves between them.[49] With the end of the Confederacy at hand, Dahlgren expressed his intention to return to Natchez, and Thomas Willingham was apparently looking for further investments in South Georgia. They agreed on a price, and Dahlgren signed the deed for his 750 acres on 30 March. He needed the money, and Willingham arranged to pay him $75,000,[50] probably in Georgia bank notes. The Dahlgrens were welcome to remain at Soldier's Home until they could make arrangements to return to Natchez.

Many obstacles faced travelers in Georgia after Sherman reached Atlanta and crippled it as a railway center. To wreak their vengeance on the Rebels, his men pulled up railroad tracks, heated the rails, and bent sections around the trunks of nearby trees. Bridges were torched. Only a few locomotives were left to run on whatever tracks remained. In May, Eliza Andrews watched Jefferson Davis and his cavalry escort stop briefly in Washington, Georgia; the president and his men were outlaws fleeing capture. She also watched streams of demoralized Confederate soldiers, hungry and footsore, stumbling on the road to home. Among those who had stayed with General Johnston in North Carolina and fought at Bentonville against General Sherman was Charlie Routh Dahlgren. He had been faithful to his pledge to his father. Soon, he too would begin the long journey home.[51]

✂❧

On 4 April, five days before Lee surrendered to Grant at Appomattox, an incident occurred in Natchez that almost took the life of eighteen-year-old Bernard Dahlgren. Dr. F. A. W. Davis, a Natchez physician and friend of the Dahlgren family, sent an urgent plea to Admiral Dahlgren in Washington and asked for his immediate intercession with the forces occupying Natchez. The letter is a strong indication of the turmoil in the South:

[Bernard] had been sent to this place [Natchez] nearly two years ago on business by his Father. . . . Instead of returning home as instructed . . . he remained and after the occupancy of this place he was staying at Mr. [Haller] Nutt's [Longwood]. His house was frequented by a large number of Federal officers who spent days and nights there. They noticed Bernard, associated with him as an equal. Of course a boy of his age was flattered. They led him to the gaming table and to drinking. It was under these circumstances he took the Oath [of Allegiance to the Union]. His money all gone he said to me he wished to go home. I urged him then as I had done before to go to his Father [in Georgia]. He promised me he would do so, but instead of going to Georgia he joined a Confederate Company [of irregulars] near this place.

This morning . . . [Bernard] was brought into this city badly wounded, it may be fatally. As the personal friend of your brother [Charles] I visited Bernard . . . and was anxious to have him with my family where he could have comforts and attention that he cannot get in the Hospital. I visited General [John Wynn] Davidson who is in command of the Post and asked of him permission to bring him to my house. He said he could not grant it, that he [Bernard] had taken the Oath of Allegiance [to the United States] and should he recover he would be tried and shot [for joining the Confederate guerrillas].

Have you not the influence with the Government to prevent so sad a catastrophe [?]. If Bernard took the Oath I do not think he thought of its Solemnity. I hope this poor boy's case may not only enlist your deepest sympathy but your most earnest efforts to save his life should he recover from this wound.

Signed F. A. W. Davis[52]

It was mid-April before Admiral Dahlgren, who was in Charleston following the city's surrender, received Dr. Davis's plea for Bernard. The admiral directed his sister Patty in Washington to go directly to Secretary of War Stanton and plead for his direct intercession.[53]

The forthright Patty obviously saw Secretary Stanton, showed him the letter from Dr. Davis, and got her nephew moved from the army hospital in Natchez to the Davis home, where he was eventually nursed back to life. General Davidson was rewarded in print for this change of heart years later when Bernard's older half-sister, Sarah Ann Ellis Dorsey, cited him in her *Recollections of Henry Watkins Allen:* "I dare here to express openly my deep gratitude to General [John Wynn] Davidson for his firmness in protecting my young brother, who had been desperately wounded in a skirmish near Natchez, from the violence of a cruel mob of brutal men and negro soldiers; who would else have torn the bleeding boy in pieces."[54] In Georgia, General and Mrs. Dahlgren were not yet aware of this incident. They would not hear of the nearly fatal injuries Bernard had sustained as a guerilla until they returned to Mississippi.

❦

The Charles Dahlgrens were still isolated in South Georgia when an explosion nearly took the life of Admiral Dahlgren on 1 March 1865. While commanding the Atlantic blockade during the summer of 1863, he had been at personal risk regularly as he led attacks on Charleston's forts in a monitor from the pilothouse, the most exposed portion of the ship. After the Union occupation of Georgetown, South Carolina, a stubborn Confederate holdout, Dahlgren left the city and confidently steamed down Winyah Bay in his flagship *Harvest Moon*. He was relieved to be headed for occupied Charleston on the first anniversary of Ulric's ambush and death. The admiral was sadly preoccupied because he had been unable to recover his son's body from the Confederates and take it to Washington for last rites.

Although the bloodshed was nearly at an end, Dahlgren experienced the sudden destruction of his flagship on 1 March: "It was nearly 8 o'clock, and I was waiting breakfast in the cabin when instantly a loud noise and shock occurred, and the bulkhead separating the cabin from the wardroom was shattered and driven in toward me," he reported. At first, he thought the boiler had burst, but then he smelled gunpowder and concluded that the magazine had been hit. Finally, the explosion was found to be the work of a torpedo, even though "it had been reported to me that the channel had been swept,"[55] Dahlgren said.

A Dahlgren biographer dramatized the scene of pandemonium:

[Dahlgren] donned a peacoat and cap and went outside. Frightened men struggled to lower the boats. The admiral squeezed past them, heading down the gangway to the upper deck ladder. Wood fragments cluttered the open spaces. The fleet captain, his white nightgown billowing behind, ran toward Dahlgren. . . . Dahlgren rightly determined the *Harvest Moon* had struck a torpedo and was sinking fast. [Rescued by a tug alongside, they steamed for another ship and] the admiral transferred his flag. The *Harvest Moon* sank in five minutes. . . . [56]

☙☞

Two of the Dahlgren brothers, John and Charles, having borne arms against each other, survived the Civil War in America. Each had been spared injury and death in combat. That was hardly the story of the sons. Dutiful to the allegiances of the fathers, the sons had volunteered their names, their lives, and their honor on opposite sides. Charles Bunker Dahlgren, the admiral's eldest son, had a hazardous naval career that ended with the bloody assault on the Confederates at Fort Fisher, North Carolina, early in 1865. He was executive officer of the USS *Gettysburg* and one of two officers not killed or wounded among the heavy losses. After the war, Charles Bunker declined to follow his father and serve in the peacetime Navy. Years later, however, he was commander of the New Jersey naval reserves and furnished two ships, the *Montauk* and *Resolute,* for the Spanish-American War. He died in 1912 at the age of seventy-two.[57]

Ulric Dahlgren, the admiral's second son, was attached briefly to the Navy on special assignments for his father and then joined cavalry units in Maryland and Pennsylvania. Headstrong and fearless, he was quick to ignite in anger and to act impulsively under stress. Feeling that he had been misled on purpose by Martin Robinson, a Negro guide in Virginia—a man whom he had falsely accused—Ulric, on one leg and a crutch, was unable to ford his cavalry across a swollen stream on the way to Richmond. In a rage, he stripped extra harness from his saddle and ordered Robinson hanged to a nearby tree as punishment for false directions.[58] Ulric's own death, a few days later, allowed him little time for remorse.

General Dahlgren's oldest son, Charles Routh, enlisted with other young Mississippians in a ground swell of patriotism during the first weeks of the war. He remained faithful to his father, the South, and his comrades-in-arms throughout the next four years of fighting in Virginia.

He and his cousin Ulric came within a few miles of facing each other in the vicinity of Richmond in 1864. Charlie Routh's youthful, romantic notions of valor came to an end when he surrendered with Confederate forces under General Johnston in North Carolina in 1865. When he arrived home, he was a broken man, a youth bereft of illusions, a dutiful son not ever to know the joy, honor, and rewards of the prodigal.[59]

Bernard Dahlgren, the general's second son, never forgave the home guard in Natchez for denying him enlistment because of his age and physique. As the war progressed, he scouted for the guerillas harassing the Yankees in Adams County. Then the Federal forces in Natchez took Bernard into their confidence and shared with him their supply of food and drink at Longwood, after Llangollen was occupied. Probably under the influence of intoxicants, he succumbed to Yankee enticements and took the oath of allegiance to the United States.[60]

The general's third son, John Adolph ("Pudge") Dahlgren, at age fourteen, was in a group of young enlisted men to know firsthand the fatal day of surrender at Vicksburg. He felt ashamed of the fumbling of Confederate leaders and, along with his father, denounced their mistakes. Experiencing his first defeat at that age and being further disillusioned by Appomattox two years later when he was sixteen years old, Pudge spent his adult life breaking faith and walking away from personal relationships. His instability was marked by precipitous changes in jobs and means of livelihood and the abandonment of two wives, a son by one wife, and a daughter by another.[61] His death seems not to have been recorded but is presumed to have occurred somewhere in California after 1920.

Bernard Ulric Dahlgren
(1784–1824), Swedish and
Norwegian consul in the
United States, husband of
Martha Rowan.

Frederick William Kratz

Martha Rowan
(1787–1838), mother of
John, Charles, William, and
Martha (Patty) Dahlgren.

Frederick William Kratz

Charles Gustavus Dahlgren (1811–1888), banker, planter, Natchez militia officer, builder, and dynast.

Portrait by Washington Cooper, Tennessee State Museum

Mary Routh Ellis Dahlgren (1813–1858), widow of Thomas Ellis, married Charles Dahlgren in 1840. The debts she brought to their union would hound Dahlgren for years.

Telfair Museum, Savannah, Georgia

Dunleith, originally Routhland, built by Charles Dahlgren in 1856.

Mary Edgar Vannoy Dahlgren before her marriage to Charles Dahlgren.

Mary Edgar Vannoy Dahlgren (1840–1928), second wife of Charles Dahlgren, by Washington Cooper, at the time of their marriage in 1859.

Charles Routh Dahlgren (1841–1867), son of Charles and Mary Routh, spent four years in the Jeff Davis Legion, Mississippi Cavalry. He fought extensively in the campaigns of the eastern theatre.

Bernard Dahlgren (1847–1868), second son of Charles Dahlgren and Mary Routh, tried to enlist in Confederate service, was rejected because of his age. He spent the war in Natchez looking after Llangollen and spying on Union forces.

Tennessee Historical Society Collection, Tennessee State Library

John Adolph Dahlgren (1849–?), third son of Charles Dahlgren and Mary Routh, joined 31st Louisiana Infantry at age fourteen, captured and paroled at Vicksburg in 1863, scout for his father's wagon train in 1865, social charmer, date and place of death unknown.

Carol Baker Ruffin

Austin Mortimer Dahlgren (1856–1906), fourth son of Charles Dahlgren and Mary Routh, lawyer, business man, died in the insane asylum at Meridian, Mississippi in 1906.

Confederate volunteers at Natchez Courthouse, circa 1862.

Charles's brother, Union Admiral John A. Dahlgren (1809–1870), father of Ulric, inventor of the famous Dahlgren naval guns.

Union cavalryman Ulric Dahlgren (1842–1864), Charles's nephew, was killed after attempting a raid on Richmond, Virginia, in 1864. Shock waves went through the South when documents allegedly found on Dahlgren's body were purported to have ordered the assassination of Confederate president Jefferson Davis.

Gustavus Vannoy Dahlgren (1860–1929) was the first son of Charles and Mary Edgar Dahlgren. At age four he made the long journey by wagon train with his parents from Georgia back to Mississippi.

Charles G. Dahlgren, circa 1870, after he lost his property in the South and became a Confederate carpetbagger on Wall Street.

Bernardina Berg Avdek

Bernardina Dahlgren Berg (1878–1920), ninth and last child born to Charles and Mary Edgar. She was idolized by older brother Van until she eloped with William Berg at age thirty-four.

Llangollen, built by Charles Dahlgren in 1859, destroyed by fire 1932.

CHARLES G. DAHLGREN & COMPANY,

112 & 114 BROADWAY.

Secure Capital for Bankers, Merchants, Incorporated Companies, Manufacturers, &c.

MAKE CASH LOANS ON MARKETABLE SECURITIES, MERCHANDISE, AND EFFECT SALES ON COMMISSIONS.

INVESTMENTS MADE IN BUSINESS OF AN APPROVED ORDER. FOR PARTIES WITH CAPITAL, WITHOUT CHARGE.

We take pleasure in offering, by permission, the following well known names as our reference, together with many others

William Butler Duncan, of Duncan, Sherman & Co., Bankers, corner of Pine and Nassau Sts.
Vermilye & Co., Bankers, 19 Nassau St.
Henry Clews, Banker, 34 Wall St.
P. C. Calhoun, President Fourth National Bank.
George W. Duer, President Bank of the State of New York.
Jas. Robb, of James Robb, King & Co., Bankers, 59 Pine St.
J. D. Vermilye, President of the Merchants Bank.
Geo. H. Gilbert, of Farnham, Gilbert & Co., Bankers

F. Marquand, Banker, Equitable Building, 120 Broadway.
E. J. Blake, President Mercantile Bank.
Charles F. Secor, V. P. & W. R. R. Co., 80 Broadway.
V. K. Stevenson, Pres't Real Estate Trust Co., corner of Broadway and Thomas St.
M. Gardner, of Evans, Gardner & Co., Wholesale Dry Goods, 331 Broadway.
Jas. McLean, of Cochran, McLean & Co., Wholesale Dry Goods, Broadway, cor. Grand St.

Inman, Swann & Co., Merchants, N. Y. Cotton Exchange.
Geo. S. Hart, of G. S. Hart & Co., Merchants, 35 Pearl St.
T. C. Durant, 20 Nassau St.
Henry Young, Capitalist, 49 Nassau St.
W. C. Alexander, Pres't Equitable Life Ins. Co.
Jas. Stokes, Pres't Manhattan Life Ins. Co.
Edward A. Jones, Pres't National Life Ins. Co.
Pliny Freeman, Pres't Globe Life Ins. Co.
Clark, Walcott & Co., Bankers, 29 Broad St.

Samuel H. Howell, Jr.

Letterhead for Charles G. Dahlgren & Co., N. Y., 1872.

John Armfield Dahlgren (1870–1938), family promoter and collector. He kept an obsolete horse-drawn streetcar from Atlanta in his back yard.

Mary Edgar Vannoy Dahlgren (1840–1928) at age eighty-five in 1925, with daughter Virginia and son John Armfield on the steps of their house, built by son Van, near Manchester, Tennessee. They represented the last shaken remnants of Dahlgren's Southern dynasty.

Ellen Smith Vannoy Gardner, Mary Edgar's older sister, who presided over every family birth and death.

M͡ʀ DAHLGREN.

Consul de S. M. le Roi
de Suède & de Norvège.

Business card of Consul Bernard Dahlgren.

Seven

Leading His Family Home
by Wagon Train

When the last Confederate Congress adjourned in Richmond on 18 March 1865, its members struck out for their homes, making their way south or west by whatever means they could find. Confederate money was no longer negotiable. Transportation by train was limited and uncertain; buggies, carriages, and wagons, if available, were ramshackle. Stout horses were at a premium too high to afford except by the few travelers with greenbacks. Walking had already become the modus operandi for common soldiers like those sighted by Eliza Andrews in Georgia.

Among the lawmakers starting the long, uncertain journey home was Confederate Senator Williamson S. Oldham from Washington County, Texas. Leaving Richmond with him were Congressmen H. C. Burnett of Kentucky and J. D. C. Atkins of Tennessee. Their journey began by train, which took them as far as Greensboro, North Carolina. On another stretch, they traveled only forty-eight miles in forty-eight hours. They passed other trains at various stations along the way with locomotives out of order or with cars broken down. Finally, at Newnan, Georgia, near Atlanta, Burnett and Atkins sought transportation north to Kentucky and Tennessee. Until there was means of going west, Oldham accepted the hospitality of Arthur St. Clair Collier, who had served in the Confederate House of Representatives. This was the first of several homes that provided Oldham with a bed and food until he could resume his journey to Texas.

Fifty-six days out of Richmond, his strength by then sorely challenged,

109

Oldham was finally able to cross the flooded Mississippi. He had made it that far by wagon, horse, mule, yawl, and stagecoach. He had traveled through lawless stretches of the South where deserters, bushwhackers, and renegade bands of irregulars preyed on the civilian populace without mercy. As a high Confederate official, he dodged Yankee patrols bent on bringing him to justice. At one point, he was joined by John Bullock, a Confederate congressman with a price on his head, and Capt. Richard T. Harper, Bullock's brother-in-law. Fearing capture and internment, as was the fate of Jefferson Davis, Oldham and Bullock decided to travel under assumed names. Harper did not need this pretense because he was lucky enough to carry his parole papers with him. Later, in order to cross the swollen Mississippi, the three men built a makeshift raft at Bayou Macon.

On 12 June, after seventy-four days of hazardous travel and providential escapes, Oldham reached his home and family near Washington, Texas. He found that all organized government had been suspended and that throughout Texas "disorder, confusion, and anarchy prevailed." Yankee troops were lying in wait to arrest Confederate line officers and civilians with rank in the government. Oldham wrote later that he feared incarceration in a northern dungeon, so he crossed the Rio Grande to avoid arrest. He joined a number of other Confederates in Mexico, including Generals Cadmus Marcellus Wilcox, John Bankhead Magruder, Sterling Price, William Polk Hardeman, and Thomas Carmichael Hindman. In Mexico, he found time to recount his journey from Richmond and complete his "Memoirs of a Confederate Senator."[1]

Six weeks after Oldham began his long trek to Texas, General Dahlgren consulted whatever maps and atlases he found in Albany and devised a route by which he could take his family and servants home to Marydale. He planned to lead them along the post roads of southern Georgia, Alabama, and Mississippi. The Federals had engaged in less pillage in these areas than in the northern part of each state. The record of that journey of thirty-five days and 545 miles is set down in daily entries in a small, leatherbound volume, approximately 4 by 6 inches; the pages are lined but not numbered. All entries from 5 May to 9 June are in pencil and many are so smudged that they are virtually impossible to read. Yet most of the people and places can be identified and a narrative unity is established through the daily entries. It was a journey of risks, treacherous but imperative, a passage of hope for the fifty-four-year-old Dahlgren, his twenty-five-year-old wife, his children, and several servants. Daring, courageous, and ultimately heroic, it was a mission that twenty human beings, white and black, felt compelled to undertake—to return after two years to a home that might no longer exist. For General Dahlgren, whose country now lay prostrate in defeat, the weeks ahead would affirm his tenacity as a leader and his courage as head of his family.

Dahlgren's chief traveling companion and guide, Dr. Tully Stewart Gibson (1831–1870), was born in Jefferson County, Mississippi, and was related to the large Gibson family of Port Gibson. His father was Gibeon, a planter with holdings in Warren County, and his aunt was the wife of Jefferson Nailor, who ran successfully against Jefferson Davis in 1843 for the state legislature in Warren. Another relative was Brig. Gen. Randal Lee Gibson (1832–1892) of the 13th Louisiana Infantry, which he led at both Shiloh and Chickamauga.

After receiving a medical education, probably at one of the Kentucky institutions, Tully Gibson was practicing medicine in Claiborne County by 1858. When Mississippi seceded in 1861, Gibson joined the Sunflower Guards as a first lieutenant (later promoted to captain). In 1862, he participated in a number of eastern engagements from Seven Pines to Fredericksburg. While on furlough as recruiting officer in Mississippi in 1863, he married the widow Anna A. Crane on 11 March in Sunflower County. Shortly afterward, he returned to duty.

As Company I in the 21st Mississippi Infantry Regiment, the Sunflower Guards saw action in ten battles in Virginia and Maryland during 1862 and 1863. The unit went on to Gettysburg, where Gibson, then a captain, was severely wounded in the thigh. He was sent to South Carolina to recover. Partially restored to health, Gibson returned to Mississippi as a conscript enrolling officer in January 1864. Unable to return to active service, he was retired from the army under General Order No. 34 on 10 April 1864.[2]

General Dahlgren and Dr. Gibson would have been friends in Mississippi before the war. It is not clear exactly when Gibson joined Dahlgren in Georgia, but Dahlgren's diary notes that Gibson began the journey from Albany with the Dahlgrens and remained with them until 4 June 1865, when he is mentioned for the last time, presumably returning to Sunflower County.

Dr. Gibson, age thirty-three, and John Adolph Dahlgren, age sixteen, who had been paroled at Vicksburg at age fourteen, were indispensable to the success of the Dahlgrens' journey of 545 miles and thirty-five days. They rode the best horses and served as outriders for the carriages and wagons that followed. Gibson and Pudge Dahlgren galloped ahead as scouts to report on the condition of the roads, bridges, and fords that they would have to cross. They sought out friendly farmers willing to sell or barter needed supplies; they bargained with blacksmiths for repairs to the wagons and carriages. Both were armed with pistols against highwaymen, stragglers, and army deserters. The diary does not record any confrontations that required the use of arms, although the party traveled daily with dangers and hardships as part of a mass migration of agitated humanity.

As a businessman and banker, Dahlgren had spent his active life dealing with money in one form or another—banknotes, drafts, bills, checks— or in real estate, cotton, and slaves. Setting out on the journey across the South in 1865 with Confederate notes that proved worthless and a small amount of reserve in Georgia State bills, he had wisely anticipated some of the perils in getting his family back to the Marydale plantation. He loaded six wagons with provisions that he could use to barter with farmers and blacksmiths along the way. The general would become a huckster. He took bags of salt, which he exchanged for meal; bundles of thread, which he swapped for fodder and bacon; yards of shirting, which he sold for cash. He assumed the responsibility of twenty human beings, white and black, and the animals that pulled their vehicles over 550 miles in the heart of the moribund Confederacy.

The following excerpts are reproduced from Dahlgren's diary verbatim and without apology. The diary is unparalleled as a day-by-day account of the turmoil in the defeated South during May 1865. It has an immediacy not achieved by retrospective accounts written after the events, such as that of Williamson Oldham. Miraculously preserved and painfully deciphered, the diary is crucial to the Dahlgren saga.

Excerpts from the Diary of Charles G. Dahlgren,
5 May–10 June 1865

May 5—Friday morning left Soldier's Home* 8½ miles below Albany at 7 oc, my carriage, barouche, chariot, buggy & 8 mules. Mary, Self, [sons] Mortimer, Rowan, Van, McWhorter, [servants] Hannah, Rachel, Irene, Miles, Nelson, Adolphus. William R. [Robinson] to Columbus . . . overtook people 4 miles beyond Albany . . . Pudge, Dr. Gibson . . . camped 11 miles from Albany—traveled 20 miles.

May 6—Left camp. Robin's wagon injured . . . delayed 5 hours . . . stopped 12 o'clock dinner . . . camped right on Nochway river [Echawaynochaway]. Travelled 16 miles. [36†]

May 7—Left camp. Robin broke down. Reached Cuthbert 12 oc. Camped 5 miles beyond Cuthbert. Travelled 20 miles. [56] Confederate money refused by every one. Mr. L. at carriage shop made no charge for use of his shop tools & timber. . . .

May 8—Left camp at 8 oc. Crops poor, wanting rain, stopped 12 oc 6 miles from Eufa[u]la . . . heavy shower . . . staid in deserted cabin [crossed over Chattahoochee River] . . . reached Eufa[u]la 6 oc . . . camped on Abbeville Road 1 mile from town . . . broke Peter's Jersey wagon,‡ Nelson driving, broke my carriage twice, Miles driving. Lige's foot [Elijah's?] got entangled in wheel, nearly

---

*Soldier's Home was the name the Dahlgrens gave their plantation in South Georgia. This transcript was made with the generous help of Alma Kellogg Carpenter of Natchez.

†Numbers in brackets refer to the total miles traveled from Albany.

‡The Jersey wagon was light and straight-sided, with four supports for the canvas roof; there were roll-up side curtains; it was usually driven in the lead position by the wagon master, with a footboard for the driver.

broke it to pieces . . . saw Mr. Collins R Road agent . . . no letter from Col. Mitchell* nor money . . . Mr. [James] Harrison [Quitman County planter, 1787–1870] said Mrs. Johnson wished to go to Miss . . . called to see her but she was not ready. Mr. H. had sold out 1 March all his property for 240,000—was in Confed. money—in 90 days: the contract being in writing. I told him I thought he was bound & of course ruined. He has two sons living at Shreveport . . . Sam Harrison and Col. [William] Harrison in Confed. service [6th Louisiana Cavalry, 1829–1914] . . . [I] have promised to write to them. Wm. Robinson did not come as expected—and directed. Camped near Col. [David P.] Lewis, Representative in Congress†—wrote Col. Mitchell . . . travelled 22 miles. [78]

May 9—Left camp 8 oc . . . teams [left] at 4AM, heavy rain all night—Saw Dr. [W. M.] Nichol [of Nashville] in Cuthbert, had no tidings of Col. [Sterling] Cockrill‡ . . . supposed gone to Texas . . . was going to Nashville . . . roadway crowded with paroled soldiers from Lee's army . . . mended my carriage & Jersey at 12 oc. Camped at night 1 mile beyond Clayton . . . water very deep on road . . . a man passed in buggy reported Mr. [William] Robinson on the road on foot . . . left Adolphus & Pudge to wait for him . . . joined us at night with letters . . . Mr. Parsons going to Atlanta . . . Dr. [J. P.] Ford going to Nashville . . . [which he and Mrs. Ford had fled in April 1863 after a year of Federal occupation] . . . travelled 23 miles . . . weather cool & pleasant . . . children & all well. [100]

May 10—Left camp . . . weather pleasant . . . roads rough . . . bridges in bad order. . . . Confederate money totally refused . . .

---

*Probably Col. Julius Caesar Bonaparte Mitchell (1819–1869), 34th Alabama, who lived near Montgomery and Eufaula, Alabama.

†Lewis appears in *Biographical Register of the Confederate Congress*.

‡Sterling Robertson Cockrill (1804–1891), Nashvillian, whom Dahlgren would have known at Beersheba Springs, Tennessee.

would buy nothing . . . stopped at 12 oc . . . after dinner Hannah's team broke down and several others . . . crossed Hobdy's bridge and procured the use of Hobdy's shop to repair wagons . . . ten wheels out of order . . . serious job to repair them . . . travelled 20 miles [120]. Mr. [John A.] Hobdy was very kind and afforded all assistance . . . busy all day . . . people all well, mules in good order . . . weather fair.

May 11—Busy at repairs to wagon . . . for two months had ordered wagons in order [at Albany] and after starting found all out of condition and unfit to travel . . . very fortunate that Mr. Hobdy had several or the wheels could not have been repaired . . . very heavy rain after dinner . . . Mary and children kept dry in camp . . . the news of Lincoln's assassination [14 April] is confirmed, creating great excitement . . . traded 4 bundles of thread to Mr. Hobdy for 50 bundles fodder & 10 lbs. bacon . . . barter the only means of trade . . . no money to be had.

May 12— . . . [F]inished wheels . . . left camp at 11 oc . . . stopped at 8 oc . . . fed mules . . . 5 pm Robin broke one of his wheels to pieces . . . had to stop at shop to repair . . . worked hard all afternoon . . . weather very cool after rain . . . people all well . . . procured some wood to mend with and fix repairs . . . reports that Gov. Vance* & Alex Stephens† had been arrested and taken North . . . country filled with paroled soldiers . . . found that bridge over one of the creeks was washed away and had to turn down another road . . . travelled today 15 miles. [135]

May 13—Left camp at 2 PM . . . reports that [Andrew] Johnson Pres. of US has been assassinated . . . returned soldiers committing great depredations on the road . . . all greatly dissatisfied with conduct of war . . . many leaving for Texas [where Confederate

---

*Gov. Zebulon Baird Vance (1830–1894) of North Carolina; not arrested by Union troops until 13 May.
†Alexander Stephens (1812–1883), vice president of the Confederacy; arrested on 11 May at Liberty Hall; incarcerated at Fort Warren, Massachusetts.

forces had not surrendered] . . . travelled 11 miles . . . road crowded with returned soldiers from Lee's army . . . some committing depredations on the people . . . some leaving for Texas . . . [T]ravelled 11 miles. [146]

May 14—Left camp . . . weather pleasant . . . all well . . . Peter let his mules break two spokes out of a wheel . . . detained us much . . . all through carelessness by not putting link on wheel . . . Nelson ran against stump and broke single tree . . . all resulting from culpable carelessness . . . [reports of] the death of And. Johnson . . . soldiers from [Samuel Wragg] Ferguson's Cavalry* report having seen Pres. Davis at Abbeville in May with Ferguson and Breckinridge† . . . and that the enemy had advertised a large reward for him . . . if this be true his capture is certain . . . roads very bad . . . camped at 6 o'c near mill . . . repaired wagon and carriage . . . travelled 22 miles today . . . lost time by bridges being destroyed. [168]

May 15—Left camp . . . weather pleasant . . . roads tolerable . . . overtook many soldiers on their way home from Lee and Johnston; reported that Alabama returned to the Union 11th inst. . . . no forage or provisions of any kind upon the road to be procured . . . the enemy having destroyed or taken all to be had . . . country in terrible condition from enemy and robbers & deserters & others . . . stopped at 10 o'c 7 miles from Greenville . . . a band of ten men said to be upon the road robbing all to be met with . . . stopped at McKenzie Mill . . . traded 10 lbs. salt for 3 bushels meal . . . many soldiers going home to Miss. . . . travelled 24 miles . . . camped 1 mile from Greenville very late . . . 11 oc before got to rest. . . . [192]

May 16—Weather pleasant . . . a run-away negro stole one of

---

*Brig. Gen. Samuel W. Ferguson (1834–1917); commanded a brigade of cavalry as Davis's escort.

†Maj. Gen. John Cabell Breckinridge (1821–1875), Confederate secretary of war.

Freeman's mules; some soldiers told of it and after a long search for him (Diamond), Dr. Gibson & Pudge went for him & bought him. The man wanted as much as old Bob for his trouble, which of course I could not do, as Confederate money was of no value. I paid him $17 in Georgia State money. The roads were travelled by the enemy and certainly were as bad as they could be . . . making travel very slow and laborious—16 miles. [208]

May 17—Left camp at 5 oc . . . roads better . . . traveled 7 miles, had to stop to repair wagon . . . detained 3 hours . . . stopped 12 o'c to dinner; reported that Jeff Davis had been taken . . . generally believe that a large reward had been offered for him; saw soldiers from Ferguson's Cavalry [Mississippians] . . . had been disbanded at Forsythe [Georgia] and paroled and gone home . . . reached Pine Apple . . . travelled and camped 21 miles from Yellow Bluff & all well . . . mules getting tired. . . . [T]ravelled 21 miles. [229]

May 18—Left camp at 4 am . . . rained last night . . . very damp . . . roads very bad and heavy . . . teams much fatigued . . . found note from J. A. Smith of Woodville that he would join me at Lower Peach Tree . . . he belongs to Cleburn's Escort . . . travelled 16 miles to dinner; met J. A. Smith on the road . . . had returned from Northern prison; reports confirmation of Lincoln's death and reward for apprehension of Jeff. Davis . . . [Gen.] Breckinridge . . . C. C. Clay* & others . . . Davis [mistakenly] supposed already [in] Miss . . . rain . . . camped at Black Bluff . . . very hard rain at dark . . . no ferry at Black Bluff . . . compelled to go to Lower Peach Tree ferry . . . tents very dry and comfortable . . . all well . . . children slightly unwell . . . travelled 21 miles . . . from Albany to Alabama river 250 miles. . . .

May 19—Started some [wagons] for ferry, some for corn at

---

*Clement Claiborne Clay Jr. (1816–1882); U. S. senator and Confederate senator; Confederate agent in Canada in 1865; falsely accused of involvement in Lincoln's assassination.

Mr. Horne's, who would only give 1 bushel corn for 4 lbs. sugar . . . compelled to do so as needed corn . . . soon after Mr. Gullett came & offered pound [sugar] for bushel of corn . . . of course I accepted it . . . corn & provisions plenty; but farmers not willing to sell them . . . this part of the country has never been travelled by the enemy & of course has plenty . . . total demoralization exists from desire of gain. Mary & children went to Dr. Mc-Cloud's to dinner & were very kindly received . . . he owns a plantation on Bayou Boeuf . . . Franklin Parish, Louisiana . . . at 4 pm started teams, called for Mary . . . crossed the Alabama River . . . camped west side of Alabama river . . . travelled 8 miles. [258]

May 20—Cool & pleasant . . . wagons & people all over by 10 o'c . . . paid Dr. McCloud 30 lbs. sugar for ferry mule . . . soldier from Miss. reported that Jeff Davis & Breckinridge* had crossed the Miss. at Big Black about 10 days ago . . . started at 2 o'c . . . part of road very bad . . . travelled 7 miles . . . country nearly bare of forage & provisions. [265]

May 21—Left camp 6 o'c . . . weather pleasant, roads tolerable . . . part of way very hilly . . . country broken and not productive . . . no provisions to be had of any kind . . . many soldiers passing down Alabama river . . . reported large number of negro soldiers are being sent to Mexico . . . stopped one mile from Macon . . . very few persons . . . & but few soldiers compared with other roads . . . camped 4 miles beyond Macon . . . travelled 19 miles. [284]

May 22—Cool & pleasant . . . slight showers . . . one bushel meal left . . . no mills to grind . . . country badly off . . . people very selfish and mercenary . . . Elijah broke his wagon & Jamie his carriage . . . stopped 12 oc 6 miles from Coffeeville . . . camped one mile from town . . . persons at landing trading for cotton . . . corn impossible to be obtained . . . everyone fearful of famine &

---

*Neither Davis nor Breckinridge got anywhere near Mississippi before being apprehended by Union troops.

distress . . . Mobile fully in possession of enemy* . . . said to be also at Bladen Springs† . . . travelled 18 miles . . . distance 302 miles.

May 23—Warm . . . went to several mills but could procure no meal; left Pudge yesterday at Mill to have corn ground; joined us at 4 PM with 10 bushels . . . all that could be ground; was unable to procure but 10 bushels of corn for 10 yards sheeting . . . 1 lb. sugar was demanded for 1 lb. butter & the same for a horseshoe . . . could not procure corn from anyone . . . Banker [?] trading boat at the Landing . . . said to have committed great outrage: they left suddenly as it was reported that some of Wheeler's cavalry‡ were coming who would have stripped the boat . . . crossed all over after dinner . . . camped 3 miles from river in pretty place. [305]

May 24—Left camp 7 oc . . . Mr. Thompson from Bladen came over to see me: he purchased my cattle 2 years ago [1863—when C.G.D. left Mississippi for Atlanta] . . . Springs not open yet . . . many negroes killed; some by enemy for deserting & some by our people for going to enemy . . . reported that 10,000 negro soldiers had been sent to Mexico . . . roads very broken . . . hilly and rocky . . . told that Mr.— has corn . . . stopped 12 o'c . . . an old man 80 yrs old came down to see us and told us that we would be compelled to go 5 miles around the bridge . . . found the road very bad and hilly & full of rain and nearly broke all the wagons . . . camped near a house where the man refused water from his well . . . took the water . . . wagons much delayed by bad roads . . . travelled 18 miles. [323]

May 25—Cool & pleasant . . . left camp . . . Richmond broke a spoke of his wagon and a bolt of my wagon . . . had to stop to repair . . . roads very bad from lack of work & nearly all the bridges

---

*Note that Dahlgren still refers to "the enemy."
†Bladen Springs is in Choctaw County near the Mississippi line.
‡The troops of Maj. Gen. Joseph Wheeler (1836–1906) of Alabama were notorious for pillaging.

washed away . . . causing a large amount of unnecessary travel over very bad roads . . . several persons on the road report the capture of Pres. Davis* & that they saw and conversed with him . . . impossible to procure corn anywhere . . . no fodder to be had . . . compelled to travel nearly 30 miles North in order to cross Buckatunna [River] . . . stopped 12 o'c 10 miles from DeSoto . . . plenty of corn in country but exorbitant prices demanded . . . camped 12 miles from DeSoto near Capt. Trother† . . . saw him in regard to corn . . . refused to exchange except 1 bushel for 2 lbs. sugar . . . travelled 16 miles. [339]

May 26—Cool & pleasant . . . sent two teams to Capt. Trother for corn . . . obtained 50 bushels at 2 lbs. sugar per bushel . . . sent one team to procure 25 bushels meal at same rate . . . my carriage broke down & detained me very late . . . overtook Capt. Smith at 10 oc night near church . . . the spirit of greed appears to have taken possession of every one here without regard to the mode of acquiring is the only object now apparent . . . great distress exists among families of soldiers, who made no crop last year & are too late to make one this year . . . travelled 8 miles . . . distance 348 miles . . . Pudge and Mr. Parker went to Waynesboro.

May 27—[Rowan's birthday—3 years of age—JAD. Note added later by John Armfield Dahlgren.] Very cool for time of year . . . left camp . . . travelled on very good roads . . . camped 2 miles beyond Shubuta at 12 o'c . . . saw papers confirming capture of Pres. Davis: proclamation of Gov. [Charles] Clark‡ calling upon State to return to Union; also Gen. [N. B.] Forrest§ address calling upon all to lay down their arms . . . all east of Miss. have surrendered; [food riots caused] great apprehension in Mobile with loss

---

*Jefferson Davis was captured near Irwinville, Georgia, on 10 May 1865.
†An Alex Trother was an early settler of Clarke County, Mississippi.
‡Charles Clark (1811–1877), Confederate brigadier general; elected governor of Mississippi in 1863.
§Lt. Gen. Nathan Bedford Forrest (1821–1877), commander of Confederate Cavalry in Tennessee and Alabama.

of life . . . much trouble with negroes there . . . especially negro soldiers . . . sent word to Gen. McRae* by a man going there . . . the enemy have never been thro here & provisions are plenty, but people very mercenary and unwilling to sell except for gold and silver . . . notes of all kinds are refused . . . nothing but gold taken . . . travelled 18 miles [367] . . . wheels of three wagons broken . . . compelled to stop and repair.

May 28—Cool & pleasant . . . detained all day repairing wagons . . . refused the use of several shops tho' we had our own mechanics, tools and coke . . . & provisions generally refused . . . tho' plenty in this country, as the enemy have not been through here . . . crops look very well . . . much better than in other States . . . many negroes ran away to enemy . . . roads very good, tho' needing repairs . . . one man refused to sell corn as he wanted it for his hogs . . . fodder not to be procured at all.

May 29—Cloudy and very cool . . . wheels all finished yesterday . . . started early . . . demand was made for pay for use of shop & timber for spokes . . . being sick, could not attend to it, but agreed to do whatever Capt. Smith or Gibson had bargained . . . left my carriage on the road to be repaired . . . overtook wagons at 12 o'c . . . Capt. Smith denied promising any pay for use of their timber . . . the chief object of the whole country appears to be desire of gain; yet the country has never been injured nor suffered from the enemy . . . travelled 23 miles. [390]

May 30—Very cool . . . camped last night near a church . . . passed 5 churches today . . . roads very bad . . . great difficulty in finding the way as people appear totally ignorant of the roads or distances . . . roads have not been worked since the war . . . crossed

---

*Colin John MacRae (1812–1877), native of North Carolina; cotton commission merchant in Mobile; general of militia; member of Mississippi legislature in 1838; financial agent of Confederate government in Europe; postwar partner of Judah P. Benjamin's brother in mercantile business in Honduras, where he died.

Hastehatchie at Rabomo bridge . . . passed by two men in buggy going to Tensas Parish . . . stopped 12 o'c 14 miles from Taylorsville . . . camped in Pines nearly 11 miles from Taylorsville . . . corn & forage not to be had . . . red bugs very bad and annoying to children . . . travelled 17 miles . . . distance 407 miles.

May 31—Morning cool . . . children all sick from change of water . . . reached Taylorsville 12 o'c . . . many going to Louisiana . . . one of Capt. Smith's horses fell lame . . . he traded him for $50 greenbacks . . . Taylorsville has store & one house . . . apparently little business . . . a man & wagon passed going to Bayou Sara . . . all reports go to confirm the capture of Pres. Davis. One returned prisoner reports [Lawrence S.] Ross Brigade Texans being crossed over last week after he left Vicksburg . . . Miss. river said to be high but falling . . . camped in old field near a soldier of 4th Miss. Regt . . . travelled 18 miles . . . distance 425.

June 1—Cool & pleasant . . . left camp 7 AM . . . crossed Bayou bridge . . . several planters refused to sell corn for any price . . . & have always refused Confederate money . . . corn is in the country but cannot be had . . . some are distilling whiskey as more profitable and of course refused to sell . . . lucre appears the only thing they care for . . . camped 12 o'c 3 miles from W[estville] Mills . . . endeavored at every place to procure corn but none would barter or sell . . . all said plenty of corn further on . . . yet all had more than they needed . . . they had hid their corn in the woods & left but little in their cribs* . . . totally dead to all action save their interest . . . roads very good . . . teams had no fodder for two weeks . . . nor can any be obtained . . . travelled 19 miles . . . distance 444.

June 2—Cool & pleasant . . . left camp . . . travelled over very good roads . . . yesterday broke John's wagon . . . detained repairing it . . . some persons refuse the use of their shop to work in

---

*This made sense at the time—to hide the corn from hungry Confederates as well as Union soldiers, tax collectors, and bushwhackers.

. . . Lige ran away and nearly ruined my wagon . . . broke one of the bolts of his carriage . . . had to stop and repair . . . stopped 12 o'c at Westville Mills . . . camped 4 miles from Guntown . . . road good but very dusty . . . broke one of the wagons & lost much time . . . a distillery at Westville makes 45 gallons per day . . . good whiskey . . . sold last month at $85 per gallon . . . now at $4 greenbacks or $2 silver . . . all paid in Confederate money is lost . . . travelled 22 miles . . . distance 466 . . . camped 4 miles from Pearl [R]iver.

June 3—Warm & dry . . . crops suffering for rain and very dusty . . . traded thread for corn, eggs & chickens . . . corn in abundance . . . crossed Pearl River at Georgetown ferry . . . paid 2 bundles thread for ferry . . . Elijah & Freeman wagon broke . . . had to stop for repairs . . . stopped at church at 12 am . . . detained till 5 o'c for wagon. . . . Saw [A. B.] Stewart of Adams [County] troops who left [son] Charley at Greensboro, North Carolina, travelling home with Gen. Bate* . . . also, a servant of T[homas] Percy [Jeff Davis Legion] who said he left [son] Bernard at Pine Ridge [near Natchez] in March and then spoke of going to Louisiana . . . Wade Hampton† & all of army [of] Virginia had surrendered . . . John's wagon broke one of the wheels, again delaying us till 12 o'c . . . all very tired . . . travelled 21 miles . . . 487 miles. Sunday

June 4—Warm & very dry . . . country suffering . . . no rain for 6 weeks . . . left camp 7 o'c . . . Smith stopped at Hazlehurst— to take Rail for Jackson to see about money . . . left Pudge to take charge of the horses till Smith returns tomorrow . . . Dr. Gibson gave him a note to Mr. Buell in Union Church, where he will stay

---

*William B. Bate (1826–1905), Tennessee-born Confederate major general, commanded a division of the Army of Tennessee in North Carolina in 1865. Elected governor of Tennessee in 1882; served two terms.

†Wade Hampton (1818–1902), wealthy South Carolina politician; lieutenant general and commander of cavalry in North Carolina in 1865. Inherited several plantations near Natchez from his father and ran them successfully before the war.

till tomorrow . . . the best roads we have seen . . . travel slow as John's wagon is broken down . . . saw considerable amounts of cotton belonging to the Confederate Govt, being hauled in by Federals who have forbidden any persons to haul cotton until their own is hauled . . . camped 12 o'c 30 miles from Port Gibson . . . saw Dr. West, Dr. [?] from Texas who report that [General] Kirby Smith* had made two million in cotton . . . travelled 22 miles . . . 509 miles.

June 5—Warm . . . left camp at 7 o'c . . . saw the first appearance of plantations of any size . . . land and country very different from any in Georgia or Alabama . . . better crops, finer growth of timber . . . improvements and general appearance all showing a superior quality of soil and land . . . roads also better from rock & stone . . . but dust 6 inches thick making travel very unpleasant. . . . Saw Weldon on place of Col. Jefferies† making some crops . . . the rumor of capture of Pres. Davis appears to be confirmed . . . called on Col. Jefferies, whom I met in Atlanta with his negroes . . . he had broken his leg by a fall . . . had 30 negroes left on the place . . . the enemy had ruined it and last week had accidentally burned his gin house with 200 bales of cotton . . . he had been to Port Gibson to procure indemnity for his loss . . . the Federals are hunting up all the Confed Govt cotton in the country . . . numbers of wagons hauling it in to be shipped to New Orleans . . . camped at 6 mile creek . . . travelled 18 miles. . . . [527]

June 6—John's wagon totally broken down & Elijah's also . . . had to wait to repair it . . . left the teams and started to Rodney to look for places to cross river [Mississippi] . . . met Capt. Roberts just from New Orleans . . . stated that Pres. Davis was certainly a

---

*Edmund Kirby-Smith (1824–1893), Floridian who, as full general, commanded the Confederate Trans-Mississippi department. Rumors alleged that Kirby-Smith, in his capacity as commander, had seized cotton for government use and sold it for his own profit. The charges were, of course, false.
†Probably Nathaniel Jefferies of Port Gibson, Claiborne County, Mississippi.

prisoner . . . overtook Col. Whitfield* of Whitfield, Texas Legion, paroled, on his way home . . . he thought that none of the Confederate soldiers would fight for Lincoln† . . . stopped 12 o'c near Mrs. McGills who sent for me to dinner . . . entertained very respectably . . . kept on to Rodney . . . could find no boat nor ferry . . . the Commandant of Post had no transport nor means of assistance . . . the place garrisoned by negro troops . . . very much dilapidated and destroyed . . . little or no business doing . . . went to Edgar Woods‡ to spend the night . . . Capt. Hunt§ had returned . . . Mr. W. had just returned from New Orleans . . . learned that [my son] Bernard had been shot and seriously injured in a fight with the enemy because he had refused to surrender to them . . . and had much difficulty because he rejoiced at Lincoln's death . . . if any chance of escape or resistance he was perfectly right not to surrender . . . the impression appears to gain ground that [Andrew] Johnson & Mexico will fight . . . travelled to Rodney . . . 30 miles . . . distance 557 miles.

June 7—Left Mr. Woods . . . learned that Col. Hinchel‖ was in jail in New Orleans for supposed complicity in killing a Lessee in Issaquena County. . . . Mr. W. had escaped damage from the war & lost no property . . . left Mr. W. to meet the people . . . went by Colemans . . . they had passed on to Rodney . . . overtook them 6 miles from Rodney near Oakland . . . very glad to see Bernard who had come from Mr. [Charles Brown] Percy's after me . . . he was recovering but had been badly wounded in skirmish, having been shot through the body & rump . . . otherwise was very well . . . grown very much . . . 6 ft. 2 in. high . . . looked

---

*Col. John W. Whitfield (1818–1879), 27th Texas Cavalry; appointed brigadier general in 1863; served in Mississippi during most of the war.

†This seems a slip of the pencil. He probably meant Andrew Johnson and a fight with Mexico, as rumored.

‡Probably E. A. Woods, Port Gibson, Claiborne County, Mississippi.

§Probably a member of David Hunt's family, prominent in Natchez.

‖Probably E. Hinchel of Raymond, Hinds County.

very manly . . . no news of Charley . . . saw Mr. Watson . . . country badly overflowed in Tensas greatest ever known . . . was unable to procure any flat or skiff and no ferry boat at Rodney . . . made crossing about impossible . . . camped near Oakland College. . . .

June 8—Clear & warm . . . went to Rodney . . . saw commandant [of] Post . . . asked him to aid me in crossing but he had no boats . . . garrisoned by negro troops . . . traded off shirting for sugar . . . yard for pound, & sold some at 35¢ per yard . . . Rodney nearly deserted . . . no business of any moment doing . . . dilapidated & falling to ruin . . . saw Mr. Garner who promised to lend a skiff . . . sent to others . . . some promised . . . others refused . . . fearing injury from the enemy . . . some have aided the cause all in their power . . . others have done nothing from fear of compromising themselves . . . others have been speculating in cotton & making all they could from the distressed state of the country . . . started in the evening to Bruinsburg . . . camped on the hill at Freelands on the road travelled by Gen. Grant's troops . . . sent to many neighbors, all of whom refused skiff, except Mr. Buckner* . . . heard from Marydale . . . the whole country said to be under water . . . camped on river bank & commenced to cross over in skiff . . . sent over some of the people . . . took one of the wagons apart & sent them over the river . . . had but one skiff and of course very slow work . . . found two men at Bruinsburg with 84 bales of cotton belonging to Capt. Smith, boating to New Orleans . . . a boat from Pennsylvania came down Bayou Pierre with cotton & hay at Bruinsburg . . . two other smaller boats also came down & staid there . . . negroes & white men from them came ashore & had a very demoralizing effect on the servants . . . mixing with them all night & instigating them to much villainy & insubordination

---

*William Aylett Buckner (1794–1886), attorney and cotton broker, business partner of Frederick Stanton, Natchez; owned Airlie but lost most of his fortune during the war. His wife Charlotte Ferguson bore him twelve children, one of whom, Edward, was killed at Shiloh. Only their son William survived his parents.

. . . very little cotton or other business was doing and all seemed very dull.

June 9—Rained hard all night . . . very damp & unpleasant . . . the Grey Eagle came about daylight for cotton to N. Orleans . . . very little cotton going in . . . freight very scarce & low—lower than ever known—one says there are 175 boats at New Orleans waiting freight and that the Govt has 125 more to sell . . . more than can find employment. . . .

June 10—Bargained with boat to cross over [to Louisiana] my teams & people for $75 in greenbacks.

Post Script [C.G.D.]

Very few trips or journeys have been made such as this, with large family, wife, and young children. [In ink, much later]

General Dahlgren not only kept a log of the mileage traveled each day, he also noted the distances between key points:

	Distance in Miles
Georgia	
Soldier's Home to Albany	9
Cuthbert	43
Alabama	
Eufala	26
Clayton	21
Louisville	10
Hobdy's Bridge	8
F____ Bridge	15
Troy	11
F____ Bridge	5
____ Bridge	12
J____ Bridge	5
Greenville	25
Pine Apple	27
Black's Bluff	30
Peachtree	9

Macon	22
Coffeeville	23
Mississippi	
Shubuta	45
Taylorsville	55
Westville	41
Georgetown	21
Hazlehurst	16
Grand Gulf	5
Rodney	61
Total	545 miles

Exactly how Dahlgren calculated his distances is difficult to judge. It is quite likely that he had one of the early odometers attached to the wheel of his carriage or one of the wagons.

By 1860, J. H. Colton of New York had published generally accurate maps of Georgia, Alabama, and Mississippi that showed railroads, "common roads," and rivers but no mileage. Dahlgren might have procured in Atlanta maps of the three states that were included in *Johnson's New Illustrated Family Atlas* (New York: Johnson & Ward, 1864). His diary indicates that local people in remote areas often gave poor or misleading directions.

Modern readers of General Dahlgren's account of the family's odyssey in 1865 might pause at the postscript and be struck by its obvious understatement. Searching their imaginations for more details, they might ponder particulars that the blunt lead pencil failed to record. They learn about the bad roads, broken wagon wheels, indifferent farmers, and bands of highwaymen, some of whom were deserting Confederates. We experience Dahlgren's need to barter when Confederate bills were refused. There is the daily search for corn and fodder to exchange for the sugar, salt, bundles of thread, and bolts of shirting on the wagons. Since the need for cornmeal is often mentioned, one can assume that mush, hoecakes, and parched corn were the staple foods for thirty-five days, except on the two occasions when the Dahlgrens were invited to a family table along the way. The horses and mules were in daily need of corn and fodder.

Dahlgren made no reference to game or fish, if indeed there was time to look for either. Wild greens gathered along the roadside—poke sallet, dandelion, and lamb's quarter—were common in the slave diet and welcome as sop for the hoecakes. The general noted stopping for dinner at midday or later, but these are the only references to a meal. Neither does he mention milk for the children or meat to fill the hungry boys. The older children could survive on hoecake and some bacon occasionally, but Edgar, called McWhorter by his father, was barely a year old. It is quite possible that Hannah, his black nurse, following a practice accepted in that day, pulverized the bread in her own mouth and pushed it into the child's like a mother bird feeding her gaping young.

In addition to the diary entries, General Dahlgren kept ledger pages on which he itemized the goods and provender used for barter that he carried in each of the six supply wagons. These were the staples that would travel. The wagons were manned by his teamsters, who doubled as mechanics when the wheels cracked or a singletree broke. His drivers were Freeman, Robin, Wellington, Richmond, John Handy, Peter (in the Jersey wagon), and Alfred. Each looked after his own mules—fed, watered, trimmed their hooves—and talked patiently to them when the pull was uphill and the fodder was running low.

On 10 May, Dahlgren was lucky to find Hobdy's blacksmith shop when repairs were needed. Hobdy let the mechanics use his premises, and he provided extra wheels for those that could not be repaired. Although he would not take Confederate money, he was willing to barter several farm items, much needed by the Dahlgrens, for items on their wagons: their thread for his fodder; salt for wheel spokes and meal; sugar for barley corn, eggs, shucks, corn, and bacon; more sugar for eight chickens, oats, and fodder. With their diminishing supply of bacon and salt pork, the Dahlgrens found Hobdy's provisions welcome but soon consumed. From that time on, there was a daily search for corn—shelled for the mules and ground into meal for twenty human mouths. Corn sustained them, man and beast.

A number of other questions arise. What were the sleeping arrangements for the Dahlgrens, the children, the male and female blacks? The
general refers to a tent as a fixture in camp and says that it kept Mary
Edgar and the children dry in a downpour. But did the servants sleep
under tents or under the wagons with strips of tarpaulin? On 8 May,
during heavy showers, they were lucky to spend the night in a deserted
cabin. Barns, corncribs, and cotton houses also would have been welcome,
the farmers permitting, but Dahlgren makes no reference to any of these
makeshift accommodations. Although the servants probably scooped up
mush with shells and drank out of gourds, many questions are not answered. How did pots, pans, and cooking cauldrons get scrubbed when
water was scarce? Had they all slept in their clothes for thirty-five days?
How did faces get purged of the dust of the open road? How were
little Edgar's diapers kept clean? What were the proprieties when twenty
travelers answered the call of nature?

The key to their survival lies not only in their resourcefulness but in
their determination to outlive the hardships. And they were not alone
on the back roads. As historian Bruce Allardice, author of *More Generals
in Gray,* points out, "So little of worth has appeared in day-by-day
accounts like Dahlgren's. Yet imagine 200,000 Confederate soldiers, and
at least an equal number of refugees, traveling by horse or mule or on
foot across a ravaged land. At least 10% of the South's entire population
was on the move at one time—in the midst of spring floods, away from
harvests and crops. The drama and the logistics of it all are staggering."[3]

One can fully recognize the degree of deprivation when comparing
Dahlgren's account with Williamson Oldham's memoirs. They comple-
ment each other dramatically, two voices recounting the harrowing details
of virtually the same story. Dahlgren's diary is the more direct, the more
immediate account because he recorded it at the end of each day while
he was facing the trials and feeling the fatigue in every muscle. How did
he manage to move the pencil between his fingers in the dark uncertainty
of each evening after a day of challenges for the entire wagon train?
Oldham lacked the encumbrances of a hungry family, servants, stubborn
mules, and broken wagon wheels. Oldham, unlike Dahlgren, recorded
his odyssey after the fact during the relative tranquility of his later sojourn

in Mexico. His prose is substantial, occasionally eloquent. Although both his account and Dahlgren's honor the physical tenacity and scribal competence of the two travelers, Dahlgren's has the edge in dramatic intensity.

Another mark of the Dahlgren odyssey is the respect of the followers for the leader. Perhaps because Dahlgren and his wife shared a strong confidence in each other, their children and servants made every effort to complete the journey. Not only did the bedraggled travelers survive the obstacles, but Dahlgren found time to jot down the details. The wonder is that he recorded no casualties. By the time they arrived in Rodney, Mississippi, they must have looked like nomads with their sunburnt faces, tired eyes, and spattered clothes. After three days, they finally found a friend in Aylett Buckner. He offered his boat to ferry them in relays across the Mississippi to Saint Joseph, Louisiana, 15 miles from Marydale for the sum of $75 in greenbacks. Where was David Richardson, Marydale's overseer? Had he fled like the others of his stripe in fear of black retaliation?

On the night of 8 June, the Dahlgrens camped on the hill at Freelands' on the road traveled by General Grant's troops. (This is the historic Vicksburg Campaign Trail, now proposed as a national landmark.) In the distance, they could see the magnificent columns of Windsor, the mansion of Smith C. Daniell II. A prime symbol of the antebellum South, Windsor had been spared and still rose in grandeur. Union Col. Henry Clay Warmoth had peered at the Windsor edifice and called it "the most magnificent I ever saw. The house could not have cost less than a hundred thousand." Other soldiers "gaped in awe as they passed Windsor with its 22 gigantic Corinthian columns."[4] It was not yet a brooding ruin.

From what they had observed on the roads from Georgia, the Dahlgrens were prepared for inevitable changes at Marydale, with much of the plantation reportedly under water. Although it was too late to hustle for seed and open furrows for cotton, they could probably plant a late garden for the kitchen and hope to hold off starvation. They might be able to barter with the people in the cabins for some staples and vegetables from their gardens.

Why, one might ask, the return to Tensas Parish instead of Natchez and Llangollen? Were the Dahlgrens too proud to appear in Natchez threadbare in a muddy carriage pulled by a horse so gaunt that his hip bones protruded and followed by wagons of ragged children and servants? Son Bernard had written during the previous year that the Yankees had engulfed Natchez and moved troops into Llangollen. He had done what he could about the furnishings there before going to Marydale. At the plantation, the family could be together and wait for Charlie Routh to make his way home from his regiment in North Carolina. Not of the least importance, Marydale would provide work in the fields for the Negroes and shelter in the cabins.

Were any of the Negroes at Marydale and The Oaks still living in the cabins? Perhaps a handful—the old and infirm and the children who tried to follow their liberators and were driven back because they were a nuisance. Could Dahlgren manage a living for those who had made the trip with him from Georgia? When Son Bernard wrote to his mother in April 1864, he spoke of the faithful Llangollen house servants: "Julian & Phoebe are well—they have behaved just the same as though they never heard of freedom—they ask to be remembered. Mammy [Dinah] died last week. I had her buried in that lot of yours which has no fence around it, where that child was buried. I had every thing done as well as could be—she was buried with respect and decency."[5]

The lost War of the Rebellion, however, had destroyed the old feudal dispensation throughout the South. A case in point is noted in Dahlgren's diary entry of 8 June, when he was trying to cross the Mississippi at Rodney and return his charges to the plantations. Along the river, gangs of freedmen were working for wages on the docks and celebrating their liberation. They urged Dahlgren's Negroes to join them in the drinking and merrymaking. Whites from the steamboats had also joined in the revelry. Dahlgren surveyed the scene and denounced its "demoralizing effect on the servants . . . mixing with them all night & instigating them to much villainy & insubordination."

After years of subjection—lately in isolated South Georgia—Miles, Nelson, Adolphus, John, Elijah, Freeman, and Peter, along with Hannah, Rachel, and Irene, reached their "freedom road" on the banks of the . Mississippi. There they declared their liberation for the first time since

Lincoln's proclamation two and a half years earlier and began to celebrate emancipation openly and with noisy revelry.

Even if Charles Dahlgren had been a benevolent master and his people had followed him home without questioning, he was now obliged to come to terms with changes that he could not control. On 8 June 1865, he was finally forced to concede the end of slavery—for his people as well as for himself.

Only four years before, Mary Edgar Dahlgren was twenty-one and mistress of Llangollen and wearing taffeta gowns from New York and gloves of Irish lace. Only four years ago, nearly to the day, her husband had been bouncing their baby Van on his knee while he waited delivery of his uniform from the tailor in New Orleans. It would bear the three gold stars of a brigadier general on each collar. By contrast, the same man, gaunt now, with heavy beard and tired shoulders, held the reins of the horse that strained to pull the muddy carriage. The woman beside him with a sunburned face and wisps of matted hair probably wore a dress of homespun, stained and wrinkled and frayed at the hem. The parents had tried to soothe the young boys and keep them from crying over the stinging bites of ticks, mosquitos, and chiggers. Their churning stomachs, brought on by changes in drinking water, had dehydrated their bodies and sapped their strength.

As the Dahlgrens prodded the tired team down the muddy, overgrown track to the Marydale quarters, they did not intend to bow to a new, punitive order. If they wrote later of the thirty-five days on the road from Soldier's Home to Marydale, there are no accounts in the surviving papers. They had established a bond each with the other, an insoluble union consummated in silence. It embraced the will and spirit and fortitude of two people who would go on living after being hounded by the forces of doom at every turn in the road. They were set on teaching themselves and their sons to forget those somber days of deprivation. They would absolve themselves of the tyranny of self-pity. They had learned the difference between living and not dying.

❧ Eight ❧

Survival without Recovery

Those planters who left Natchez during the war and returned to their homes following the Confederate surrender shared the same humiliation as the returning soldiers who tried to take up their lives again. The last days of the war and the surrender of the Adams Troops near Goldsboro, North Carolina, on 18 April 1865 are described in a memoir of Volney Daniel Fowler, a comrade of Charles Routh Dahlgren in the Jeff Davis Legion. He recounted the journey back to Natchez: "The terms of our surrender allowed us to keep our horses, pistols, and swords. We were given a wagon and two mules to pull it. That wagon contained our assets, our capital, our wherewithal to huckster our way home." Like General Dahlgren, Fowler and his men bartered what they had, including "the latest style of Confederate russet shoes," for two months across South Carolina, Georgia, Alabama, and Mississippi. Also, like the Dahlgrens, Fowler eventually heard the news of Lincoln's assassination. He wrote: "I felt that our only championship in that day of bitterness was to come from that man who had controlled Northern sentiments throughout the war and that he was preparing to heal the bleeding sores of the South."[1]

At the hamlet Washington, just outside Natchez, Fowler "was confounded at the tableau there exhibited." He found companies of Negro soldiers in U.S. uniforms patrolling the streets, prowling troops destroying property, and the chaos attendant to the Freedmen's Bureau. "Natchez had changed from gentleness and peacefulness to agitation and boisterousness." So there was wisdom in Dahlgren's decision to avoid the concentration of strife in Natchez and take his family back to the relative quiet of Marydale. He was convinced of his decision when they arrived at Rodney and encountered a garrison of Negro troops and saw the demoralizing effect that they had on his servants.

Among the Northern civilians who traveled in the South during 1865 was journalist Whitelaw Reid, a native of Ohio. Reid was a passionate Republican, antislavery and anti-South. As a correspondent in Washington during the war, he had been widely read for the clarity and accuracy of his dispatches. He had reported on Shiloh and Gettysburg and was one of the first newspapermen to appear in Richmond after its fall. Because of his endorsement of party-line views, Reid was selected to visit the South in the company of Chief Justice Salmon P. Chase and report on conditions there during the weeks following Appomattox.

Reid made other visits, which he describes in *After the War: Tour of the Southern States, 1865–1866.*[2] He wrote well, and his reportage of what he found by interviewing all classes of Southerners is of value. He had a good ear for the speech patterns from the Tidewater to Louisiana to the Uplands. He was also fairly successful in recording the dialect of the former slaves, although the long narratives in that idiom seem ponderous today.

Reid ended his book with a pitch to Northern capitalists to come south, invest their money in buying or leasing plantations along the Mississippi, and reap up to 50 percent in profits from their investments in cotton: "Whoever contemplates going South, in time for the operations of 1867, should not delay his first visit later than November, 1866. Between October and January last, the prices of lands throughout the South, either for lease or sale, advanced fully fifty percent!"[3] Reid provided readers with a breakdown of expenses that included wages for Negro labor, provisions for their families, corn and hay for the mules, and the purchase of farm equipment.

At age thirty, Reid was so convinced of his projections that he hopped on the bandwagon of the Southern revival himself. He borrowed money, journeyed again to Natchez, and invested in three plantations across the river in Concordia Parish, Louisiana. His experiences there with laborers, drivers, and overseers, although not directly identified as Reid's, provide the specifics for some of the most telling episodes in his book. But the disillusionment following the fantasy was not long in coming.

As Reid's editor also points out: "Floodwaters and army worms dispelled his dream and brought him close to financial disaster." Reid's experience with the Negroes also changed his attitude: "I have now about 300 of these beings under my control. They work well; but life among them is a fearful thing for one's rose-colored ideas. The present generation is bad material to develop. We shall do better with the next."[4] He was distressed at the passion for whiskey and "the lack of virtue" among them.

There is no record of precisely what the Dahlgrens found when they returned to Marydale in June 1865. From the accounts of other planters on both sides of the Mississippi, the plight of the returning owners was severe. Many found that the Federal government had leased their property to Northerners who hoped to take advantage of huge profits in cotton. The record shows that in the area of Vicksburg alone there were 136 plantations leased to new operators—113 to Northern whites and 23 to Negroes.[5] The object of the leases was "to line the banks of the Mississippi River with a loyal population and [secure] the uninterrupted navigation of the river, at the same time to give employment to the freed Negroes whereby they may earn wages and become self-supporting."[6] One negative response to the plan came from humanitarian James Yeatman of the Western Sanitary Commission in Saint Louis: ". . . [T]he parties leasing plantations and employing freedmen do it from no motives either of loyalty or humanity. The desire of gain alone prompts them, and they care not whether they make it out of the blood of those they employ or from the land."[7] Ironically, Yeatman concluded, that greed was the aftermath of peace.

One case that combined economic exploitation with a misguided zeal for social reform was that of A. T. Morgan, a Union soldier from Ohio, who joined his brother Charles after their release from the Union army and went to Yazoo County, Mississippi, to make their fortunes. They brought with them "substantial capital" and enough farming experience to strike it rich in "a wonderful country." Their disastrous experiences as lessees are detailed in *Yazoo: or, On the Picket Line of Freedom in the*

South. A. T. Morgan was made a carpetbagger sheriff and tax collector in Yazoo County, where he was resented and reviled. He was unable to make the fortune he first imagined. Death threats to him and his mulatto wife and a depleted bank account finally drove him back to the North. Whatever commitments he had to social reforms had ended in disillusionment.[8]

Other lessees in the Delta areas experienced flooding during the spring of 1866 and soon regretted their haste in signing agreements. To his credit, President Johnson eventually ordered the return of the plantations to their owners, but the levees had been so neglected and the cotton lowlands so inundated that hope for crops in 1866 vanished.[9]

∝℘

One brief reference provides a clue about what conditions the Dahlgrens found when they returned. It comes from the diary of Charles's brother John, who wrote that "he has plenty of land but that is not available." This was the dilemma of scores of planters, including Dahlgren, at the time. Their plantations had been leased out from under them.

Governor Henry W. Allen of Louisiana, a bachelor, moved to Mexico City in June 1865, after borrowing five hundred dollars. There he began publishing a Confederate newspaper called *Mexican Times.* Saying that he preferred exile to punishment by the Northern victors, Allen, a classicist, quoted Aristotle: "Banishment is desirable, because a banished man has the choice of places in which to dwell." Welcomed by Empress Carlota at Maximilian's court, Allen received a subsidy to publish his newspaper and promote emigration from the South to Mexico. His efforts were short-lived, however, because death from old wounds and a weakened heart closed his career on 22 April 1866.[10]

Allen's friendship with Sarah Ann Dorsey, General Dahlgren's stepdaughter, resulted in her biography, *Recollections of Henry W. Allen,* published the year of his death. The book contains many colorful details about life in Tensas Parish during the 1850s when Allen was an honored guest of the Routh family and other plantation aristocrats during holidays and extravagant celebrations.

Although a few Southern families settled in Mexico, the rebellion against Maximilian, his death by a firing squad, and the banishment of Carlota to France were deterrents to immigration. The planters looked elsewhere—to Cuba, where slavery was still legal, and to Brazil, where it was also legal and where the government was offering foreigners special inducements in land grants and promises of new roads. The Brazilians thought that the Confederates, with their agricultural expertise, would be able to effect a revolution in Brazilian farming. The plow, they expected, would finally replace the hoe.

To investigate opportunities in Brazil, a group of Southerners sent Dr. J. McF. Gaston of Columbia, South Carolina, on an exploratory visit, which included extensive traveling.

A former brigade surgeon in the Confederate Army, Dr. Gaston was also a planter and businessman. He published a detailed narrative, *Hunting a Home in Brazil,* in Philadelphia in 1867. The subtitle reveals Gaston's mission: *The Agricultural Resources and Other Characteristics of the Country. Also, the Manners and Customs of the Inhabitants.*

It is a readable treatise, scientific for its time, and filled with details of agriculture, food, slave rituals, dinners, bastardy, females riding astride, and petitions to the court of Emperor Dom Pedro II. Gaston attempted a realistic appraisal of the country and listed the many opportunities that it could offer Southerners chafing under carpetbagger rule at home. He was frank about the lack of sanitation in the cities, loose morals of the clergy, and the proliferation of mahogany-back roaches at public hostels, but agriculture and industry would flourish with Southern know-how and the continuing labor of slaves. Dr. Gaston concluded: ". . . Though slavery may be destined to cease in Brazil at some future day, by gradual emancipation, yet the mastery of the white man will never be erased entirely from the people. There is a dignity and hospitality . . . that correspond to the lofty and generous bearing which characterized the Southern Gentleman in former times."[11]

A number of families from South Carolina, Tennessee, and Texas sold their holdings for what they could get on a weak market; gathered their wives, children, and servants; and bought passage on one of the steamers leaving Mobile, New Orleans, or Charleston for Rio de Janeiro. At Villa Americana in Central Brazil and at Santarem on the Amazon, they hoped to show the world that the pioneer spirit of Southerners was still alive, in spite of the South's defeat, and would be heralded abroad with sympathy.

Many of the Confederate families who immigrated from 1865 to 1870 can be identified today by surname. Many others caught in the Brazilian dream, no matter how hard they attempted to make it work, went down in a few years to a second defeat 10,000 miles from home. By 1888, when the government abolished slavery, an old feudal system was again undermined. Land without its husbandman and he without his hands became the heaviest of burdens. This was a load that the backs of the *Confederados* could not sustain for long. Today, their descendants sing their praises for their courage, and each generation reverently decorates the graves of old Southern names, such as Thompson, Williams, and Calhoun, with tropical flowers and Confederate flags. Although they had survived for a spell, they had never recaptured the prosperity of the Old South.

General Dahlgren had been to Brazil during his Navy days.[12] Perhaps that experience was enough to convince him to look elsewhere. If all did not go well during the remaining months of 1865, he considered his chances as a cotton broker and business agent in Toronto.[13] The Canadians had chafed under British domination for decades and would be likely to welcome the Southern secessionists.

From June until November, General Dahlgren and his family remained at Marydale and tried to assess their chances for survival. Everything needed mending, weeding, shoring up, repairing, sharpening, or coddling back to use. If they raised a cotton crop, there was no working gin or rafts to float the cotton to market, and they would have a long wait before collecting from the factors in New Orleans. Food for the table was scant, meat a luxury. There was no corn for the hogs, so they ran wild to root for themselves, only to get leaner and harder to catch. Nor was there any comfort in learning that some of Dahlgren's once affluent neighbors around Lake Saint Joseph had been burned to the ground.

Charles Routh Dahlgren was discharged from the Confederate Army in Greensboro, North Carolina, on 29 April 1865 and was ready to make his way home in June. Suffering from ascites, he had been sent to Howard's Grove Hospital, Richmond, in May 1864 and remained there until 26 September, when he was allowed to return to duty with Company A, Jeff Davis Legion. His health had taken him out of action as early as 1862, but he had always returned to duty and was with General Johnston when he surrendered to General Sherman in Greensboro on 18 April.[14] He was attached to the 4th Tennessee Cavalry at the Battle of Bentonville. During that final engagement, his regiment lost about one half of the total casualties. After being paroled, he accompanied Maj. Gen. William B. Bate home to Tennessee as a member of Bate's honor guard and then made his way south to Louisiana and his family. Charlie had kept his vow to his father to bear arms until the war was over.

For his brothers Berney, Pudge, and Morty, Charlie brought the sword of a Union colonel whom he had killed in Virginia.[15] He had served most of the war as a private and left as a corporal. Although he was only twenty-four years old, he had lost several teeth and looked at best a dozen years older. As he asked about his cousin Nanny Hollingsworth a flash of hope crossed in the tired gray eyes. She was well and wanted him to call, his father told him, giving his shoulder a gentle whack.

They all talked about the death of Ulric and hoped the body would be returned to his father now that the war was over. They wrote to Uncle John in Washington and asked him to send a photograph of Ulric for the mantle.[16] Admiral Dahlgren obliged with a miniature and a brief note of affection for them all.[17]

In June a Union sympathizer living near Richmond revealed the location of Ulric's body and made arrangements to send the casket to Admiral Dahlgren. "He lost no time in having proper examination made, in order to verify the remains of his lamented son."[18] But because of the intense heat that summer, the admiral was advised to postpone the obsequies and burial until cool weather. Meanwhile, alert officers of the detective force working in behalf of the admiral were able to obtain ". . . the coat worn by Colonel Dahlgren when he fell, his watch, and the golden ring for which the finger had been so brutally severed. The artificial leg was also recovered. The coat was pierced by four bullet-holes, on the left side and rather towards the back, showing clearly that the fatal volley had been fired [at Ulric] after he passed and not directly at him as he approached."[19] The restless, hard-riding, vengeance-driven young warrior, a model for a colonel's uniform, lay in repose until the state funeral was arranged in late October.[20]

Meanwhile, Admiral Dahlgren was relieved of the command of the South Atlantic Blockading Squadron on 23 June. He returned to Washington to make arrangements to marry the wealthy widow Madeleine Vinton Goddard, age forty, who had a grown son and daughter. Without telling his children of his plans and fearing their disapproval—Mrs. Goddard was a pious Roman Catholic—the admiral stole away to New York City and was married by the Reverend J. W. Cummings of St. Stephen's Church "according to the usages of the Roman Catholic Church."[21] The witnesses were Joseph M. Bradford and the groom's sister, Martha M. Dahlgren, who had lived under his roof and brought up his children. His grown sons by Mary Clement Bunker, Charles and Paul, referred to their new stepmother as "that Jesuit" and never quite forgave their father for his second marriage.

◌ৎ ৡ◌

The news of the admiral's new wife soon reached Marydale and Natchez as General Dahlgren—he would always retain the title—tried one source after another to finance the recovery of his plantations. Either the banks in the South lacked funds to lend or they considered Dahlgren a risk because of his financial troubles during the 1850s. It was common knowledge that Llangollen, completed in 1860, still had a mechanic's lien on it. Other debts also plagued him and might have driven a man of less steel to retreat from the fray and run west.

Part of his indebtedness included three notes held by Stephen Duncan, perhaps the richest individual in the Natchez area. During the 1850s, Duncan's net worth was "conservatively estimated at almost $2 million, including $829,907 in slaves, $400,000 in lands, $479,500 in bonds and stocks, and $200,000 in personal notes."[22]

Preserved are two letters from Dahlgren to Duncan about a debt contracted before the war. From New York the wealthy Duncan, who was a Unionist and had left the South in 1863, threatened to encumber all of Dahlgren's holdings in Tensas. Because of the war, Dahlgren pleaded an abatement of interest on the loan. When Duncan died in 1867 at age seventy-nine, the debt remained outstanding.[23]

Duncan also had invested heavily in the North, and his ledgers show that he reaped the benefits of diversification. A crafty operator, like other "patricians" in the Natchez district, Duncan "lived a portion of the year in New York or New England and profited from the marketplace arrangement of free labor just as [he] did from the paternalism of the plantation."[24] He had learned how to prosper in a dual economy.

Nor could Dahlgren hope for revenue from the property at Beersheba Springs. The note that he had signed with Colonel Armfield in 1860 was still outstanding. Although Beersheba Springs had been an idyllic refuge for Southerners during the era before the war, it was overrun alternately by contending military forces and sacked by guerillas from 1861 to 1865. During the summer of 1863, Bettie Ridley Blackmore and her husband George, with several family members, refuged at Beersheba Springs in the Murfree cottage. They had traveled by surrey and buggy and were accompanied by a wagon of "eatables" driven by a teamster. "Twelve souls in all," Mrs. Blackmore wrote in her journal. On the way, they were plagued by balking horses, worn-out harness, an overturned surrey, and at least one broken wheel. To complete the trip, they were fortunate to hire a sturdy ox wagon and team.

When the Federals under Gen. William S. Rosecrans occupied middle Tennessee, the rumor circulated that they intended to burn the Beersheba hotel and cottages in order to smoke out the Confederates. The mountain people and the bushwhackers reacted by descending on the village, breaking into the cottages, and carting off household furnishings "to take care of them." Seized by the illiterates were Bishop Otey's theological library, as well as Rolf Loundres's miscellaneous library, along with china and furniture. Colonel Armfield, to counter the pillaging, "sent word to any of us who desired articles to go & get them and leave the money with the superintendent [Ryan] at the hotel," Mrs. Blackmore wrote. On other occasions, she added, the Federal cavalry troops "were very attentive to us. Cousin and myself hid our husbands always—sometimes in the black-jacks, and another time in the kitchen loft." The ladies rocked silently on the gallery but feared their husbands' horses might stomp and neigh in the woods lot behind the house and give their deception away.[25]

A neighbor, Mrs. Lucy Virginia French, observed in her diary the damage to Dahlgren's property during the war by gangs of mountain marauders: ". . . [A] crowd of ill-looking men, and rough, slatternly women were stalking and racing to and fro, eager as famished wolves for prey—hauling out furniture, tearing up matting and carpets." She noted that one of the pillagers had fallen down in a fit at the dining room door and "they were deluging the contorted frame with cold water outside, and endeavoring to pour the stinging corn-juice inside—because under all circumstances alcoholic assistance is the one idea of a true indigent." The man had drunk from a jug marked "POISON" in the Dahlgren larder, believing the label was a way of protecting the owner's liquor. The smell had been too seductive to resist, when in fact, the contents were "a corrosive sublimate in alcohol."[26] Beersheba Springs was no place for the Dahlgrens to attempt recovery. So the cottage was sold to Miss Fannie Thompson of Nashville for $2,000.

Dahlgren made another hopeful trip to New Orleans, only to find an economy still stagnant and depressed. It was then that he finally turned to the North for help. The first step for him—as for all Southerners of his class in 1865—was to petition Washington for a pardon and the return of his enfranchisement. He had to swear allegiance to the United States, ask forgiveness in writing, and be pardoned before he could return to business. On 23 September 1865, with endorsements from William L. Sharkey and J. Madison Wells, provisional governors of Mississippi and Louisiana, respectively, Dahlgren wrote to President Andrew Johnson "to obtain the benefit of the pardon offered in your proclamation of 29th May last." Dahlgren swore to the Amnesty Oath of the State of Mississippi on 20 July 1865. In his appeal to the President, he stated: "I have never held any civil appointment from the Confederacy, nor any military office except a junior appointment under General Beauregard which the authority nullified and refused to confirm: though I did hold office as Brigadier-

General under the State of Mississippi: but not after June 1862. My application is based as being liable to the 13th clause, or the $20,000 exemption."[27] Southerners were eligible for pardons if they had not held a public office or the rank of general in the Confederacy or who, in 1865, had assets of less than $20,000. Dahlgren was saved the embarrassment of itemizing his dwindling assets.

In his endorsement of Dahlgren, on 24 October, Governor Wells made a point of reminding President Johnson that Dahlgren was "an esteemed citizen of Louisiana . . . and a relative of the Commodore and visits Washington on business of his own." In the appeal to Johnson, Dahlgren himself cited his brother "for my standing." But there was no reply as October came and went. Official Washington, with a flood of applications, had apparently shuffled Dahlgren's papers aside and ignored his plea.

☙

On 29 October 1865, the remains of Ulric Dahlgren were brought to the Council Chamber in Washington City Hall where they lay in state until noon on the 30th. Draped in an American flag and flanked by a guard of honor, the casket was taken to the Rev. Dr. Sunderland's church on Four-and-a-half Street, where the memorial had been preached the year before. In the procession were President Johnson, members of the Cabinet, distinguished clergymen and guests, and the family. General Dahlgren was not among them. Feeling in the North was still so high that his presence was hardly welcome, even if he could have afforded the journey. The Rev. Henry Ward Beecher of Boston delivered the sermon, the entire text of which was printed by *The New York Times* the following day.[28]

After the obsequies, Ulric's casket was escorted to the station, given a military salute, and transported to Baltimore, where it was transferred to the Philadelphia depot. Again, the major newspapers reported the details, by which means they trickled south. Accompanying the remains were Admiral Dahlgren and his youngest son, Paul, who had left the Naval Academy at Newport and entered West Point by an appointment made earlier by President Lincoln. In Philadelphia Ulric's body was taken to Independence Hall, where it again lay in state, honored with an oration by the Rev. J. P Wilson, and was finally accompanied by the Marine Band to Laurel Hill Cemetery and the family plot. Paul recorded the family's mourning in his diary;[29] the newspapers referred again to the martyrdom of a Union hero.

❧

Still having no response from his petition for a pardon, General Dahlgren decided he should visit Washington and present his appeal in person. With his brother's political influence, he hoped to find a shortcut through bureaucratic delays. His route from Natchez to Washington was probably through Jackson and north to Grand Junction by train, then east through Northern Alabama, with a stop at Huntsville; then Chattanooga to Knoxville, Tennessee; and north to Virginia and through the Shenandoah Valley via Lynchburg to Washington. It was a necessary ordeal, with uncertain schedules, crowded cars, and soot sifting over clothes from the smokestack. The journey, as far as Chattanooga, was a leg of the trip that the Dahlgrens had taken in 1860 to Beersheba Springs via Tracy City, Tennessee.[30]

The fashionable household of Admiral and Mrs. Dahlgren was not prepared for the visitor who appeared at the door on 9 November 1865. The admiral noted the arrival in his diary: "When I came home to my surprise found my brother Charles sitting quietly in my study; have not seen him for 9 years; comes for a pardon, having been a rebel for four years. He looks very seedy and says he has not more than ten dollars— plenty of land but that is not available. So I have to get his pardon; rather hard after all I have done & suffered for four years in putting down the Rebellion; one affliction after another."[31]

Charles Dahlgren wrote a daily account of the trip east and the people whom he met; he acknowledged the offers of his brother to help. He expressed, as well, his appreciation for the six weeks of hospitality provided him by the second Mrs. Dahlgren. The only member of the family to turn a hostile tongue on him was his sister Patty, bitter over his disloyalty to the Union and still mourning the loss of her young nephew Ulric. Because the diary is a prime document detailing the turmoil in Washington in the months after the war, verbatim selections are reproduced below. The diary also charts Dahlgren's schemes for the South's recovery, as well as his own.[32]

Excerpts from the Washington Diary of Charles G. Dahlgren, 9 November 1865–8 January 1866

Nov. 9—John called to see Mr. [William H.] Seward* with my application for pardon & left the papers with the Secy of State, who promised to attend to it . . . much difficulty and delay attends all business with any of the Departments.

Nov. 10—Addressed note to Baron [Edouard] de Stoeckl, Russian Ambassador [Envoy], in regard to casket & also his guns . . . weather very cold and very early for this latitude.

Nov. 11—Still cold. Judge Sharkey called to know when I was to return home as his sister Mary Thomas was very desirous to go with me. . . . I could not say.

Nov. 12—Met T. A. Murdock of Vicksburg . . . he was after claims for cotton . . . complains much of delay . . . tho' that is common.

Nov. 13—Elections in N York and N Jersey have gone very largely in favor of Republicans . . . have made great differences in matters here. . . . Southerners all consider it unfavorable to them and have gone home. . . . Mr. Seward stated that he had a Southern Levee every night till these elections and that night was the first Northern attendance that he had. Wilson and others were there.

Nov. 14—Still cold. Called to see Mrs. Thomas who leaves tomorrow for Mississippi . . . she had not succeeded with her claim being for cotton taken by Federals . . . but it was thought she

---

*William Henry Seward (1801–1872) was Lincoln's Secretary of State. Although he was not directly involved in granting pardons, he was a close friend of Admiral Dahlgren's.

would do so upon proper evidence . . . stated she saw nothing but bitter feeling toward the South.

Nov. 15—John saw Mr. [James] Speed* . . . stated that my papers had been made out and sent to Mr. Seward for signature.

Nov. 16—Weather quite pleasant . . . too mild for season.

Nov. 17—John wrote to Secy Stanton,† who stated that my pardon would soon be ready . . . very great change of feeling has occurred here toward the South. . . .

Nov. 18—Venniger Holtz from Louisiana claims a steamboat taken by Federals . . . advised him to procure a pardon as a matter of safety.

Nov. 19—Recd letter from Mary . . . only second one since I left home. . . . I have [sent] 13 letters to her . . . tho' some having been sent to St. Joseph may not have gone there and have been lost.

Nov. 20—Recd letter from Mr. [Richard H.] Gordon . . . they are all well but in great dread from many robberies and murders committed at Nashville and around there.

Nov. 21—Visited Capitol, the two wings nearly completed . . . making a very large magnificent building but not commodious and very badly lighted. The dome is one of the finest I have ever seen, but the statue on top is placed with her back to the West, and as all approach is from the West all the effect of the dome is lost. The object was to have the statue of America facing the East. Very proper in theory but bad in effect. [The statue is Freedom, not America.]

Nov. 22—Very large sale takes place of surplus stores and supplies belonging to Government . . . bring fair prices . . . I was chief purchaser. [Was he buying on credit? On Brother John?]

---

*Appointed Attorney General by Lincoln in 1864; resigned in 1866 over Andrew Johnson's Reconstruction policies.

†Secretary of War Edwin M. Stanton, fired by Andrew Johnson in 1868 in a test of the Tenure of Office Act and, ultimately, the chief cause of Johnson's impeachment by the House of Representatives. Johnson was exonerated by one vote in the U.S. Senate.

Nov. 23—Still delayed waiting for my pardon . . . great difficulty exists in regard to them . . . several have been revoked after delivery for reasons I could not ascertain. John recd note from Secy Stanton, saying that my pardon had been completed and if I would call today could receive it . . . as the note was sent after office hours, it was impossible to obtain it . . . sorry for that, as I wish to examine everything as Departments are not very exact in matters of importance.

Nov. 24—Called with John to see Mr. Seward, who stated that my pardon had gone last night to Gov. [William] Sharkey [in Mississippi]. . . . I endeavored to open conversation with Mr. Seward as to what the States were required to do before they could be restored to their rights in the Union, but he turned the conversation, unwilling to enlarge upon the subject . . . in reply to my question he stated that Gov. Sharkey was Governor of Mississippi and that Gov. [J. Madison] Wells* was Governor of Louisiana, but under military law. As he refused further conversation I could learn but little that I desired to be informed of . . . met there Admiral Farragut† and Commander [William A.] Parker‡ . . . had not seen the former since 1832. He was Lieut. on the *Hudson* under Com. Creighton on the coast of Brazil while I was there, and when the *Boston* under Capt. [B. V.] Hoffman . . . ran away from that station and went to New York because Creighton wished to detain the *Boston* after the time of her crew was up, for which Hoffman was court martialed & sentenced to be dismissed from the service . . . but released on account of service in war of 1812 . . . when he served on the *Constitution* under Stewart and was prize [junior] officer of the *Cyane* and brought her safely home.

---

*James Madison Wells (1808–1899) was elected governor of Louisiana in November 1865.
†David Glasgow Farragut (1801–1870), Admiral, USN.
‡Midshipman 3 July 1832, rising in rank to commander on 28 June 1861, died on 24 October 1882.

. . . [James S.] Palmer commanded the *Iroquois* as his flagship of the squadron which demanded the surrender of Natchez when I commanded there in May 1862, which I refused and never did deliver the city. [This is a misleading statement. Finding there were not enough men under arms to defend the city, Dahlgren turned it over to the civil authorities and Mayor John Hunter surrendered Natchez.]

Nov. 25—Saw Gov. Dennison* Post Master General and presented petition for Post Office at St. Joseph & [appointment of Robert] Murdock Postmaster . . . said he would consider the matter and give me answer Monday. He was very polite and courteous and seemed desirous to accommodate . . . asked after boats on the river. I stated 4 fine boats ran between Vicksburg & N Orleans, one that had come out since the war the *Magenta* was as fine as ever was had.

Nov. 26—Walked to Georgetown . . . staid home & wrote letters to Mary, Charles, and others.

Nov. 27—Called at White House . . . impossible to see President [Andrew Johnson] . . . crowd very great. Called on Mr. [James] Speed, Attorney General. He stated that orders had been [given] for no more pardons to issue to anyone for any account as the conduct of the States was unsatisfactory and until that change[d] no further pardons could issue. I urged my cases, but with no effect, apparently. Finally he said they would be thought over, Gen. [William T.] Martin included.†

Nov. 28—Cabinet day . . . could not see President . . . called on Secy State . . . stated the Atty Gen arranged all matters in regard

---

*William Dennison (1815–1882), ex-governor of Ohio, appointed Postmaster General in 1864.

†William Thompson Martin (1823–1910), Natchez lawyer and Confederate major general. He married (1854) Margaret Dunlop Conner (1836–1921) of a prominent Natchez family and resided at Monteigne. Martin began the war as Captain of the Adams Troop in 1861, served with J. E. B. Stuart, and was ordered west after Antietam.

to pardons and did not know what to say or what he could do.
. . . Called at Gen. [Oliver O.] Howard's* Bureau of Freedman
. . . had gone to New Orleans & Vicksburg to examine Freedman's Bureau.

Nov. 29—To Treasury Dept . . . inquired of tax upon cotton
raised in 1861 but sold in 1864 . . . members of Congress are
beginning to arrive from various parts of the North as Congress
meets soon.

Nov. 30—Called at White House and after much delay and
waiting at 4 P.M. saw President, asked him if the States of the
South recognized (1) the new Slavery Amendment to the Constitution . . . (2) abolition of slavery . . . (3) repudiation of War Debt
. . . (4) allowing to Freedmen to contract for wages—permission
to sue in Court their own color, to testify in cases where interested,
and were protected in life, limb & property. . . . If anything further
was necessary for their [states'] restoration of civil authority and
rights in the Union. He replied he did not see that anything more
was needed—in reply to question of stating that in writing if I
would address a note to him . . . he excused himself on the ground
of lack of time . . . he asked if the Delegates from the South would
press for seats in Congress and attempt to make a party in Congress.
I told him I thought not, for if so inclined it would be useless
against such a heavy majority as existed against them. He said the
majority might be too large. I asked for pardons for those I had
brought petitions for. He asked how many there were. I told him.
He asked if I had a list. . . . I told him I had not, but would
procure it.

Nov. 30—Saw Mr. Speed. Left petitions for pardon with clerk
to be examined & filed. Addressed Gen. Howard on subject of
Levees . . . called on him with card from John . . . had long interview . . . he appeared willing to do all in his power and promised

---

*Oliver Otis Howard (1830–1909), Union major general, commander of the
Army of Tennessee. Postwar head of Freedmen's Bureau.

to examine petition and referred it to Col. [William] Fowler*
AAG—promised that full orders had been given for restoration of
all my property and if not done to notify him and it should be
attended to at once.

Dec. 1—Recd official letter in regard to sale of land for taxes
. . . sent it by mail to Gov. Wells . . . could not see President . . .
Cabinet day . . . met Gen. John C. Brown† of Tennessee, Mr.
[John] Overton‡ and Col. Sterling Cockrill . . . the latter had been
pardoned. . . . The other two applying but without much hope
of success at present. . . . Col. Cockrill stated that his negroes had
all returned from Texas and were on the plantation . . . that Dr.
[John] Waters§ had rented his plantation for $12,000 per annum
. . . Mrs. Waters had obtained possession of home in Nashville
and would probably stay and live there.

Dec. 2—Saw Col. Withers‖ of Miss . . . agent of the State for
pardons . . . offered letters to capitalists [in] North to procure
leave to commence planting . . . saw Post Master . . . procured
duplicate of Murdock's appointment [as postmaster, Saint Joseph,
Louisiana] in case of delay or failure of original. Called at White
House, could not see President. Saw several of Southern Delegates
. . . advised no action or attempt to force admission to Senate as

---

*Brevet Maj. William Fowler, late lieutenant of the 146th New York, became
assistant adjutant general in early 1865.

†John Calvin Brown (1827–1899), Tennessee lawyer and Confederate major
general.

‡John Overton (1821–1898), colonel in the Tennessee State Militia in 1861,
offered his considerable fortune to the Confederate cause, was active in field
hospitals, disliked by Andrew Johnson, who called him "an aristocrat and oppres-
sor of the poor." He was in Washington seeking compensation for Federal
desecration of his properties near Nashville and Memphis.

§Dr. John Waters, Nashvillian, planter, and next-door neighbor of the Dahlgrens
at Beersheba Springs.

‖William T. Withers (1825–1889), Mexican War veteran, lawyer, colonel of the
1st Mississippi Artillery.

it would do no good but great deal of harm, as no party could expect to compete with the strong numbers of the other side . . . and opposition could have no effect but to bind them closer together . . . if refused admittance, retire, wait a short period & if then not admitted to go home.

Dec. 3—Wrote letters home. Saw Mr. Cockrill . . . his views coincided with mine as to course of Delegates . . . saw Gov. [William B.] Campbell* of Tennessee and Gen. [James L.] Alcorn† of Mississippi . . . they also agreed with me as the only course to be pursued.

Dec. 4—President saw my list of applicants for pardon . . . wished the Atty Gen. to certify to their correctness . . . some time ago applied for W. T. Martin . . . great difficulty as he was Maj. Gen. in Confed. Service . . . his pardon has been granted . . . the only one of that kind . . . addressed Gen. Howard asking for white troops to be stationed in the South as rumors of insurrections are reported, and there would be no harm in placing a few there . . . endeavored to procure order for G. M. Davis' house [Choctaw] from possession of Gen. [John W.] Davidson but Asst. Secy of War said they had not been able to get it before the Secy of War as yet. . . . Col. Withers said that Gen. [Gideon] Pillow‡ had borrowed $130,000 for 12 mos. at 10 per cent interest and 1/4 of all cotton made.

Dec. 5—Cabinet day . . . could not see the President . . . Gens. [John C.] Brown and [John] Overton left, unable to accomplish anything . . . all pardons are forbidden at present. . . . Saw Messrs. King, Ray, & Wickliff,§ St. Martin [Parish] Delegates from Louisi-

---

*William Bowen Campbell (1807–1867), last Whig governor of Tennessee; Union brigadier general.

†James Lusk Alcorn (1816–1894); brigadier general of Mississippi troops in 1861; later governor of Mississippi and U.S. Senator.

‡Gideon Johnson Pillow (1806–1878), Tennessee politician, brigadier general CSA.

§Robert C. Wickliffe, governor of Louisiana, 1856–1860, secessionist.

ana. Congress met yesterday . . . [Charles] Sumner in Senate and [Thaddeus] Stevens in house introduced and passed resolutions denying right of [Southern] States to representation and that they should be treated as conquered provinces. . . . This was done to forestall the President's message . . . visited the Navy Yard with Mr. [Sterling] Cockrill . . . saw the *Shenandoah* . . . very powerful vessel, especially from her ram . . . built in France . . . found Capt. Andrews . . . was very glad to see me . . . he had visited Natchez 12 years ago and was at Routhland . . . he had changed very much . . . thinner & much older . . . was escorted by Capt. Gunther who had commanded on the Miss River and spoke of losing part of his command at Ellis Cliffs, not dreaming that I was in command & by my orders that he was so fired on . . . he was very polite . . . had command of the *Waxsaw*.

Dec. 6—President ordered pardons for those applied for . . . took it to Atty Gen . . . promised to have it tomorrow . . . called to see Gen. Grant . . . had left at daylight for the South . . . saw Gov. Sharkey and delegation from Mississippi . . . they had called to see President . . . had been ten days from Vicksburg . . . very long trip . . . President's message delivered to Congress yesterday . . . takes ground that the States were never out of the Union and that the war was based on the ground that [they] could not go out . . . resolutions passed that no [Southern] Representatives should be admitted . . . this makes hostility between President and Congress for the two views are diametrically hostile to each other . . . very few Southerners here . . . all gone home . . . addressed Gen. Howard at length on subject of hiring Freedmen . . . he appears willing to do all in his power . . . stated that they were feeding several hundred thousand freedmen for whom there could be found no labor.

Dec. 7—Procured from Atty Gen. requisitions for pardons . . . went to Dept. of State . . . saw clerk & Col. Withers who had them all made out . . . those for Mississippi delivered to me & others for Louisiana sent by mail to Natchez . . . found that a pardon [for me] had been granted upon my first application in

August . . . the last pardon being spelled wrong, I took the first dated October and gave up the latter . . . certainly very singular carelessness . . . that my pardon had not been sent as stated by Mr. Seward . . . & then that there should be two pardons issued at the same time . . . Gen. Howard, Comm. Freedman Bureau, reported to Secy War in favor of my application for building Levees . . . the first time that has ever been done . . . hitherto opposed by all branches of the government and all aid refused.

Dec. 8—John went and introduced me to Mr. Stanton, Secy War, and spoke to him regarding Levees on the Miss River . . . Mr. Stanton said that he had not seen the papers nor thought of it, but would look at them and do all he could. . . . *Much* excitement in Congress . . . all members from the South [were] refused their seats and admittance to the Senate or House . . . resolutions introduced that those States should be viewed as conquered countries and treated as territories . . . the feeling against the South very strong and bitter and becoming more so daily . . . all of the Delegates from the South are here, but none have taken any active part except the members from Tennessee . . . [Horace] Maynard* endeavored to make a speech but was refused a hearing.

Dec. 9—Called upon Gen. Howard, who had reported to Secy of War favorably to my application for Govt to assist in building Levees. . . . Mr. Stanton said he had examined my application & had consulted the President, who had consented to build the Levees [on] the Mississippi and in order to arrive at the matter properly would dispatch an officer to make the examination . . . that [Maj.] Gen. [A. A.] Humphreys would be instructed to proceed at once to the Miss. river. . . . In reply to my inquiry, if he could go to work without waiting for other orders, the Secy stated that Gen. H. would be impowered to begin work without further instructions if satisfied of the propriety . . . Gov. [Robert C.] Wick-

---

*Horace Maynard (1814–1882), Tennessee Unionist, elected to U.S. Congress in 1865.

liffe said that Gen. Canby was fully informed and prepared to work upon the levees, as he had fully investigated the subject. . . . The Secy said that he would appoint Gen. Canby* if we desired . . . as the Secretary had selected Gen. Humphreys,† we prepared to let him take his own solution . . . in reply to question from Gov. Sharkey, as to whom and how, the cost should be repaid by the States. . . . The Secy stated that they had not come to any decision on that point and therefore would leave it an open question . . . to which I immediately assented, as a matter of no importance compared with the object in view . . . and remarking that we might now consider the levees as built and urging upon the Secretary the importance of time, from the usual rise of the river . . . and thanking him for his courtesy we left . . . before the Secy expressed a desire to have interview with Gen. Alcorn, Senator from Mississippi, as reference from myself to question in Louisiana . . . who could render any aid or assistance in forwarding the desired work . . . to which I assented. By request of Gov. Sharkey I went to see Gen. Alcorn . . . found him and sent him to Mr. Stanton . . . telegraphed Gov. Wells at New Orleans what had been done & directed the message repeated back—which was done—the message sent to New Orleans & repeated back in one hour & forty minutes. . . . The most extraordinary dispatch ever known, the Legislature being in session . . . it was very important for me to have reply from Gov. Wells, but had no answer up to late last night . . . the building of the Levees is the greatest point of the day. . . .

Dec. 10—Home all day writing letters . . . no letters from home. . . . They must have miscarried from irregularity of mails. . . . Having succeeded in all of my affairs I am only waiting the answer of Gov. Wells to leave and return home.

---

*Edward Richard Sprigs Canby (1817–1873), Union major general.
†Andrew Atkinson Humphreys (1810–1883), Union major general; appointed chief engineer of the Army, regular brigadier general, 1866.

Dec. 11—Notified Gov. Wells that I was waiting reply [about levee repairs and construction] . . . called on Gen. Howard . . . he had not been able to answer my application in regard to [directing] the Freedmen . . . his absence has caused much delay . . . the Govt are compelled to support a large number [of freedmen] and it would be better to hire them out to Planters.

Dec. 12—Much excitement in Congress about Southern Delegates . . . they have not been admitted and will not be . . . the Radicals are fearful of losing their power and do not wish to admit any from Southern States. . . . Submitted proposition to Gov. Sharkey to lay before President Johnson in regard to restoring civil authority . . . Gov. Sharkey approved & promised to take steps in relation thereto . . . though from appearance of affairs in Congress doubted if President would take any action as the majority of Republicans was so very heavy . . . being over two thirds of both houses.

Dec. 13—Congress is doing nothing of any moment, and I do not think will . . . their chief object appears to keep out the Southern delegation . . . telegraphed again to Gov. Wells for answer to my dispatch certainly very strange none has yet arrived.

Dec. 14—Saw Gen. Humphreys . . . told me that under orders from War Dept he would leave for Mississippi River tomorrow with Engineers to commence work upon our Levees. . . . He had formerly been engaged in examining that river and seems well acquainted with it . . . John describes him as an excellent officer . . . stated that his orders were to call on Gen. [Edward Richard Sprigs] Canby for all labor needed to do the work & gave him letters to Gov. Sparrow, Dr. Bowman, Capt. Farrar . . . he agreed to stop the bayou at Lake Providence before any other work was done . . . that being of great moment.

Dec. 15—Saw Gen. Grant . . . said that he always thought the Levees should be rebuilt by the Government . . . that Gen. Humphreys had left for the South with orders to call on Gen. Canby for labor to build the Levees, which should be promptly furnished . . . that he knew of no other source from which the levees could be built except from the colored regiments and should be promptly furnished. In reply to my questions, he said that ten thousand should be supplied if demanded by Gen. Humphreys, as the Levees should be built . . . telegraphed Gov. Wells to the effect of Gen. Grant's conversation and requesting an answer as I never received any reply to my former dispatch [to Gov. Wells concerning his cooperation in the Levee project] . . . he is very careless on a matter of such extreme moment . . . directed Telegraph officer, if anything came for me to send it to New York care Ira Smith & Co., 370 Broadway, as I could not wait here any longer . . . made all my preparations to leave in the morning for Philadelphia.

Dec. 16—Weather very cold . . . left Washington at 11-1/4 oc for Philadelphia. . . . John gave me letters to several [financiers] in Boston and authorized me to draw upon him for money . . . his conduct has been very noble . . . all of John's family, Mrs. Dahlgren, her children Vinton and Miss Romaine [Goddard] & Eva [Dahlgren] have all behaved with great consideration and kindness in every respect . . . the only exception has been Martha [Patty], whose conduct has been infamous ever since I have been in the House. I did not hold any communication with her, nor speak to her, on leaving . . . and never again will under any circumstances acknowledge her, or hold the slightest intercourse with her . . . her villainy is of the most unparalleled description. . . . Admiral Farragut and several officers were on the cars, which were much crowded . . . no change of cars, all streams are bridged, except Susquehanna . . . the Locomotive & cars there cross on top of ferry boat having Rail Road tracks for cars to run upon . . . very inconvenient but the bridge will soon be completed . . . arrived at Philadelphia at 6 P.M. . . . went to Girard House . . . very clean & comfortable . . . fare very good.

When Dahlgren left Washington, he was satisfied that federal help would be forthcoming for the restoration of the levees. It would be the first step toward successful farming and economic recovery in a stricken

South. State agencies were depleted and incapable of raising the necessary funds. The diary reflects Dahlgren's dogged efforts in interviews with President Johnson, General Canby, Generals Grant and Humphreys, and Governor Sharkey of Mississippi to put his scheme into action. Profiting directly would be laborers from the unemployed population of freedmen. His proposal would help put the planter back on his feet, invite capital from Northern investors, find employment for the Negro troops, and take thousands of homeless families off the government dole.

The chief dissenter in the South was Governor Wells of Louisiana, who refused to answer Dahlgren's telegrams asking for his cooperation. Nevertheless, the diary records that Dahlgren left Washington sanguine that there would be funds for repairing the levees when the new Congress met in the summer. His next move was to travel on to Philadelphia, New York, and Boston armed with assurances about the levees in order to attract capitalists who might be willing to lease or buy tax-ridden plantations or to form partnerships with their owners for a percentage of the profits. His friend Dr. John Waters had reportedly leased his holdings for $12,000 per annum. It was rumored that Gen. Gideon Pillow had borrowed $130,000 at 10 percent interest and one fourth of all cotton made. The report was only slightly exaggerated, for Pillow's biographers cite a loan of $125,000 from Watts, Given, and Co., New York.[33]

Not all of Dahlgren's time in Washington that December was taken up in getting a pardon for himself and several of his friends or in giving interviews that he hoped would bring an understanding and benevolent treatment of the South. The social side of his nature began to revive. He was struck by recollections when he met Admiral Farragut. They had reminisced about their first meeting in 1832 when Dahlgren was a young sailor just turned twenty-one. He had joked with James S. Palmer, whose flagship *Iroquois* had trained her guns on Dahlgren and demanded the surrender of Natchez. He strode with curiosity around the Navy Yard, looked at advances in naval armaments, and admired the *Shenendoah* that had been built in France for the Confederate Navy. He went his gregarious way basking in the attention of his late antagonists. Exchanging amenities, he found them as polite as warriors of the classic mode. They had all fought hard, won each other's respect in arms, and now saluted and walked off abreast to swap tales in the nearest saloon.

It was almost as though they had shrugged off Shiloh, Pickett's Charge, the burning of Atlanta, and the sunset flow of blood in December just a year ago at Franklin. They wanted to forget that infantrymen had perished with frozen feet and seamen were still roiling in salty shrouds. For now, they would roll back four years and find means of diversion. They would act again as young men with firm flesh and steady gait. They would address each other in jesting tones and maintain the spirit of good fellows. They would not let the past distemper their talk or sully their recovering spirits.

In addition to the military, Dahlgren kept running into Southerners who had come to Washington for pardons, compensation for war damages to their property, or recompense for their losses in cotton, buildings, and even a steamboat. He had a natural feeling of fellowship with other Southerners when they met on the streets of Washington, each hoping for a hearing of his claims and an early endorsement. Several, including Generals Alcorn and Martin, had made the journey from Mississippi. Dahlgren had known firsthand, or known about, Tennesseans like Generals Overton and John C. Brown when he visited Nashville or Beersheba Springs. He also had a surprise meeting with Sterling Cockrill, a coinvestor with him at the resort in 1859.

The Southerners sighted each other on the steps of the Capitol, spoke in guarded tones about the Radicals in Congress, and invented strategies for Southern representation again in the body politic. In short, it was a time of unexpected camaraderie for Dahlgren and his peers as they huddled together in their dusty suits and wrinkled collars. They indulged in personal news, talked about their families, and exchanged bits and pieces of "crossroads history." There was relief in retailing gossip from back home, finding satisfaction in the recent bad luck of a political rival, or joking about Yankee red tape in handling the chaos that was paralyzing the country at the end of 1865.

With the support of Admiral Dahlgren, Charles had held court in the capital city; he had carried his reconstruction arguments all the way to

President Johnson. His natural temerity, along with his gift of rhetoric, had kept him moving through the bureaucracy to the top. He still believed in the South's survival and recovery.

In Philadelphia, where he had spent his youth, Charles visited familiar scenes and the graves of his forebears. The newest grave (and not yet settled) was Ulric's among the granite shafts of three generations. He called on Nancy Watson, a cousin whose financial lot was as stricken as his, and left her a small token. Her son was permanently crippled from wounds at Sharpsburg, Maryland.[34]

In his diary, Charles also recorded a number of sympathetic attitudes expressed to him about the defeat of the South: ". . . saw Mr. Ingersoll . . . he was very much disappointed at the sudden yielding of the South: as it now amounted to a perfect submission to the Radical party. . . ."[35] Mr. Ingersoll's remarks gave Dahlgren an opportunity to lash out at Confederate leaders and their mistakes: "I explained that [the South gave up] from the total lack of confidence in [Jefferson] Davis or in any of the leaders or Generals . . . that the latter were certainly the most incompetent ever known . . . nor would any other be appointed while Davis had any control or authority. . . ." Then came Dahlgren's summary of what he had heard from Northern moderates about the South: ". . . [A]lthough none upheld the action of the South in attempting to secede, yet many regretted very much the condition of her affairs . . . as much more would have been obtained by different management . . . even up to the period of Commissioners' visit to Lincoln . . . for if obliged to yield, it certainly would have been far better to have compromised with gradual emancipation [of the slaves] than to have been driven out with nothing. . . ."[36] Thus the voices of reason and compromise spoke up ex post facto—after four years of section versus section in the bloodiest internecine conflict in history.

In New York, the general found that not all his business associates from his prosperous years had profited by the war. He called on his friend Ira Smith of 370 Broadway, for whom he would later name one of his twin sons, and found Smith and Company trying to settle accounts and close the business. He was moved to hear of the deaths of familiar tradesmen whom he had patronized. Among them were Cullen the

bootmaker and Stuart the watchmaker—"the best of their profession."
He called on C. G. Newcomb and was hardly prepared for the surprise,
for Newcomb paid him a balance of $81 that he had owed since 1860.
His friend then confided that he had lost heavily on a number of debts
due him from the South.[37]

Trying to stretch his brother's credit "in probably the most costly
city in the world" gave Dahlgren pause as he experienced the postwar
inflation and extravagance displayed in the New York shops and mercantile houses that he had known before the war. The resources of many
old friends were depleted, and the new capitalists turned a deaf ear to
his argument that a productive South, with investments and a little time,
would return the favors and bring prosperity to both sections. He found
no one in New York willing to take the risk. Dahlgren did not mention
calling on Dr. Stephen Duncan, 12 Washington Square, about two notes
owing to Duncan that had come due in 1864 and 1865, with another
due in January 1866. He probably intended to discuss them later by
correspondence when he found investors for his crops.

Dahlgren arrived in Boston two days before Christmas with a heavy
snow on the ground. He put up at the Revere House and went immediately to call on capitalist Robert Bennet Forbes (1804–1889), former sea
captain, China merchant, shipowner, and a friend of Admiral Dahlgren's.
Forbes was not in; so he called on General Burt, a land company agent,
and was promised help. But he found that even with "much capital here
it is difficult to be had, as people [are] afraid of Southern security."[38]

On the day after Christmas, he went again to see Forbes. He was
politely received and given a letter to John Murray Forbes, a younger
brother. "They are very cautious and easily alarmed," Dahlgren concluded
after the meeting. Other businessmen "appeared not to understand the
state of affairs and are really ignorant of the condition of things [in the
South] or they would soon invest there."[39] With Southerners land poor
and pleading at their gates, the Northerners had the advantage of naming
their own prices. Dahlgren argued that they could earn profits in sugar
cane, rice, and timber, in addition to cotton, but his rhetoric was not
immediately effective.

If they were willing to deal at all, the Northern banks demanded "stiff terms," as one observer pointed out: "They wanted participating planters to pay 10 percent annual interest on their loans, sign over the mortgages on their lands, divide the profits from their crops, consign all crops to the mortgaging agency, and pay the 'customary commercial commissions.' "[40] Although R. B. Forbes seemed to show more interest in Dahlgren's proposals than anyone else, he hesitated about making final decisions on his own. So, according to Dahlgren's diary, he and Forbes went public with a notice in a Boston newspaper in the hope of attracting additional investors:

> . . . [P]ut advertisement in paper for money and interest in crops. Mr. Forbes advertized that he would take [invest] one fifth of $30,000 if others would take the residue . . . several persons called to see me . . . all very anxious and desiring to go South or to invest their money . . . many wanted to send sums from $5,000 to $25,000 and send their children with it to obtain salary . . . this I refused as I had no office nor salary to give them . . . many others who were violent abolitionists or Radicals were very desirous also to invest or do anything to make money . . . but I refused all such conversations. . . . [41]

Unwilling to yield to the opportunists, Dahlgren was finally able to strike an arrangement with R. B. Forbes and two of his associates, Jeffries and Cunningham. They agreed "to take the $30,000 on condition of one-sixth of the crop, deducting $60 per bale expenses."[42]

Other planters whose property was near Dahlgren's plantations were beginning to rent their acreage to outsiders at extremely low figures because of the depressed market. "Robert Carter . . . leased Vidalia . . . in Concordia Parish to Benjamin Teel for $7,000" in 1866, down from the $12,500 agreement of the year before. "Eliza Sanderson let out Overton, 15 miles southeast of Natchez for $1500. Thomas R. Shields received $1,000 for Hermitage." Neither lessor nor lessee could be sure of any profits ahead, even at these figures.[43]

When the contract was signed with Forbes and funds for the crop of 1866 assured, Dahlgren made his way south on 8 January. He had achieved promises in Washington that the levees would be repaired and his property restored to him. Meanwhile, he would try to block the sheriff's sale for delinquent taxes that had piled up for four years. He had much to report to Mary Edgar and the boys and the other planters in Tensas, including his interview with President Johnson. He wanted to take back to them what they needed most—reassurances and a countenance of hope—but he would not mislead them about the Radicals in Congress and their schemes for punishing the rebellious South.

It was well for Dahlgren and the other planters that they could not predict the instruments of loss in their fields in 1866 and 1867—defective seed, excessive rain and flooding during the spring, long droughts in summer, and destructive army worms. One observer reported that "in a few days the fields [invaded by the worms] were blackened like fire had swept over them."[44] What cotton there was would be inferior and languish at sluggish prices in 1867. Returning to his fields in January 1866, Dahlgren could not know that most of the deck had already been stacked against him.

❦ Nine ❧

Another Move,
Another Start at Sixty

In January 1866, Charles Dahlgren might have looked at his dusty account books and reflected on the bumper years of his plantations for the decade 1850 to 1860. The figures showed him what he might achieve again if he could get a running start. He assumed, after the journey to Washington and the assurances of Andrew Johnson, that the federal government would rebuild the levees with the labor of freedmen and keep the river at bay. He hoped that the Radicals in Congress could be convinced that a rehabilitated South was vital to the economy of the nation, bringing profits to the victors as well as to the defeated. He had plenty of support from home.

Before him now were his figures on Glenwood Farm: 1,990 acres, which had produced 68 bales of cotton and 1,500 bushels of corn in 1850, total value $14,426. Marydale, with 5,700 acres, had produced 600 bales of cotton and 5,000 bushels of corn in 1856, total value $70,000. This figure did not include $1,000 for ten yokes of oxen and $4,200 for sixty horses. The 168 slaves at Marydale had been valued at $76,600.[1] By 1860, the plantations had increased in value to $245,000 and the slaves to $192,000.

Dahlgren could also look at his file of deeds and review a number of transactions like the the one in 1857 when he conveyed 1,076 acres in Tensas to his stepson, Thomas LaRoche Ellis. The price of $49,560 was for the land, buildings, and appurtenances. Included were eight mules, six yokes of oxen, hogs, wagons, plows, and 3,500 barrels of corn. Ellis was to pay the first note of $10,900 on 1 January 1859; $10,400 on

1 January 1860; $9,000 in 1861, and so on with a final payment in 1863.[2] When the war began and Thomas LaRoche went off to the Confederate Army, his payments lapsed. His service was very brief; he fell ill and died of consumption while on furlough in Tensas on 2 February 1862.[3] His young widow, Appoline Ingraham Ellis, was not able to meet her husband's obligation to his stepfather, and the 1,000 acres were added to the other idle properties with delinquent taxes in 1866.

Following their December visit in Washington, Admiral Dahlgren wrote to Charles in New Orleans on 20 February 1866. The older brother acknowledged Charles's partial payment of the loan to travel in the East: "The money is all right and I hope you *have not* returned it before you could do so conveniently . . . though it was not in my power to go further. . . . Several things have pressed me just now. My allowance to [Sister] Patty of $300 per ann . . . [and] other expenses not personal had cleaned me out at the time."

Then, responding to Charles's plea for his help in the recovery of Llangollen from Federal troops, the admiral wrote: "I saw [Edwin] Stanton soon after receiving your note today. His answer was in fact a declination to interfere. He said no judgment could be formed here and that the authorities *there* must decide [on any compensation for use by Union troops]. . . . I will take an opportunity to see Gen. Grant who may be able to do something."[4] Meanwhile, Charles went to New Orleans several times to court other sources of capital for his crops.

In early spring 1866, lacking funds to hire hands, Dahlgren put his older sons Charlie Routh, Bernard, and Pudge to the plow and the younger boys, Mortimer and Van, to the kitchen garden. (Rowan was only four years old and Edgar two.) The older boys labored alongside the blacks who were living in ramshackle slave houses. They agreed to work for a garden plot and $10 to $15 per month. Mary Edgar managed the house, sewed, and taught the children. The bountiful life that she had experienced in Nashville and Natchez had been swept away by the time she was twenty-three years old. At age twenty-six, she could not look beyond a hope to survive.

As though four years of war were not enough, the Mississippi River ravaged the land and crops in the spring of 1866 and again in 1867. In

June 1868, Dahlgren wrote Pudge in Toronto: "At present misfortunes hang heavily on our country. We were overflowed this year, three years in succession, and since the subsiding of the waters it has rained so continually as to make all crops impossible to be grown & now the worms have made their appearance & doubtless will destroy all the cotton."[5] The tax collector, however, was never idle with his notices stamped "DELINQUENT."

On 15 April 1867, Mary Edgar gave birth to her fourth child, another son who was named Charles Ulric for his father and his cousin Ulric.[6] Then, on 23 April, son Charlie Routh and Nannie Hollingsworth, a first cousin once removed, were married in Natchez by Dr. Joseph Buck Stratton, their cousin by marriage.[7] The celebration was quiet but cheerful. Both sides of the family took pride in Charles's long service in the war, but they were concerned about his trouble with ascites and the toll that the war had taken. They had reason to be apprehensive. Six months later, on 6 November, the loss to the family and the new bride was recorded by the faithful Dr. Stratton in his diary: "Charles R. Dahlgren, cousin of my wife, a young man just grown and married, died last evening at Lake St. Joseph, suddenly, and his body is to be brought down tonight in the packet for interment."[8]

Charlie Routh was twenty-six years old and the heir apparent in the Dahlgren dynasty. His father was deeply stricken but acted quickly two weeks later. On 18 November 1867, the general went to court in Tensas Parish to have his next three sons, all under twenty-one, declared majors in the courts of Louisiana. Bernard was twenty; Pudge, eighteen; and Mortimer, eleven. They could now do business legally as adults, including ownership and sale of land and signing of mortgages.[9] Then came another blow on 29 July 1868: son Bernard died of fever at Marydale. Once again the dynasty was bereft.[10]

General Dahlgren had used the legal means of transferring land to a minor son at least once before. In July 1863, on the day he bought the tract of 101 acres from Daniel Melton in DeKalb County, Georgia, the general signed the property over to John Adolph, then age fifteen, and took a mortgage on it.[11] The maneuver raises some questions that the record fails to answer. It would appear, however, that Dahlgren used

Pudge as a safeguard against any demands by creditors. Legally, if the property stayed in his son's name, the general's creditors could not move in without a good deal of trouble and expense.[12] The property in Louisiana, if conveyed to Pudge and Mortimer, could be protected with the same maneuver.

℞℞

Another move occurred to Dahlgren in early 1868. Tottering on bankruptcy in Louisiana, he began to explore business opportunities in Canada, as had a number of Confederates. He sent son Pudge to college in Toronto and asked him to investigate their chances there. With an athlete's bent for fencing, military drill, and boxing, in addition to a lot of personal cunning, Pudge was the anointed son to carry out his father's business. "I intend to give you an education, my dear boy," his father wrote, "for I can give you nothing else." Once Adolph had completed his regimen of studies, father and son would team up to outmaneuver the tax collector and the army worm.[13]

The one available letter of this period, a copy preserved in a letter book, is from General Dahlgren to Pudge and reveals the father's protective attitude toward his son. The general, at age fifty-seven, opens his heart and expresses his convictions, religious and political, to the son in Toronto. It is a declaration meant to reflect the wisdom and affirm the authority of the patriarch. If Adolph was too young and too spirited to follow the maxims of his father, the document is nonetheless of interest for its piety. "Never omit Sunday church as you were raised . . . remember he who is false to God will be false to man . . . if any approach you with any dishonorable offers, strike them to the earth as you would a viper. . . . I am the third generation that has been stripped of my property by adherence to principles." He recounts the story of his maternal grandfather James Rowan, who lost his estate in Ireland; then he tells of his own father's losses in defiance of Napoleon's puppet Bernadotte in Sweden. Finally, he describes his decisions that brought about his own losses:

I could have procured rank in the North, which Jefferson Davis refused me [in the South] and wealth of which I am bereft—and position which I do not possess—but it had no influence with me to possess those things. I believed the South was right and I remained true to my principles and now after all my trials & hardships, after my reduction from wealth to poverty & compelled to live in a conquered country, I stand as firm, unflinching, & unchanged as at first. I would unhesitatingly do the same thing. Tho' it is coupled with the sorrowful knowledge that our misfortunes are our own fault. Could I have carried out my plans, I could have saved our country. . . . [14]

It is relevant to recall the general's aborted career in the military of Mississippi during 1861 and 1862—to contrast his lack of leadership then against his assertions to Pudge in 1868. He had convinced himself that if it had not been for the stubbornness of Jefferson Davis, he could have saved the South. One wonders if Pudge was convinced. Yet the young man might have been moved by his father's belief in freedom of choice and his moral responsibility in declaring "our misfortunes are our own fault." His father, as many fathers appear to their sons, was a man of conflicting assertions. But the general reaffirmed to Pudge that he had exercised freedom of choice and would accept the results.

The letter of 1868 urges Pudge to enroll in a curriculum of mental and physical studies that would sustain him for life: "The Scriptures & Holy History . . . Mathematics, Algebra, ancient and modern History, Latin, French, Spanish, German, Reading, Grammar, Writing, drawing, music (flute). . . . Swimming, riding, fencing, shooting, rowing, dueling, boxing, gymnastic exercises, drawing. Then with a voyage to learn navigation and a course at Military School to learn maneuvers & science."[15]

To the general's credit, his own education had included a commendable grasp of the subjects that he outlined for Pudge. Several were acquired in wide reading, others in voyages as a young man, and many in close perusals of military manuals. Dahlgren's prose style was marked by a gift for rhetoric. If he had been born with a less volatile nature, the general might have been a successful educator or the commandant of one of the South's military academies. After the war, Robert E. Lee became president of Washington College in Lexington, Virginia. Such positions carried a more professional dignity than lending one's name to an insurance company, as Jefferson Davis did for a while, or joining the Louisiana State Lottery, for which Generals Beauregard and Early acted as commissioners during the 1870s.[16] Dahlgren, however, still physically strong and mentally alert, looked for recovery in trade, broker-age, and private banking. In them lay the challenges for his vigor and competitive spirit.

෬෪

The letter of 1868 suggests that the general, after being victimized by floods and tax collectors, was serious about a new life for himself and his family in Toronto. He asked Pudge to cast about for business opportunities and to investigate suitable housing for the family. The same letter closes with a message: "Tell Gen. Early I will write to him." Jubal Early, however, after three years of expatriation in Canada, returned to his native Virginia and cast his lot again with the South.[17]

Jefferson Davis, after his release from Fortress Monroe and ten years of uncertainty, including residence in Canada, also turned South again to live at Beauvoir as the guest of Sarah Dorsey on the Mississippi Coast. There, he would not be demeaned by writing insurance policies but would find time to complete his memoirs. One Southerner, Thomas Yeatman of Tennessee, a stepson of Senator John Bell, went to Paris, married a French woman, operated a girls' school, and remained in France to bring up another generation of Yeatmans.

After the school term of 1868 ended in Toronto, General Dahlgren was so short of funds that he wrote Pudge to return home. Like the once mighty John Routh and the heirs of the Routh estates in Tensas Parish, Dahlgren was about to be sold out for taxes. That blow finally struck on a dark day in November when the Seventh District Court in New Orleans ordered the sheriff of Tensas Parish to seize all the Dahlgren properties. The nineteen tracts, ranging from 40 to 1,600 acres, totaled

7,866 acres and included Marydale and The Oaks. On 17 November, the sheriff "advertised said property for sale to take place at the Court House door in St. Joseph on Saturday the 2nd of January AD 1869." As was customary, the notice was placed "in three public places in this Parish for more than thirty clear days," and the sale was held at the appointed time and place.[18]

The general remained in New Orleans and sent Pudge to act in the proceedings. Having read the writ advertisement, appraisement, and certificate of mortgages, Sheriff James M. Gillespie pronounced the estate for sale. Stepping forward to bid was son John Adolph Dahlgren, in the amount of $15,732, "which being the last & highest bid or offer made therefor, and two thirds of the appraised value, I [Sheriff of Tensas] struck off & publicly adjudicated the same to him." The sheriff spoke in behalf of the court, and the 7,866 acres went for $2 an acre, or two thirds of the appraised value of $3. By ironic contrast, the census recorder in 1860 had estimated the value of the same property as $245,000. It had made Dahlgren 700 bales of cotton in 1859 with the labor of 187 slaves at Marydale and 23 at The Oaks. That was exactly a decade before, when his real estate in Adams County (Natchez) was valued at $75,000 and his personal property at $10,000.

The question arises as to how Pudge was able to come up with $15,000 to purchase the property in 1869. It is known that Dahlgren had stayed in touch with R. B. Forbes of Boston and that Forbes sent his agent and attorney, Henry A. Pierce, to New Orleans to negotiate for the property, or at least the Oaks tract of 1,000 acres. The next deed, Adolph Dahlgren to Forbes, 12 March 1869, reveals that the general had executed three promissory notes against the property in February 1866 after his meeting with Forbes in Boston: the first for $10,000, payable November 1866; the second for $5,000, payable December 1866; and the third for $5,000, payable January 1867. At the time Dahlgren was hopeful about repayment by the end of each year after the crops were sold, the hands paid, and expenses settled. That was not to be the case, however, with three bad years in a row, and by 1869 he had apparently not been able to make as much as the first payment.

Then, on 14 March 1869, a total of six notes against the property were handed over to son Adolph Dahlgren at a cash valuation of $12,500, "as estimated in value by all parties," and The Oaks went to Forbes for $12.50 an acre and without encumbrances. Adolph Dahlgren, listed as vendor in the deed, would not be twenty years old until May. He declared for the record that "he is neither tutor, curator of minors, interdicted persons or absentees and that he is unmarried."[19] With his bravado and cunning, Pudge had intervened for his father, sold the property, and satisfied the sheriff, if not the remainder of his father's creditors.

Before the sale, Charles Dahlgren had asked his brother John to send him the balance owing him from their mother's estate ($649.50), to which John added his own share as a gift, making a total of $1,299. By that time, Charles had Mary Edgar and six children to support. The admiral had noted in his diary on 1 January that in addition he sent Charles a personal check for $200 and would like to send more because of his "great destitution."[20] It was a fine gesture, of course, but not really a sacrifice because the admiral was married to a wife of considerable means and living in a magnificent house of four stories at 1325 Massachusetts Avenue, near Thomas Circle, in Washington.

About the same time, Admiral Dahlgren wrote to their sister Patty, the third wife, since 1867, of the very wealthy Matthew Parsons Read. They were childless and living in luxury on Madison Avenue in New York City. The admiral told Patty that brother Charles's children were reduced to wearing linsey-woolsey (a coarse fabric of wool and cotton) and that there was seldom meat on the table. The general had also reported to him that his son Austin Mortimer, at age twelve, had not yet learned to read and write.[21]

The plight of the southern Dahlgrens was so severe that Madeleine, the admiral's wife, was moved to compassion. John wrote to Charles that he and Madeleine would be glad to take two of the boys into their Washington household for two years and see that they were instructed "at least in the ordinary elements of English education."[22] The admiral added a note to the effect that if Charles sent the boys they were to come as they were, not try to find money for new clothes. The gesture was appreciated but came to naught. Admiral Dahlgren wrote in his diary on 26 March that "their mother is unwilling to part with them."[23]

Mary Edgar, however, kept communications open between Louisiana and Washington. In late April, she sent a plea to the admiral, who, in turn, forwarded it to sister Patty and Mr. Read in New York. Her letter was so telling of the family's plight that even the adamant Patty was moved. She wrote to John, and John reported that "on the 1st August Mr. Read will by change of investment have $10,000" and he proposes paying off the mortgage on Llangollen so "the party holding mortgage on the house" will not foreclose.[24] At long last, Patty had been moved to compassion and had manipulated her husband into keeping a roof over the heads of Charles and his family for a little longer. Then, another loss came in June. Little Martha Jane, age four months, died of summer fever. She had been Dahlgren's hope of a little girl in a household of noisy, rowdy boys.[25]

The admiral and Madeleine, aware of Martha Jane's arrival, sent Charles and Mary Edgar a check for $50 on 4 May 1869, with a note: "Madeleine has seen Senator [John S.] Harris [of Louisiana] who promised to give Charles a $1200 a year job if he applies, as is the custom." The general probably did not apply because he had already decided to gamble on leaving the South.[26]

In addition to his losses and the deprivation forced on his family, Dahlgren had only to look in Adams County and observe firsthand the plight of other families. There were numerous women who had lost their husbands in the war and whose children were left with no support. By 1867, the Board of Aldermen was regularly receiving petitions to help destitute widows and indigent children. The lists reflect the far-flung military service of Mississippians during the four years of conflict. They show the casualties sustained by local families in every major theater of the war—Virginia, Maryland, Tennessee, Mississippi. Several fathers had died in Yankee prisons. One list records thirty-six petitions for help. Another list names sixteen children in St. Mary's Asylum whose parents or relatives had been in Confederate service. Still another names twenty-three children in the Orphans Asylum "whose fathers perished in the Confederate cause."[27]

αℬ

If the social upheaval and economic straits that plagued the South in the late 1860s seemed a Biblical judgment to a number of Southerners, General Dahlgren tried to find relief through compromise with Washington. His conversation with President Johnson in November 1865 indicated as much, and his diary reflects Johnson's verbal agreement to the return of Southern representation in Congress, steady employment of ex-slaves for subsistence wages, and federal subsidies for the South's depleted farms and broken levees. The President, however, was locked in a power struggle with Congress that came to a head on 5 March 1868 when the House, led by Thaddeus Stevens, brought impeachment proceedings. The unprecedented trial in the Senate ended with the dismissal of all charges by one vote and Johnson finished his term in office. Dahlgren fully supported Johnson's measures for the South and regretted the punitive acts of the Radicals. Martial law was still in effect, and corrupt appointees from the North governed the major municipalities. Miscreant carpetbaggers had the nod of the Federal troops whom they followed to the South. It was not until 1877 that military occupation was generally withdrawn.

In contrast, the dazzling prosperity that Dahlgren observed in New York City in late 1865 was to increase during the next decades. The oligarchy of robber barons—men such as Cornelius Vanderbilt, Jay Gould, John Pierpont Morgan, Joseph William Drexel, John D. Rockefeller, and Andrew Carnegie—amassed such wealth in so few years that they seemed to command heaven along with earth. William ("Boss") Tweed (1823–1878) dominated New York City through fraudulent contracts, kickbacks, and a following of faithful grafters. The Civil War had brought the Industrial Age to new heights; it was an age of factory hirelings in mill towns, labor strikes, and a loss of confidence in elected leaders. Just as the cotton gin had earlier advanced the economy of the Deep South and brought with it the cry for more and more slave labor to keep up with the machine, the industrial economy in the North called for more hirelings at more machines to create more articles for a public persuaded to buy what they did not always need or might have produced as well at home. The era was flamboyant, as well, marked by social pretensions born of money and producing artificial patterns of behavior.

One of its seriocomic observers, Mark Twain, dubbed it the "Gilded Age." The wives of the robber barons vied with each other, season after season, to stage the most extravagant balls in the most lavish settings that wealth could create. Their object was to outdo the competition in expenditures, outshine the pretenders, and, most of all, to amuse the jaded with fresh outrages that would jar loose the forked tongues of gossip.

From a distance Charles Dahlgren and his family would watch the admiral's two younger sons by Madeleine marry into the Drexel clan and reach the top of the economic ladder. John Vinton and Eric Bernard married, respectively, Elizabeth and Lucy Drexel, daughters of the wealthy Joseph William and Lucy Wharton Drexel. John and Eric rose to favor in the society of the *haute monde* in New York, Newport, and the watering places of Europe. Although John died young from tuberculosis, his son, John Vinton Jr., and his brother Bernard were never to forgo any of the excesses of the Gilded Age. Wealth, or the lack of it, had driven a wedge between the next generation of Dahlgrens, North and South.

❧

During the autumn of 1869, the Charles Dahlgrens decided it would be prudent for Mary Edgar and the younger boys to move to Nashville because they had lost both Llangollen and Marydale. The older boys, Charlie Routh and Bernard, lay in unmarked graves in the Natchez City Cemetery. Arranging a house next door to theirs on Vine Street, Mary Edgar's older sister, Ellen Vannoy Gardner, and her husband, Edwin S. Gardner, were in a position to help. Ellen had presided over the birth of Van at Beersheba Springs and was busy now with preparations for another Dahlgren baby in March. Soon after Christmas, General Dahlgren left the crowded household and retreated to Atlanta to look for opportunities there as factor, commission agent, or salesman.[28]

Charles could leave with good conscience because Ellen Gardner was a woman who would handle his brood and run the house with a firm hand. To help were three servants, Kitty Black, age eighty; Mahaly Black, age thirty; and Mary Black, age nineteen. They appear as part of the Dahlgren household in the Nashville census of 1870. Dahlgren does not list any real estate holdings in Nashville, only personal property valued at $8,000. His wife's property was listed at $1,500. They had managed to save the jewelry, the Cooper portraits, and some of the family silver. The property at Beersheba Springs was reclaimed by Colonel Armfield for forfeited mortgage payments and unpaid taxes. The hospitality of the Gardners proved a haven for Mary Edgar and her children.

While they were in Nashville, the general was stunned by the news of Dr. Tully Gibson's death in Mississippi. Gibson, their companion and outrider on the long journey home in 1865, had been shot down by a Reconstruction sheriff in Sunflower County on 4 January 1870. His death reflected the anarchy in Mississippi when Gen. Adelbert Ames was appointed provisional governor of the state on 15 July 1868. Ames named irresponsible followers, white and black, to positions of local authority. The result was a catastrophic takeover by forces antithetical to civil law and order.[29]

The corrupt regime had begun acts of vengeance against former slave-owners on 2 January 1869. Incited by their unscrupulous leaders, the former slaves banded together and rioted in Sunflower, Newton, and Hinds counties. One of the leaders, William Combash, said that he was sent by Governor Ames to "redeem his people from thraldom." In Sunflower County, he enlisted followers bearing arms, estimated at four hundred. Combash, a slave born in Maryland, had been sold south before 1861 for a series of thefts. He had escaped and returned North to join a black infantry unit in Philadelphia during the war. In 1865 he went back to Mississippi and was elected a representative from Washington County to the Black and Tan Constitutional Convention of 1868.

The white men of Sunflower County, led by Dr. Gibson, had organized an armed force to put down Combash's followers. Gibson's men also showed their opposition to the carpetbagger sheriff, J. J. Gainey, who held office under the protection of U.S. soldiers. The final clash between Gibson's followers and those of William Combash was recorded by Benjamin G. Humphreys in his autobiography:

The white men organized for defense and advanced to Beck's Ferry where Combash fell back to the old Archer place and formed his line. The white men commanded by Captain Gibson pursued him. . . . Combash fired on Gibson's skirmishers and Gibson ordered a general charge. A regular Rebel yell went up as his boys advanced firing. Soon the black line of Combash disappeared in the cane-brakes, and order was again restored throughout the country.[30]

There were three blacks left dead on the field—William Combash mean-while had escaped to the canebrakes. According to the *Vicksburg Herald* (9 January 1870), Sheriff Gainey gave Gibson assurances that he would not attempt to take him if Gibson remained quietly at his home on the Yazoo River and dispersed his men.

The sheriff did not keep his word. On the morning of 4 January 1870, Gainey, accompanied by six Federal soldiers, rode up to the Gibson home at breakfast time. He called Gibson out to the front porch. Gibson seeing that he had been betrayed, met the posse with his Navy repeater in hand as he opened the door. Then, the deputy "drew up his gun to fire," as reported in the *Herald*. "But quick indeed must have been the man who pulled a sooner trigger than Tully Gibson." The bullets from the pistol found their mark, and the sheriff crumpled. Two of his aides also fell when Gibson unloaded his gun.

Other soldiers, stationed at Gibson's gate, advanced "and fired a volley upon Gibson . . . one ball striking him in the head. . . ." It was reported that the soldiers "dragged him by the heels . . . robbed him of his pocket book and pistol . . . reviled and insulted the ladies." Thus, the captain of the Sunflower Guards, a soldier who had risked his life in Confederate engagements in Virginia and was wounded at Gettysburg, became a victim of Reconstruction lawlessness at the steps of his own home. He was thirty-seven years old. The *Herald* reported further: "He was naturally of a somewhat reserved and moody temper, but since the deaths of his first wife and little son by a steamboat disaster in '65 he has been more than usually so." He chose not to be captured and subjected to a military trial—none of whose officers he believed to be his peer.

The story of Gibson affirms the tensions during the months after the war when both the conquerors and the conquered perpetrated spiteful acts of vengeance against each other in a South torn and chafing under military rule.

ℭ ℘

In 1866, Admiral Dahlgren had begat twins on his new wife Madeleine. The boy and girl had come into the world with every advantage and comfort in a prosperous household. Four years later, 9 March 1870, Ellen Gardner in Nashville addressed her brother-in-law Charles Dahlgren about the arrival of his own twin boys:

> Dear Mr. Dahlgren,
>
> I write to you the first moment of leisure to announce Mary's confinement and safe delivery of Twins—Boys—we were preparing to walk to Ma's [Mrs. Jane Ward Vannoy, widow of Mason Vannoy]. She was taken about 5 o'clock. Dr. Briggs was engaged to wait upon her but she was in such haste that we could not get a Dr. in time. The nurse she had Delivered her of the first one and I saw that another one was coming. I had runners in all Directions. We succeeded in Getting Dr. Jennings in time for the second *one*. She was very ill indeed. I never witness[ed] such suffering in all my life and hope I [never] see anybody have Twins . . . but Dr. Jennings told me he would get [her] safely through and he did.[31]

Mrs. Gardner's letter underscores the pain that accompanied childbirth in nineteenth-century America.

Her letter goes on to report the effect of twins on the mother and the older children under the Dahlgren roof. "Mary was greatly troubled at having two, and I was grieved myself, but today they look so healthy and pretty Mary says she would hate to lose one." Very much displeased with the squealing boys was the older half-brother, Austin Mortimer Dahlgren, age fourteen. Also obliged to make room for the twins were their brothers Van, age ten; Rowan, age eight; Edgar, age six; and Charles

Ulric, age three. When the general joined them again, the household would number nine, not counting servants.[32]

The general's reaction to the twin boys is preserved in a letter, dated 12 March at Atlanta, to his wife:

> My dearest Mary:
>
> I have just recd Mrs. Gardner's letter informing me of the arrival of twins. . . . I am very sorry, because they are more difficult to raise than single children: however we must only do our best and make good men of them. . . .

Then follow two pages of instructions for his wife. Dahlgren wrote as though Mary Edgar had not already brought four sons successfully into the world:

> Attend very carefully my letters of how to do and especially about eating: eat plenty and often and not to overload the stomach. See no company till the third week. Sit up as soon as you can: as it is weakening to lay long in bed. Eat good strong food, you must keep your strength up. . . . Do not have any noises, but be perfectly quiet and still . . . no company til the third week, and then not many of them. . . . Don't worry darling til you are perfectly well and then not much at the time. . . .
>
> Much love, your affectionate husband. Goodby dearest.[33]

This nineteenth-century father, fifty-nine years old at the time and writing to a wife of thirty, was a male presuming to have all the answers for a mother of twins. Yet, in spite of her stern husband's solicitations, Mary Edgar Dahlgren brought the boys to maturity and later gave birth to two daughters, for a total of nine children.

The elder twin was named Ira Smith for Dahlgren's business friend in New York. The second, named John Armfield in honor of Colonel Armfield of Beersheba Springs, was called Johnny to distinguish him from his older half-brother, John Adolph (Pudge). Both Johns signed their letters John A. Dahlgren, although the older was called either Adolph or Pudge by his familiars.

Having no success in establishing a business in either Atlanta or Nashville and responsible now for a wife and seven sons, Charles Dahlgren left the South in 1870 determined to try his chances for recovery in New York. The city and its boroughs were attracting a number of ambitious but threadbare Southerners because of their prosperity. Stranded empty-handed on a desolate landscape in the South, Dahlgren felt the move was right for himself and his family. The South was hopelessly beset with too many postwar problems—economic, racial, political—to reclaim prosperity during his lifetime. Born a Yankee, he would return to a place where fortunes were still made and where he and his sons would be able to escape carpetbagger rule, the sweat of the fields, and the disastrous whims of nature. In 1870, a land-based dynasty was no longer a prospect for Dahlgren and his two sets of sons.

Other Southerners, dubbed "Confederate Carpetbaggers" by historian Daniel E. Sutherland, scattered in many directions, but they went especially to Chicago, Boston, and New York. Although James D. B. DeBow, editor of *De Bow's Review,* the South's leading economic journal, estimated that twenty thousand Southerners had settled in the New York–Brooklyn area before and after 1865, the figure proves to be an exaggeration, according to Sutherland. Yet he finds that the census of 1870 pinpoints 136 immigrant families from Virginia, 62 from Tennessee, 56 from Kentucky, 43 from South Carolina, 43 from Alabama, and 40 from North Carolina. In his examination of the 1880 census, Sutherland identifies approximately 1,068 individual Confederates who moved north between 1861 and 1880.[34]

Unable to afford the cost of keeping a family in New York, General Dahlgren moved his brood from Nashville to Winchester, Virginia, in December 1870, put Mary Edgar in a house that belonged to her Kenton relatives in a pleasant neighborhood, and went on his own to live in rented rooms in New York for $4 or $5 per week.[35] For the next six years, Mary Edgar ran the house, put the older boys in school, and welcomed her husband home for holidays. Their daughter, Virginia, was born in Winchester in 1873: at last a little girl who might be nourished past infancy.[36] Mary Edgar adapted to the new domestic situation and moved her membership from Natchez to the Presbyterian Church in Winchester. Son Mortimer, enrolled at Shenandoah Academy, did well once he was settled and became a good example for the younger boys. With one ploy or another, Pudge was making his way in New Orleans. Mary Edgar and the general agreed that he was old enough and resourceful enough to take care of himself.

What his parents did not know was that Pudge had entered into a relationship with May Clifford of Saint Joseph and married her secretly on 19 August 1868. A son, and the general's first grandchild, was born to them in 1872 and given the name Franklin Clifford. Pudge had broken away from his father's piety and was racing off on an adventurous course of his own.[37]

❧ Ten ❧

Eighteen Years
a Confederate Carpetbagger

fter calling on a number of New York business friends—bankers,
merchants, and insurance agents from his former days of prosperity—General Dahlgren lost no time in hanging out his shingle
and looking for clients. He set up an office at Nos. 112 and 114 on
Broadway in the heart of the mercantile and banking district. His imposing letterhead read *Charles G. Dahlgren & Company*, which offered
"Secure Capital for Bankers, Merchants, and Incorporated Companies."
He announced that he would "make cash loans on marketable securities,
merchandise, and effect sales on commissions." Further, the letterhead
read, "investments made in business of an approved order, for parties
with capital, without charge."[1] The words reflect a confident financier
with experience in his profession.

A second look at the letterhead and the claims it made might suggest
a venture too promising for a wary investor. To any skeptics expressing
a lack of confidence, however, Dahlgren furnished a printed list of the
names of twenty references who could be consulted as to his reliability
and banking experience. Cited "by permission" were some of New York's
most powerful bankers, real estate brokers, dry goods merchants, and
life insurance executives. Dahlgren had known some of them like V. K.
Stevenson, dubbed the father of railroads in Tennessee, before the war.
Others, who were also from the South or had lived there, were William
C. Alexander of Virginia; Thomas W. Evans, whose business was chiefly
with Southern merchants; and John H. Inman, a North Carolina native

who had been in the Confederate Army and was prospering with the firm Inman, Swann and Company and the New York Cotton Exchange. James Robb, banker, was described by a Philadelphian as "a very rich man and large operator in N. Orleans some years ago, whom I knew very well and who is now in N. York." Dahlgren almost surely knew Robb before the war and had his confidence.[2]

Yet there is a question. Were these affluent businessmen participants in Dahlgren's schemes or merely passive onlookers who lent him their names in a gesture of helping a stricken acquaintance in his efforts toward recovery? Dahlgren said that he was using their names "by permission." One can deduce, therefore, that they placed their trust in his abilities to make a comeback.

There is also the possibility of some backing from Matthew Read, his sister Patty's rich and aging husband. Such help would have been an ironic turn of events in view of the long estrangement of Patty and Charles. They were not speaking to each other in December 1865 when Charles visited the admiral in Washington. On the other hand, Patty had shown her concern for Mary Edgar and the boys during their hand-to-mouth existence in 1867 when she persuaded Read to put up $10,000 to save Llangollen. Family histories often turn up paradoxes of this kind, and the Dahlgrens had already displayed their share.

One finds, after looking at the ambitious Southerners in the North after the war, that Dahlgren's appearance on lower Broadway was not an exception. Historian Sutherland's analysis of the businesses flourishing in the financial district adds considerable light:

> . . . [I]t became possible as early as 1867 to tour lower Manhattan via southern stores, shops, offices, banks. James D. B. DeBow set up the business office of his *Review* . . . [he] spends much of his time in New York, and when he is away, his brother and a platoon of Confederate friends handle affairs. At 380 . . . stands Evans, Gardner and Company, operated by two affable good-humored southerners from North Carolina and Tennessee who seemingly hire none but former rebels.[3]

Although he does not include General Dahlgren at 112 Broadway—probably because the censuses show Dahlgren was born in Pennsylvania—Sutherland devotes five pages to the Southerners and their businesses during his "stroll" in the financial and mercantile district.

One can surmise that General Dahlgren managed to get a place on lower Broadway in 1872 by a combination of grit and cunning. He was then sixty-one years old and at home with old friends and a number of successful acquaintances in the business world. He was set on making enough money to bring his family to New York, where he found opportunities that were not open to him in the South. He accepted the challenge to drive hard in a competitive marketplace.

Although Admiral Dahlgren had been stricken at his home and died there in 1870, Charles was most certainly aware of the rising success enjoyed by the admiral's older sons, Charles Bunker and Paul. Charles was an engineer in charge of a silver mine in Mexico and presumably on his way to wealth. After a few years in the U.S. Army, son Paul became the political nominee in 1873 of Hamilton Fish, Grant's Secretary of State, for the post of consul general in Rome. This was a postmortem gesture to the admiral. After his appointment, Paul married Annie Rutherford Morgan, daughter of the Reverend William F. Morgan of St. Thomas Episcopal Church in New York. The wedding was noted in the social columns and was followed by the couple's honeymoon voyage across the Atlantic on the *Abyssinia* for Italy.[4] In contrast, Charles's older sons, Pudge and Mortimer, showed few indications of prosperity. Van and the younger boys were hiring out for menial jobs in Winchester and helping their mother buy groceries with their earnings.

If the general was jealous of his nephews' successes, the feeling could not have lasted. He read in *The New York Times* of 28 March 1876 that Paul Dahlgren, the young consul general, was dead in Rome from "an overdose of prescription medicine." The combination of drugs for a chronic heart ailment and excessive alcohol had killed Paul at age twenty-nine. He was estranged from his wife, who had returned to America with one child while expecting another. Deeply depressed, Paul was found dead by a servant after refusals to unlock his door to his physician.[5]

ॐ ॐ

After they had lived apart for six years, the general was able to move Mary Edgar and the children to New York in September 1876. He put them up first at 182 E. 93rd Street and then moved them to 225 McDonough Street, Brooklyn, in 1878. In May 1884, they moved again to 294 Macon Street and then to 330 Decatur Street.[6]

Although presumably advantageous, the moves could hardly have been easy on Mary Edgar and the children. Brooklyn offered compensations, however, if the sons could find time to take advantage of them—schools, public, private, and endowed; City Library, Brooklyn Institute, and several private libraries; music in the public schools, at the Lyceum, and at the Grand Opera House. Churches numbered more than four hundred in Henry R. Stiles's history of 1884. They included Roman Catholic and most of the recognized Protestant denominations—Quakers, Reformed Presbyterians, and German Evangelicals. Listed with the Methodists were the African Bethels, Primitive Methodists, and African Weslyans. In short, Brooklyn was a heterogeneous and cosmopolitan city.

The Dahlgren boys would occasionally go to Manhattan, either by ferry or the new bridge, to the circus and entertainments in Central Park. At home there was no dearth of events sponsored by the Brooklyn athletic associations.

General Dahlgren was now listed as a public accountant at 37 Park Row in *Goulding's New York City Directory*, 1876–77. He would have been qualified as a bookkeeper because of his years as a Natchez banker and businessman. His frequent appearances in the courts of the South and the East, both as plaintiff and defendant, had given him a wide experience with legal proceedings, and, as trustee, he had settled a number of estates. Not surprisingly, by 1881, he is listed as a lawyer at 34 Pine Street and in 1885–86 as a lawyer at 63 Broadway. He had absorbed enough law to be admitted to the bar, and it is very likely that he was approved in much the same manner as was Roger A. Pryor of Petersburg, Virginia, another Confederate carpetbagger.

General Pryor and his wife, the former Sarah Agnes Rice, had been almost destitute in 1865–66: "There was no hope for lucrative occupation," Mrs. Pryor wrote. "He had no profession. He had forgotten the little law he had learned at the university. He had been an editor, diplomat, politician, and soldier, and distinguished himself in all four. These were now closed to him forever! There seemed to be no room for a rebel in all the world."[7] Then, a sympathetic Yankee in Richmond, Gen. George Lucas Hartsuff, sent word to the Pryors by one Captain Gregory: "Madam, there is a future before your husband. New York is the place for him." Reluctantly, Pryor agreed to go north after hocking his watch and buying a new suit to replace "the threadbare uniform of Confederate gray."[8]

The Southern community welcomed Pryor, a gentleman with education and bearing, and he was soon employed by Ben Wood of the *New York News* for a salary of $25.00 a week. A letter to Mrs. Pryor reported Wood's advice to him on a particular occasion: "General, why don't you practice law? You would make $10,000 a year." Pryor answered, "For the best of all possible reasons—I am not a lawyer." Then Wood answered: "Neither is C, nor T; yet they make $10,000."

With Wood's encouragement, Pryor began reading law and reviewing cases in a friend's office. His account of the examination for the bar indicates the way Southerners stuck together and promoted each other's interests. The story, as reported by Pryor to his wife, undoubtedly runs parallel to the circumstances by which General Dahlgren passed the bar and began advertising his services in 1881. Pryor wrote:

. . . [T]he Hon. John B. Haskins—my former associate in [prewar] Congress—was appointed to examine me as to my knowledge of Law. Under his lead we went to a restaurant. When seated he proceeded, with much solemnity of manner, to "examine" me. He asked me, "What are the essentials of negotiability of a note?" This question I was prepared to answer, and did answer to his satisfaction. After a "judicial pause," he asked gravely, "What will you take?" [order for lunch] This also I was fully prepared to answer—and entirely to his satisfaction. He asked me no other question. He was apparently satisfied with the good sense of my last answer. We returned to the Court, and he reported in favor of my application![9]

In spite of his highly informal entry into the legal profession, Roger Pryor went on to a lucrative career as attorney, business executive, and diplomat. General Dahlgren, as banker, bookkeeper, and lawyer, also found a variety of ways to support his family in a Yankee marketplace.

୧୨

News relating to Pudge reached the Dahlgrens in November 1875. Having broken his relationship with May Clifford some time in 1872 after the birth of their son Clifford, Pudge went to Nashville, where he was known as Adolph. He stayed with the Edwin Gardners and ingratiated himself into the society of some prosperous households on High, Vine, and Spruce Streets. After several weeks, he concentrated on the family of Felix Demoville at the corner of Church and Vine. Demoville was a well-to-do druggist with an established wholesale business. He also had several single daughters. Adolph set his cap for Bettie, the oldest, age twenty, and won her hand. They exchanged vows on 11 November 1875 at St. Mary's Cathedral, with P. A. Feehan, Bishop of Nashville, officiating. The couple received the blessings and congratulations of a large company of family and friends.[10] Following their honeymoon, Adolph was taken into the Demoville business as bookkeeper and treasurer. His ingratiating ways, a direct inheritance from his father, had served him well.

If the Catholic hierarchy had investigated the marriage of Adolph to May Clifford and found it invalid, the tribunal was silent and approved the union with Bettie Demoville. (In 1877 a marriage license was issued for May Clifford Dahlgren, under that name, to D. C. Hughes in Louisiana.) Adolph had maneuvered himself out of one relationship and into another of advantage. The Dahlgrens in Brooklyn were probably relieved that, at age twenty-six, Pudge had settled down, acquired a wife from a family of standing in the community, and now had a position of responsibility in Nashville. The next year, Adolph gave General Dahlgren his second grandchild, Mary Bettie Dahlgren, a beautiful dark-haired girl.[11]

୧୨

A letter with encouraging news reached the Charles Dahlgrens in New York early in 1877. It was from the general's stepdaughter, Sarah Ann Ellis Dorsey, a widow after the death of Samuel Dorsey. Aware of the straitened circumstances of the general's family and in need herself of a male arm, Sarah Ann invited her half brother, Mortimer Dahlgren, then almost twenty-one years old, to come to the Mississippi coast and help manage her extensive plantation. No matter how long she had held General Dahlgren at arm's length, Sarah Ann would attempt to do her best for Mortimer. After all, they were brother and sister, with the same mother. This was also a gesture that Sarah Ann, a childless widow, could make to their mother's memory, for Mary Routh had asked in her will that her Ellis and Dahlgren children "love each other, let no difference of name separate them . . . the strong to help & aid the poor and weak."[12]

Mortimer left Brooklyn, stopped in New Orleans for new clothes at sister Sarah's expense, and then began a prosperous life on the Gulf Coast. He read law with Gen. Joseph R. Davis, the nephew of Jefferson Davis; looked after his sister's business; and became something of a social lion at parties in Biloxi and Mississippi City. Details about Mortimer are revealed in letters that he wrote home—his witty observations on the visitors at Beauvoir and the grand life of former days that Sarah Ann attempted to maintain. Mortimer was ever mindful, however, of the hard times that he had left behind in Brooklyn and the plight of his father's household. He ended one letter hoping "the sun of prosperity may soon burst through the breaking clouds and shed his brightest beams upon you all, after such a long, dark night of adversity."[13]

The major change at Beauvoir was the arrival of Jefferson Davis after his hostess offered him help in writing a history of the Confederacy. Sarah Ann set aside a wing of the house for Davis, with library and living quarters. Her servants attended him, and Mortimer played host to the visitors who stopped at the gate to pay homage to the fallen president. For Christmas 1877 at Beauvoir, Sarah Ann invited guests who had been prominent in the Confederacy to join Davis. Among them were Gen. Jubal Early, Gen. Joseph R. Davis, and Maj. W. Thomas Walthall.

Sarah Ann entertained the company with a feast reminiscent of the holidays at Elk Ridge in Tensas Parish—delicacies "from sea, land, and air." Mortimer reported that on a silver salver was perched a large stuffed "peacock (which had been skinned so as to preserve the beautiful feathers . . . the longest of which measured five feet . . . and arranged as alive)." The body of the peacock was "nicely roasted and stuffed with oysters."[14] For Mortimer, having spent most of his years in a lean household, the display was incredible. He wrote to Brooklyn that the peacock "was a dish that is rarely ever prepared except for Kings." The feast at Beauvoir that Christmas was Sarah Ann's nostalgic recreation of the abundant years in the Old South.[15]

After dinner, there was a reception in honor of General Early with hundreds of candles, pine knots, and chandeliers blazing—"only to be reflected back by sparkling eyes and brilliant gems upon the necks and fingers of their fair owners."[16] Social-minded as he was, Mortimer was clearly in his element. He wrote a toast in verse to General Early and recited it to the merriment of the company. His letter also described the music and dancing. Everyone joined in the Virginia reel, even the "gentlemen who had not danced for *twenty years,* and none under sixty-five or seventy."

Mortimer's reports brought much satisfaction to his family in the East, particularly when he included a quotation from a letter Sarah Ann had written to a friend: "Mortimer is as good as ten *girls,* besides being a *boy,* which is better still; I don't know how I could have gotten along without him."[17] This was the Mortimer who, in 1869 at age twelve, had not learned to read and write well. As General Dahlgren reflected on this son, he was pleased with how much he had matured. The general also must have mused that Mortimer's talents had so won Sarah Ann that she would make Mortimer her heir to the domain of a thousand acres and all the amenities of Beauvoir House. So at Christmas 1877, with Adolph married and keeping books for his father-in-law in Nashville and Mortimer flourishing in Biloxi, the Dahlgren banner was raised again in the South.

∂℘

Brooklyn in the 1880s was an expanding city of substantial homes and good neighborhoods. Commuting to lower Manhattan was easy after the completion of the Brooklyn Bridge over the East River in 1883, and the cost of living was modest in comparison with New York. Stephen Percy Ellis, the general's stepson, was living at 1038 LaFayette Avenue in Brooklyn and writing for a newspaper.

In 1880, the household at 225 McDonough Street was recorded by the federal census: Charles G. Dahlgren, 70; Mary, 40; Gustavus [Van], 19; Rowan, 18; Edgar, 15; Charles, 12; twins Ira and John, 10; Virginia, 7; Bernardina, 1. The older sons had found jobs that helped with their upkeep and with family expenses. The twins were in school but regularly contributed their earnings as yard boys.

The census did not list live-in help, as was the case in Nashville in 1870. There might have been Irish girls when the Dahlgrens could afford them. It was a busy if not affluent household, bustling with offspring ranging in age from nineteen to one.

By the time the Dahlgren twins, Johnny and Ira, were fourteen years old, they were earning wages as industrious handymen in the Bedford-Stuyvesant neighborhood adjacent to home. They were earnest about following the example of their older brother Van, who had worked since he was thirteen and educated himself at the same time. Prompted by their father, the twins kept account books. Some of Johnny's ledgers have survived and give evidence of the boy's industry and determination to help his mother with his upkeep:

Summer of 1885

INCOME

May 26	294	Macon St.	.20
	283	Macon St.	.25
May 27	292	Macon St.	.75
May 28	296	Macon St.	.65
May 29	294	Macon St.	.35
May 30	241	McDonough St.	.25
May 31		Raining	

For the same period the EXPENDITURES

May 23	Oil can	.08
May 23	Oil for mower	.06
May 23	Haircut	.30
May 23	Cake	.01
May 27	Ma	.75
May 28	Ma	.65
May 29	Ma	.35
May 30	Ma	.25

Apparently, after deducting such expenses as oil, wood screws, and occasional help—plus personal expenses for such items as clothing, tooth powder, haircuts, spice cakes, Sunday School, and a trip to Barnum's Circus—Johnny handed over about a third of his weekly earnings to Mary Dahlgren.[18]

With Mary Edgar on his arm, the general led his family to the Second Presbyterian Church at Clinton and Remsen Streets on Sunday. Dr. H. J. Van Dyke, late of Nashville's First Presbyterian Church, saluted the troops marching at the heels of the stern *paterfamilias*. Johnny was asked to help with a Sunday School class while still in his teens. In his later years, he recorded his mother's church affiliations from the time she was a bride in Natchez to Winchester, Brooklyn, Atlanta, and finally Manchester in Tennessee. The chronology of churches is roughly parallel to the family's migrations from 1865 to 1922.[19]

∂℘

In June 1878, Mrs. Jefferson Davis came to Beauvoir on the Gulf Coast for a visit with her husband after receiving an invitation from Sarah Ann Dorsey. Mrs. Davis made the trip in spite of having written to Davis on April 18: "There is one thing, my dear husband, that I have to beg of you. Do not—please do not let Mrs. Dorsey come to see me. I cannot see her and do not desire ever to do so again. . . . Let us agree to disagree about her. . . ." Varina Davis had come to resent Sarah Ann Dorsey for her aggressive manner and for the help that she was giving her husband that Varina was unable to give.[20] Her publicized presence at Beauvoir later that year, however, would do much for appearances. It was meant to be a short visit, but Varina's stay was extended to several weeks because an outbreak of yellow fever prevented her return to Memphis. The same epidemic took the life of her son Jefferson Davis Jr.

A number of cases of fever were also reported on the Gulf Coast, and, for some weeks, Mrs. Davis herself was ill. Davis wrote to their daughter that her mother was "nursed with unwearied care" by Mrs. Dorsey. Although Mrs. Davis had a smoldering resentment of Sarah Ann Dorsey, she was forced to accept her hospitality and did not rejoin her daughter and son-in-law in Memphis until late December.

After Varina left, in February 1879 Mrs. Dorsey had a private discussion with Davis. As a result, she entered into a formal agreement to sell Beauvoir to him for $5,500, the total sum to be paid in three installments. After a diagnosis of cancer, she moved to New Orleans and placed herself under the care of a physician. She had discussed the sale and her new will with others, including General Early during his visit to Beauvoir,[21] but not with members of her family—certainly not with her sister Inez Ellis Peckham and her half brothers Mortimer and Adolph Dahlgren.

At Beauvoir, Mortimer sensed the change in command at once and revealed as much to the press:

> . . . [I]n February, Jefferson Davis began to undermine me. . . . Mr. Davis gradually—though not offensively, at first—began assuming the management of the place while I was absent at my office [in Biloxi]. . . . He stalked around the place domineering and despotic. . . . I saw him on one occasion kick a crippled negro down a back stairs for some fancied insult. . . . Mr. Davis threatened to beat another negro for disregarding an order of his by carrying out one of mine. By this time things came to such a pass that I never knew whether my orders would be obeyed or not. Davis countermanded them.[22]

Chafing under his sister's deception and his own disappointment, Mortimer Dahlgren left Beauvoir on 25 March 1879 in spite of entreaties from sister Sarah and Davis himself to remain there and continue his law practice in Biloxi. He repeated his parting remark in a published interview: "I told him I couldn't live in his house, so I left." Now the callow young man of twelve months earlier, who had nothing but praise for the Confederate president in his letters home, was ready to confide his bitterness to the press and any others who would listen. On his way north, Mortimer stopped with his brother Adolph and wife Bettie in Nashville and then went to St. Louis to stay with his half brother Van. He hoped to practice law there but found the profession crowded. For a short period, he managed a cigar store.[23] A house and lot in Biloxi and hundreds of acres in Arkansas that Mortimer said were promised him by his sister were never conveyed. She chided him during his final visit to her bedside in New Orleans for not paying a courtesy call on Davis at Beauvoir.

Mortimer's resentment of Davis and his rancor toward his sister became known to all after Mrs. Dorsey died of cancer on 4 July 1879, at the St. Charles Hotel in New Orleans. Davis was at her bedside and is said to have repeated the Beatitudes to her after she received Holy Communion. According to an editor of Davis's papers, "She asked him to take down certain deathbed bequests to nieces, cousins, and servants, which he did with pad and pencil. She told him she owed absolutely nothing to her brother and half-brother [Stephen Percy Ellis and Mortimer Dahlgren], that she had given them cash and property in the past, that they had squandered her gifts and proved ungrateful."[24]

Sarah Ann Dorsey's will, dated 4 January 1878 and probated in New Orleans on 15 July 1879, states, "I owe no obligation of any sort whatever to any relative of my own; I have done all I could for them during my life. I, therefore, give and bequeath all my property, real, personal, and mixed . . . to Jefferson Davis . . . the man who is in my eyes the highest and noblest in existence."

All major newspapers, North and South, took notice of her will. They pointed out that the ex-president, with his interests in the Brierfield plantation in Mississippi recently restored in court and now the Dorsey bequest, would be able to spend a comfortable old age as he completed his history of the Confederacy. Sarah Ann Dorsey became a heroine to Southerners as his benefactress and amanuensis. Hints of a romance between her and Davis continued to be whispered on the gossip circuit, much to the embarrassment of sister Inez and the brothers.

Obviously, Sarah Dorsey's siblings felt cheated of a family inheritance that they reckoned should have come to them because the Dorseys had no natural heirs. The strongest contenders were brother Stephen Percy Ellis, sister Inez Ellis Peckham, and Mary Ellis, the daughter of Sarah's deceased brother Thomas LaRoche Ellis. Next were the two half brothers Adolph and Mortimer Dahlgren. Although she stated in her will "I have done all I could for them during my life," she did not spell out exactly what she had done.

The kin felt that the will ought to be contested and asked the United States Circuit Court in New Orleans to set it aside as null and void. The litigants, Stephen Percy Ellis et al., hired counsel on a contingency basis because of their limited resources.[25] The newspapers took up the story again when the family went to court against Jefferson Davis. Among those interviewed in 1879 by the Philadelphia *Press* was General Dahlgren, Mrs. Dorsey's aging stepfather, a patriarch quick to point an accusing finger at his wayward stepchild. His love for her as a little girl and the education that he had lavished on her, including a journey abroad, might have been predicated in part on her bowing to his will, or so ran the rumors in Natchez. Dahlgren countered in his interview, however, that all his favors had been met with ungrateful responses, his counsel with defiance and deaf ears. He might have cited his success, through his own efforts, in rescuing the family from bankruptcy due to Thomas Ellis's debts, but he was silent on that subject.

General Dahlgren was asked by the *Press* to recount his version of "the truth" about the late Mrs. Dorsey, and he referred to the mental aberrations that she had inherited from her Percy forebears. Her grandmother, the deranged Mrs. John Ellis, was born Sarah Percy and the general went on at length about the Percy family as precursors of Sarah Ann's mental instability. He maintained that heredity had finally rendered her incapable of composing a sane and reasonable will.

There is something unbalanced about the family, and there have been seven cases of mental derangement in their history in this country. There is a creek in Mississippi named for Capt. Percy, and one day he was found in it with a weight of iron about his neck. . . . [Another] committed suicide by opening an artery in his foot. Another descendant was a victim of idiocy. Mrs. Dorsey's grandmother (Sarah Percy, wife of John Ellis, mother of Thomas G. Ellis) died insane in my house, and there have been three other instances I could name. . . . Mrs. Dorsey had the family characteristic, which was impulsiveness. Once started, there was no holding her. Her mind was marked by that want of steady balance which is needed in a safe, sane and prudent person.[26]

In death, however, Sarah Ann got even with her stepfather when she struck back with the will. General Dahlgren ranted at his old nemesis, Jefferson Davis, and charged Davis with using undue persuasion on Mrs. Dorsey. "Jefferson Davis possessed infinite tact and cunning," the general said in the same interview. "He was polished and persuasive in his speech, but always knew when to stop talking."

In an interview with the *St. Louis Globe Democrat*, Mortimer Dahlgren dryly observed, "She seemed to be bound up in Jefferson Davis . . . [who] ought to have seen it, and not to have submitted the motives of an innocent and excellent lady to be misconstrued in the eyes of the world. She was a very impulsive woman." If Davis were a gentleman, Mortimer chided, he would not allow a lady to go as far as Sarah Ann went with her affection. Davis was no longer a friend and hero to Mortimer.

The rising tide of postwar blame toward Davis for the South's demise, the frequent enumeration of his shortcomings as president and leader, and his aloof manner were all matters for which Sarah Ann tried to compensate in her will, but she could not hold off the attacks of her kinsmen or soften their blows against the man whom she considered "the highest and noblest in existence."

Shortly after Mrs. Dorsey's death, Davis sent a number of family portraits and some of Sarah Ann's personal items from Beauvoir to Stephen Percy Ellis in Brooklyn, according to the press. Among them was the fine oil portrait of Mary Routh Dahlgren by Charles Loring Elliott of New York. The real estate, as far as Davis was concerned, was his and the will was legal. *So the court ruled.* On 10 March 1880, Davis wrote Varina: "I have the pleasure to inform you that the Court has decided in favor of the Demurrer, not only the point of jurisdiction but upon all those presented."[27] Thus, not without its stroke of irony, Jefferson Davis came into a portion of the legacy that Charles Dahlgren had rescued twenty-five years earlier for Sarah Ann Dorsey and her siblings when their father's estate was on the brink of bankruptcy. The Ellises and Dahlgrens did not appeal the case to the Supreme Court. They had struck their final blows to no avail.

Later, Varina Davis reflected on the alarming behavior of those Dahlgrens whom she had known. It was difficult for her to reconcile the mannerly young Ulric Dahlgren, a boy she had seen grow up in antebellum Washington, and the vengeance-driven Ulric who had meant to kill her husband during the raid on Richmond. Davis confessed that he had the same difficulty in trying to reconcile the two Mortimers—first, the amiable young friend in 1877 and, then, his bitter critic two years later.

∂℘

At the time that General Dahlgren denounced Sarah Ann in the press, he was described as "tall and gray, and although now nearly 70 years of age, possesses a powerful frame, a steady step, and a clear eye. Perhaps no man in New York is more rich in reminiscence . . ."[28] His talent for stories and his title of general brought a parade of young admirers to the little office on lower Broadway. He entertained them with anecdotes about his duels, the bowie knife fights, and the pistol balls in his ribs, all dating from his younger days. Although he proudly showed his scars, none of them had to do with his Confederate service. He was a holdover, an oddity, a relic of the Old South of chivalry, of tempestuous talk, and of glorified losses. The young men of the 1880s in New York who took their accounts to him were entertained by the thunder of the Old Secessionist. He held court, and his courtiers were many.

In later years, with his gift of the picaresque, Dahlgren added more and more details to his autobiography and elaborated whenever he had a listener. He referred to himself as a *Planter,* a designation that stuck with him just as *General* also stuck. His young admirers respected both titles. It was the least that the next generation could do for a superannuary of another time. The general's responses were invariably spirited and courtly, and his listeners enjoyed his rhetoric. In practice, the exchanges were the gratuities of polite intercourse between young and old.

During his eighteen years in New York, Dahlgren's audience could not have known all the details of his career in the South. They were drawn to him and his oratory and his stories. They had no concerns about verifying facts. So he created a persona, concocted a character with his name and his bearing and his imagination. Before long, his listeners came to believe the creation. He became a soothsayer looking backward as he voiced what might have been, a sage vigorously inventing his curriculum vitae.

Dahlgren's stories, "rich in reminiscence," paralleled those of Gen. Daniel Edgar Sickles, the aging Yankee leader who had lost a leg at Gettysburg. Mark Twain visited "Sickles the Incredible" on a rainy night in New York in 1906: "Now when we sat there in the General's presence, listening to his monotonous talk—it was about himself, and is always about himself . . . it seemed to me that he was just the kind of man who would risk his salvation in order to do some last words in an attractive way. . . . I noticed then that the General valued his lost leg away above the one that is left. I am perfectly sure that if he had to part with either of them, he would part with the one he has got."[29] Twain, no doubt, would have made similar comments after a visit with General Dahlgren if the two had met, and he would have likewise embalmed the old Yankee turned Confederate in playful observations.

Besides his stepson Stephen Ellis who lived briefly in Brooklyn, and nephew Charles Bunker Dahlgren, General Dahlgren had no relatives in the metropolitan area except Mary Edgar and the children. His son Van, an ambitious and personable young businessman, had been sent to Holland by a tea and coffee company and then had settled as a broker in Saint Louis. As a prosperous young executive, Van helped his family by sending his mother checks to run the house.

The Dahlgrens, however, were not included in the social circles of recovering Southerners in New York such as the Thursday Evening Club and the Nineteenth Century Club. Membership presupposed a more prosperous income than the Dahlgrens had. A chronicler of this group and a prominent member herself was Mrs. Burton Harrison (1843–1920), whose *Recollections Grave and Gay* frequently alluded to leading expatriates. Her husband had been private secretary to Jefferson Davis in Richmond and was part of his escort when Davis was captured in Georgia; Harrison also had been briefly incarcerated. A successful businessman, Harrison remained loyal to Davis and encouraged a kind of Davis cult in the North.

Mrs. Harrison wrote an amusing story about some of the down-and-out Confederates in New York who came to their door for hand-outs. "[They] induced my husband and brother to pay their way back to Dixie, reappearing directly after, in the thoroughfares of New York."[30] Yet Harrison would never refuse, in spite of his wife's warnings.

The Dahlgrens of Decatur Street, Brooklyn, had no time for social coteries. There were no Rebel drifters pleading at the door. Their ninth child had arrived in New York in August 1878—a little girl to whom they gave the ancestral name Bernardina and made room. When she was born, the General was sixty-seven; Mary Edgar, thirty-eight. Bernardina grew up in a loving but disciplined household. It was not the domestic arrangement, however, that a young Charles Dahlgren had envisioned forty years earlier when he plotted his dynastic course among the planters of the South.

In his retreat, Dahlgren was never passive and refused to accept unconditional surrender. He held onto his beliefs—"I thought the South was right"—and kept on stubbornly declaring the relevance of his vision. He had never knuckled under to the indignities of total defeat.

⊘ ⊘

General Dahlgren kept in touch with his brother John until 1870 when the admiral, age sixty-one, died of a heart attack at his home in Washington. After a state funeral that included a long oration by the Reverend Dr. Sunderland, the admiral's heavy casket, with silver-plated lid, was conveyed by train to the family plot in Laurel Hill Cemetery, Philadelphia. At the insistence of the admiral's widow Madeleine, Ulric Dahlgren's grave was opened, and the father and son were buried to-gether.[31] Madeleine, in a sentimental gesture, had exercised the preroga-tive of the widow. Because of his cannon and his years of naval service and his martyred son, the admiral would be remembered.

There is no record that Charles paid his respects in Washington. Nor did the errant brother, William, who was in France and involved in the Franco-Prussian War.[32] According to the admiral's biographer, he was honored at home and abroad for his "modern advance in the art of war. . . . Our Navy has never had a more capable and accomplished ordnance officer. . . . "[33] He had achieved, in part at least, his quest for glory and had died quietly in service. The nation's loss was also the family's because the peacemaker and adjudicator, to whom they had all deferred and had depended on, was gone.

Sixteen years later, in 1886, the aging Charles Dahlgren was still a familiar figure in lower Manhattan. At home, he was the stern pater familias of his Brooklyn household, but the long stride was slackening and his body was becoming a little bent as he made his way about town with the support of an ebony cane. He was addressed respectfully as General Dahlgren, and he still buttonholed the young men and told them stories of his friendships with Daniel Webster, John C. Calhoun, Henry Clay, Davy Crockett, Rezin Bowie, and Gen. John A. Quitman, hero of the Mexican War and a Southern crusader. The familiar names engaged his young audiences, who also asked for details of his defense of the South in 1861. Although Jefferson Davis and his advisors had ignored the defensive drawings that Dahlgren had prepared in 1861, they had remained a part of the general's paraphernalia. After the war, he sent copies of the plans to the German General Helmut von Moltke, who commented, "if they had been adopted and carried out as planned, the South would be a nation today."[34] This ex post facto commendation, whether sincerely meant or not, restored some of Dahlgren's confidence during his old age.

All references to people whom he had known in the past were reveries of times that he would not allow to be forgotten. His stories, as passed on later to the press by his listeners, were also responsible for multiple errors that cropped up in his obituaries published in Brooklyn, Atlanta, Natchez, and elsewhere. In 1886, two years before he died, he still had Natchez on his mind: those years as a young bank clerk for Nicholas Biddle; the halcyon days before the war; and, finally, his losses. He had sold, parted with, or relinquished everything but a last few acres of property in Natchez by 27 January 1868: a lot near Llangollen which he conveyed to William Ayres "subject to the mortgage and lien . . ." The price was $550.[35] That real estate transaction severed his ties with the city where he had known the best of times and could go on reflecting on them. The farm outside Atlanta was still his in title, but it carried a heavy mortgage.

Dahlgren's mind was clearly on Natchez when he wrote a letter from Brooklyn to the editor of the *Natchez Daily Democrat* that was published on 24 January 1886. It was meant to correct an article that the paper had published earlier about territorial Natchez: ". . . [Y]ou stated that the American flag was first raised on Ft. Panmure [Fort Rosalie] at the evacuation of the Spaniards. This is erroneous. The American flag was first raised upon Routhland, then the humble, one-storied residence of my father-in-law, the late Job Routh, Esq. Not only that, but it was the first American flag raised upon the great Father of the Waters." Dahlgren went on to tell how American troops had camped at Routhland, raised the American flag, and then proceeded to rout Gayoso, the Spanish commander, after which the Americans claimed Fort Rosalie and hoisted their flag. Then he provided proof and referred to his own time at the Routh estate. "In plowing up ground for my garden at Routhland, I turned up several cannon balls shot from Ft. Panmure at the troops located there, which my children amused themselves with, and which may possibly yet remain about the house."

He indulged in further recollections as he sketched Job Routh's additions to the house, his marriage to Routh's daughter, and the destruction of the house by lightning "in consequence of my wife desiring terra cotta chimney tops placed . . . above the surrounding trees . . . and affording an object for the electric fluid." Having rebuilt on the same site in 1856, Dahlgren suggested that the new house, surrounded by columns and reflecting the height of Greek Revival, should be recognized as a master-piece and "the original name of Routhland restored." The name was changed to Dunleith by A.V. Davis, but the mansion remains today a monument to the Dahlgrens' classical taste.

It can also be argued that Dunleith reflects, in its strict geometric dimensions, the character of Charles Dahlgren and the personality traits that his contemporaries associated with him. Like the man himself, Dunleith's design allows little or no variation. It is a rectangular residence of straight lines and uncompromising ninety-degree angles. The front hall runs straight from the entrance to the rear gallery. The other galleries that surround this magnificent box are equidistant from the outside walls on four sides. Enhancing the whole are twenty-six giant Tuscan columns that rise all the way to the roof. Inside, the severe straight lines of the center hall break at right angles to form, right and left, double parlors, a library, and a dining room. To the right a staircase leads to the second story with four large bedrooms of equal size that follow the same strict pattern.

By the time Dahlgren built the house in 1856, he was already marked among his contemporaries as a man of strong assertions. He was generally intractable, and his house was built on straight lines that neither yield nor compromise their integrity. As Dr. Van Dyke, his Presbyterian minis-ter, said of him: ". . . [H]e had an indomitable will with little toleration for those who opposed it" (obituary, *Brooklyn Daily Eagle,* 21 Decem-ber 1888).

By 1886, the Routhland estate had passed through the hands of Alfred Vidal Davis, Hiram Baldwin, and George Warner and then to Joseph N. Carpenter and his descendants. But throughout his recollections the old Natchezian kept the image of his pillared home in his head as he recalled the old, lost days of vigor and wealth. That was the time he remembered best: when he acquired, as a young man, the pistol balls in his ribs, the tip of the bowie knife in his skull. Those were the days when he was lean of limb, lithe of gait, and blithe of spirit. He recalled his marriage to Mary Routh Ellis and the miles of cotton rows that brought him position and rank in the South. He recalled the good years over those that had followed hard upon them.

☙

On 17 December 1888, the *Brooklyn Daily Eagle* ran a column headed by capitals:

GEN. DAHLGREN, THE SOUTHERN BRIGADIER
DYING IN BROOKLYN. HIS BROTHER WAS A UNION
ADMIRAL AND BOTH WERE CONSPICUOUS FOR
THEIR GALLANTRY—RUINED BY THE WAR.

The account that followed praised Dahlgren for leading the Third Mississippi, which "he raised and equipped out of his own pocket, clear through the war at Iuka, Corinth, Atlanta, and Chickamauga." This and nearly every sentence is riddled with errors. His Swedish background is mentioned, his two wives are correctly named, and his children are identified. The year 1860 is given as the year of his marriage to Mary Edgar, when it should have been 1859. Son Mortimer is identified as a wholesale merchant in Saint Louis, but he was practicing law on the Gulf Coast. Estimates of Dahlgren's wealth in 1860 had skyrocketed: "At the outbreak of the war he was worth $750,000 and in enjoyment of an annual income of $100,000." One statement that rings true in this fanciful mixture is "his wife is living and nurses him faithfully." As mother and nurse for her nine children and now for her husband, Mary Edgar had many times earned her laurels at age forty-eight.

Toward the end, as Dahlgren lay dying of a weak heart and complications, a young man from the *Brooklyn Daily Eagle* had come to his door to take notes from his family and his minister. What showed up in print was what they had told him—not what was literally true but what they felt ought to be true, not what the general had actually earned in honors but the honors they felt he deserved. They could reckon the height of his piled-up years from what he had told them, naming the multiple roles he had played: his apprenticeship as a fledgling banker in Natchez; his fiery clashes with rivals and his street fights to uphold the chivalric code; his command of cotton rows in Louisiana sustained by the labor of Africans in bondage; his choice of two wives who together had borne him sixteen children; his deep, manly grief (and no indulgence of tears) over the loss of Charlie Routh and Bernard in their youth, the boys taken before they could become his heirs, his dynasty shattered out of season.

And soon the fire in him was all burned out. The scars he had acquired in his youth and worn like badges of honor for the rest of his life were hardly visible now, lost in folds of pallid flesh that hung limp on bones turned brittle, chalky, somnolent.

Frequent doses of morphine helped to hold the pain at bay. The aged warrior, pale and shrunken, died at his home, 330 Decatur Street, Brooklyn, on 18 December 1888. He had reached seventy-seven years in August, tired but determined to go on living as he began his seventy-eighth year. He had lived longer than his father and his father's father, outlived Mary Routh and five of their children, succeeded his brother John as patriarch of the Dahlgrens in America.[36]

He had lived long enough to see most of his worldly stores taken away and dispersed. He had lost out with the banks in Natchez, had given up the two magnificent houses he had built on the banks of the Mississippi, had seen a war wipe away the plantations and people he had owned in Louisiana. Finally he was denied a role for himself and his sons in the affairs of the New South. He could be proud that nothing was taken without a fight—a long one as it turned out—and he not once succumbed to feeling sorry for his decisions and their consequences. Best of all, he had Mary Edgar, and he put his trust in the children to represent him and stand up for his principles in the decades ahead. They would remember, above all, his watchful guidance of the family.

His coffin was taken to the Second Presbyterian Church at Clinton and Remsen streets, where the Reverend Dr. Van Dyke conducted services in the presence of his widow and his children. Adolph was there from Nashville and Van from Saint Louis. The eulogy, quoted in the *Brooklyn Daily Eagle* on 21 December, remarked on his "steady courage" and "indomitable will" and the strength of his convictions: "Few men have lost all they owned and yet, as he, professed a steady trust in God and a patient confidence in the future. He strove to make everything bend to his will. He had little toleration with those who opposed his convictions, but he was just as severe with himself in all criticism."[37] Thus, the old general's stubborn resolves and scant regard for the opinions of others are part of his eulogy. They were characteristics so pronounced that, years later, his son Van told Dr. Van Dyke's son that he was grateful for the minister's candor in speaking of his father's weaknesses as well as his strengths.[38]

The iron coffin was temporarily removed to Green-Wood Cemetery to await shipment to Natchez, with final interment in the Natchez City Cemetery, where Dahlgren owned lots 294 through 300. He had bought the plot from the city on 22 May 1860.[39] It lies high on a sloping hillside and occupies a commanding position in the marble-strewn burying ground. He had prepared it for the casket of Mary Routh and commanded that her remains be moved there in 1860, wrenching them away from her kin in the Routh family cemetery opposite Routhland, defying her daughters Sarah Ann and Inez.

Dahlgren had ordered an iron fence forged by Wood and Perot of Philadelphia. On the gate, "C. G. Dahlgren" greets the visitor who comes today and pauses to read the inscriptions on four sides of Mary Routh's towering monolith. Her virtues are enumerated in marble and her memory preserved by a loving husband of eighteen years. In 1860, Mary Edgar, the new wife of twenty, had watched the memorial being set in place. She would have remarked on the beauty of the sentiments and the serenity of the site as she and her husband drove in the carriage back to Llangollen.

The general had not been in Natchez for nearly two decades when his casket, accompanied by his son Van, arrived on 23 December 1888. A hearse conveyed the coffin to City Cemetery, where the grave beside Mary Routh's was open in the shadow of her marble shaft. At 10:30 A.M. on the morning of 24 December, with Van and a few townspeople attending, the faithful Reverend Mr. Stratton said prayers at the grave and pronounced the benediction. The dutiful shivered in the chill of Christmas Eve and returned to their Yule logs and the merriment of the season.

General Dahlgren had been adamant when he commanded that his burial take place in Natchez. He had been too preoccupied with thoughts of Natchez in his late years not to return there. Mary Edgar and Van agreed. He was clearheaded in making his decision and stubborn to the end. That green sward with its elegant appointments in iron and marble, situated on high ground above the Mississippi, was all he still owned outright and could call his domain in 1888. It was his without threat of foreclosure, his without creditors, his beyond the rap of the sheriff's hammer, his without a last-minute scramble for collateral, his in memory, his an annuity in perpetuity, his because the small wrought iron marker standing upright in the grass assured "Perpetual Care."

And so the general lay there quietly, at last settled in the iron casket and protected by the iron pickets.[40] The years would take their toll on the Reverend Mr. Stratton and the few townspeople who had remembered Dahlgren in his prime.

After his death, Mary Edgar and the young children left Brooklyn and stayed for a while with Van in Saint Louis; Adolph and Mortimer kept trying their luck in Nashville and Biloxi. One of the twins, John Armfield, and the little girls, Virginia and Bernardina, moved with Mary Edgar to Atlanta in 1890 to live on the acres that the general had bought from Daniel Melton in 1863.

None of the family, including Van, the most prosperous, went to the expense of marking the general's grave. A large monument matching Mary Routh's was beyond their means, and anything less grand seemed inappropriate beside hers. The lean years demanded what money there was should be spent on the living.

Two descendants later took advantage of having inherited the plot, however, and made it their final resting place. Son Charles Ulric (1867–1921) and his wife Elizabeth (1864–1953) are buried there, as is their son Charles Gustavus (1904–1948). Those graves were duly marked with modest stones soon after each was buried. Ten feet away the general still lay without notice. *DAMNATIO MEMORIAE.*

Nor did the scrambled ledgers in the office of the Natchez Cemetery offer any clue to his whereabouts. Above him, the turf grew green each spring and the earth swallowed him up in due season. His grandchildren made hurried stopovers in Natchez from time to time, identified themselves to the owners at Dunleith, and then went on their way without finding and marking their grandsire's resting place.

In 1992, however, 104 years after Dahlgren's coffin was lowered into the earth, a search began among historians to find that missing Mississippi general and dignify his resting place with a marble slab of his own. The unpublished diary of the Reverend Mr. Stratton finally yielded the clue, and a steel probe driven alongside Mary Routh found the evidence.[41] There to pay him respect and homage on 18 January 1992 were members of the Natchez Chapter of the United Daughters of the Confederacy, who conducted a prayer service, and the Confederate Re-enactors from Vicksburg, who came in uniform and fired salutes.[42] Also attending were two grandchildren and a great-great-grandchild.

The modest headstone, provided by the U.S. Department of Veterans Affairs, reads:

Brig. Gen.
Charles G. Dahlgren
Mississippi State Troops
C.S.A.
Aug. 13, 1811
Dec. 18, 1888

Alma Kellogg Carpenter of Natchez, who had lived for twenty-three years with her family at Dunleith, placed a spray of red camellias on the grave. They were a bright token on a gray afternoon. The guard then broke rank, and the visitors dispersed.[43]

Greeting the assembly afterward at Dunleith were its owners, Mr. and Mrs. William Heins, whose reception extended the hour of General Dahlgren's recognition. The historians who spoke on that occasion cheered the old general for having run a full gamut of adventures, for having taken a lot of risks at almost every turn in a long life.

At times, he had been the grand puppeteer, a master manipulator, given to pulling strings and wires for social and business advantages, loving his sons and using the law to promote them to their majority before they were twenty-one, making merry behind the scenes in the competitive art of survival and obviously enjoying it, measure for measure. He had lived nearly eight decades of his century astride the tumult of the times, and he died comfortable with his doctrines. His long life had been charmed—especially charmed for one breathing so much fire and indulging in so very many contradictions.

✑ Eleven ✐

The General's Relict and End of the Dynasty

M ary Edgar Vannoy Dahlgren, who was born in 1840 and lived until 1928, could look back over more decades of the family's history than any other member.[1] As the youngest child of Mason (1790–1863) and Jane Ward Vannoy, she was linked directly to the eighteenth century. Together, her life and her father's life spanned 138 years in the annals of America.[2] When Mason Vannoy was born in Maysville, Kentucky, a western outpost in the great wilderness, George Washington was president and still had nine years to live. When Mary Edgar died in her eighty-eighth year on the Vannoy property near Manchester, Tennessee, Calvin Coolidge was president and Herbert Hoover was soon to be elected. She was five years old when Andrew Jackson died in 1845 at the Hermitage, 12 miles from her father's home in Nashville, and she was in her early twenties, married and with young children, during the last days of the Confederacy. Mary Edgar had inherited her father's physical strength and his ability to survive. The trials that she endured for nearly nine decades are proof that she was endowed with Mason Vannoy's pioneer qualities. She needed all of them at one time or another during her long life, for she had many sudden and grievous reversals.

Mary Edgar's paternal grandfather was Andrew Vannoy, a captain in the North Carolina Regiment of Continentals during the Revolutionary War; after the war, he received a land grant near Manchester, Tennessee, for his services. Her grandmother was the former Susannah Shepherd.[3]

As revolutionaries, pioneers, backwoodsmen, and defenders of the free-dom for which they fought, the Vannoys developed a strain of hardiness that would sustain them on the frontier.

Mason Vannoy was no exception. He served in the War of 1812 under William Henry Harrison and, after the war, moved to Mercer County, Kentucky. In 1818 he wooed Jane Garrett Ward of Harrodsburg and married her at the home of Jane's aunt Ellen Smith. The couple moved to Nashville in 1828 or 1830 and took up residence at what became 311 Vine Street. Mason established a carpenter shop at the bottom of the hill near the Nashville and Chattanooga Railroad depot. As a car builder and contractor, he assembled railroad cars (passenger and freight) and manufactured doors, sashes, blinds, and mantlings. He was a master craftsman, and his business prospered. By 1860, he was a man of rank in the community.[4] His son, G. B. Vannoy, had become one of Nashville's four practicing architects by 1846. Mary Edgar grew up in this prosperous household. She attended the Nashville Ladies College, from which she was graduated in 1854 after acquiring the graces of her social class. Neither family counsel nor the homilies of Dr. John Todd Edgar at the Presbyterian church could have prepared her at age eighteen for the seventy years ahead. To help her stand up to those challenges, she had the fortitude of the Vannoy blood, the devotion of Charles Dahlgren, and the love of her children.

At the outset of the Civil War, Mary Edgar's first child, Van, was nine months old. She had inherited four stepsons—who affectionately called her Ma—from Dahlgren's first marriage. In the next eighteen years, she brought up eight children of her own and lost a ninth child. During the war years, she wrote from Georgia to stepson Bernard in Natchez that the dark days were "the shadows of life & are given to try us & make men & women of us."

Another such stalwart was Phoebe Yates Pember, who spent most of the war nursing soldiers in Richmond, "boys hardly old enough to realize man's sorrows, much less suffer by man's fierce hate." Pember felt that witnessing pain and suffering had taught her "benevolence, charity, and love."

In a passage laced with wry humor, Pember described her "toilette" when she called on the Federals seeking rations for herself and her charges. She wore:

> . . . boots of untanned leather, tied with thongs; a Georgia woven homespun dress in black and white blocks—the white, cotton yarn, the black an old silk, washed, scraped with broken glass into pulp, and then corded and spun (it was an elegant thing); white cuffs and collar of bleached homespun, and a hat plaited of the rye straw picked from the field back of us, dyed black with walnut juice, a shoe string for ribbon to encircle it; and knitted worsted gloves of three shades of green—the darkest bottle shade being around the wrist, while the color tapered to the lovliest blossom of the pea at the finger-tips. *The style of the make was Confederate.*[5]

Phoebe Pember was destined to survive. She could laugh at her labors in "making-do" despite the troubled times. These resolute women of the South knew no poverty of spirit and in their ranks for the next fifty years of her life was Mary Edgar Dahlgren.

ℤ℥

Details of Mary Edgar's youthful years are included in the brief memoir that she dictated to her son John Armfield. Portions of it follow:

Some Early Recollections of Mary Edgar Vannoy Dahlgren

Let's go to Beersheba Springs [in 1860], the last summer of music in the ballroom and games in the courtyard and long sessions of cards for the men to take their minds off the election [coming up] in November. General Dahlgren and other gentlemen had formed the Beersheba Springs Company and had agreed to buy out Colonel Armfield's interests. General Dahlgren had already signed a note for $4,000 for our cottage; so we had our own place in 1860 next door to Dr. Waters and down the road from the Hardings and Basses. You know the house, John, although we had lost it by the time you came along.* I think often of that cottage and the people in it in 1860 and the perilous days that came down hard upon us in the months ahead. At least we had one summer there and were spared, by God's will, foreknowledge of the days of wrath to come.

Before the wedding in December your father made arrangements with Mr. Washington Cooper to paint our portraits in January. Times were good and Mr. Cooper had quite a following among our friends. He had also painted your Aunt Ellen and Uncle Edwin. Unfortunately, my morning sickness delayed Mr. Cooper's work on my portrait because I could not sit long at a time. He was patient about the interruptions, I recall, and was a gentleman to the core.† I'm glad you admire the portraits. I know they need a touch-up here and there. Like us, they've had to stand up to a lot of banging about. But the bride of 19 and the groom of 49 are still there as they were.

Nor has the summer of 1860 changed. At least not for me. And I think I can tell you why. The truth is that we were happy and we knew it and we thought the happiness would go on and on. General Dahlgren was so attentive that I could hardly take a step without the offer of his arm. We would cross the road and dine with the guests at the hotel when I felt like a supper away from the cottage. He liked to remind me that women carrying babies become more beautiful as the child grows. He loved to touch my cheek and say that my skin was translucent.

There were all sorts of amusements besides the balls and masquerades and musicales. Sister Ellen and your cousin Laura took

---

*See Howell, *John Armfield*, passim.

†Prolific portraitist, born in East Tennessee in 1802; popular in Nashville, where he probably painted as many as thirty-five faces a year. The Dahlgren portraits now hang above the mantel of a reconstructed Victorian parlor in the Tennessee State Museum, Nashville.

delight in wildflower walks along the brow of the mountain and came back to the cottage with bouquets of butterfly weed and sumac feathers and golden rod and wild asparagus to decorate the long porch.

The boys would sometimes leave after breakfast and go on expeditions to the caves or scale the opposite mountain or frolic in the clear cold pools in the valley. One day they killed a fox and made a sling for it. For them the pelt was not enough. Under cover of night, when all was quiet and the guests at the hotel were sleeping peacefully, those rascals dragged the carcass up and down the lane between our cottage and the hotel. They crept into the courtyard and circled it several times and then ran round the carpenter's shop and livery stable. Mr. Cagle's hounds were penned up between the two. So the boys unlatched the gate and let the hounds hit the trail with the most awful barking and yelping you can imagine. They went round and round in the courtyard and circled the cistern and played havoc with chairs and furniture on the gallery. No one could sleep, of course, and no one was sure what was happening.

Next morning the boys denied everything—allowed they were asleep in the cabin and heard nothing. General gave them a stern lecture behind the icehouse, nevertheless, his riding crop held in his right hand for emphasis.

Who were the boys? Did I forget to tell you who those pranksters were—they who kept all Beersheba awake with their midnight fox hunt? I can see their faces now, lined up like steps on a staircase, twitching with devilment. The oldest was Charlie Routh—didn't I say he was my stepson and just a year younger? Then there was Ulric Dahlgren, a nephew of the General's from Washington City. His father became an admiral in the U.S. Navy, but you know all that. Then came Bernard, the General's second son, Charlie's brother. And then the younger brother, Adolph, who was only eleven but given to as much mischief as the others. Last, there was Mortimer—little Mortimer—four years old. So four of the boys were your half brothers and the fifth, Ulric, your first cousin. You know all this.

I know I've mentioned Ellen and Laura being there. Also there were my mother and father—who were also Ellen's—and our brother McEwen. There were twelve of us in all, ranging in age from Pa at 70 to Mortimer at 4, with still another arrival expected in September.

Ulric had spent two winters in Natchez with his uncle and cousins. He was a capable surveyor and ran lines on the property across the river in Tensas as well as Beersheba. He loved horses, hunting, and fencing. At Beersheba he took lessons in fencing and French and impressed his tutors and all the younger boys that summer. He thought his real calling, however, was the law and decided to return to the East and read law in an uncle's office in Philadelphia. How we hated to see him go—tall, thin as a bean pole, flirtatious in the ballroom, a fine shot, ambitious, and always deferential to his uncle.

So the boys devised a scheme to mark the houseparty that summer and leave a record of the Dahlgrens, Vannoys, and Gardners who had assembled. They found a six foot boulder in a clearing of the pine thicket and went to work with hammers and chisels—borrowed, I think, from Mr. Cagle's shop. They hammered away all one afternoon and cut their initials on the sloping sides of the little boulder rising about two feet from the ground. The older men cut their own and their ladies' initials.

Then General Dahlgren gathered us all to the spot just as Charlie Routh was finishing the date: August 31, 1860. We all felt good about "our summer" at the cottage and happy about leaving behind "our marks" on Beersheba. Ulric thanked his uncle and me for all the good times he'd had in the South and clasped hands with his cousins. He left the following day by coach to Tracy and then by train to Nashville and Washington. You have the miniature of him in his blue uniform—the picture that belonged to Charlie Routh. They were as close as brothers—and you've the picture of Charlie in gray. Don't let anything happen to the pictures, my son, because the boys were like two brothers in different uniforms.*

It was only about three weeks after Ulric left the mountain that General stepped next door about midnight and roused Dr. Waters from his slumbers. It was my first child, of course, and General knew all the signals better than I. After all, in the eighteen years he was married to Mrs. Dahlgren he had seen her give birth to seven children, four of them to grow up. So he felt strongly that my time had come and indeed it had.

Dr. Waters delivered your brother Van by lamplight on the morning of September 22 at 4 o'clock. We named him Gustavus Vannoy. Sister Ellen was in attendance and the grandparents were waiting anxiously in the hall with General. Dr. Waters later sat on the front gallery and sipped a toddy of whiskey and sugar about

---

*The Dahlgren Stone lay choked with vines and covered with an accumulation of moss for a century before the pine grove adjacent to the Dahlgren cottage was cut over and the brush burned. Beersheba's oldest residents did not remember that it was there until the growth was cleared by Mrs. Josephine Eubanks and her grandson Nicholas King in 1987. All fourteen sets of initials, including the last two sets added in 1935, now have been positively identified:

C.G.D.	Charles Gustavus Dahlgren	1811–1888
M.E.D.	Mary Edgar Vannoy Dahlgren	1840–1928
M.V.	Mason Vannoy	1790–1863
J.V.	Jane Ward Vannoy	1800–1878
R.M.V.	Robert McEwen Vannoy	1835–1909
E.S.V.G.	Ellen Smith Vannoy Gardner	1822–1892
L.A.G.	Laura Adelaide Gardner	1843–1919
C.R.D.	Charles Routh Dahlgren	1841–1867
B.D.	Bernard Dahlgren	1847–1868
J.A.D.	John Adolph Dahlgren	1849–?
U.D.	Ulric Dahlgren	1842–1864
A.M.D.	Austin Mortimer Dahlgren	1856–1906
	(Austin Mortimer's initials are on small stone nearby.)	
E.S.G.	Edwin Sumner Gardner	1906–1980
	(A great-grandson of E.S.V.G. above)	
J.F.C.	John Foster Caldwell	1884–1965

daylight and reminded them all that he had delivered me as well. They said he was not certain of the date—there had been so many along the way—but I reminded him myself when he called in the afternoon. It was 20 years, almost to the day, between the good doctor's two deliveries. He looked down at me and held my hand and smiled in that kindly manner he was known for and whispered that he was getting a little old and found it hard to keep track of all the births and all the deaths he had been called to preside over in the last forty years.

Now that I am seventy-seven I can understand Dr. Waters. I have my good days. I have bad ones. Today was a good day for recalling what it was like at Beersheba all those years ago. You asked me and I tried to tell you what the world was like before you were born. I hope you've got it all down.

Recollections have a way of spurring us on to talk our tongues out. Then when we've said it we feel good and wonder where all the words came from in the first place.

Spoken from the lips of my beloved Mother
Mary Edgar Vannoy Dahlgren
and duly transcribed by her devoted son
John Armfield Dahlgren, Dahlgren Station,
Atlanta, Georgia. April 2, 1917.

In 1859, Mary Edgar and Charles Dahlgren had entered into a marriage contract that was recorded in Natchez on 5 January 1860.[6] It provided a sum of $25,000 to be paid from his estate to Mary Edgar at his death; there would be no joint or community property; each party was free to dispose of his or her own assets; neither was to be responsible for the debts of the other. Exactly what resources the bride brought to the marriage were not recorded, nor were the groom's. The sum of $25,000 would have been generous in 1860 for a bride of twenty. When Dahlgren died twenty-eight years later, however, finances were so altered that the sum seemed even greater, ironically, because the general's estate could not honor any part of the agreement of 1860.[7]

Mary Edgar must have learned early on, as the wife of Charles Dahlgren, that he was a man who did not usually change direction when he had made up his mind. As the wife of General Dahlgren in 1861, she knew how much he cared for her when he arranged for her and her younger stepsons to accompany him to his command on the Gulf Coast. There she nursed her own son Van and saw the baby through a case of measles. The so-called little General was hardly a year old.[8] Her next seven children were born in six different states from Mississippi to New York. It is clear that Mary Edgar always lived up to her responsibilities as wife, mother, and protector of the people who served her. She expressed no public criticism of her husband and did not use his decisions as an opportunity for bickering before the children.

If family finances were at a low ebb in 1865, they were even worse by 1869, the year that Admiral Dahlgren and his wife offered to take two of the boys into their household and provide them with "the ordinary elements of English education."[9] Apparently, the general was willing to accept the arrangement for the boys' education, but Mary Edgar was not. She wanted to keep her family intact and exercise her maternal rights. She would hear their lessons and prepare them for the academy herself. She would not allow her boys to live as poor relations in an affluent household in Washington.

Of her six sons, Mary Edgar depended most on Van, the firstborn. She loved Van to an extent that she would never love the others. He had come to her at Beersheba Springs in 1860 when there was peace in the little community—when the morning sun shone on the green hills and shadows purpled the river valley. She had sister Ellen with her, her mother and father, the devoted attention of General Dahlgren and Dr. Waters. She was happy then, at age twenty, to bring a new life into their world.

The other children came to her during the upheaval and uncertainties of the next twenty years, a different age. Together, she and the general named them—called them by the names of their kin or closest friends:

Rowan Foote, Edgar McWhorter, Charles Ulric, Ira Smith, John Armfield, Virginia, and Bernardina. The children would grow up knowing
their connections and identifying themselves with names from the family's past.

Van remained the right arm of his mother and his younger brothers
and sisters. He put up his half brother Mortimer in Saint Louis when
Mortimer fled Beauvoir after Sarah Dorsey passed over him and left her
estate to Jefferson Davis.[10] It was Van who went to Brooklyn in 1888
to accompany the body of his father to Natchez. In 1890, Van moved
his mother and the younger children to Saint Louis from Brooklyn and
looked after them until he could send them to the Dahlgren farm near
Atlanta. Because the general left no will, Edgar Dahlgren remained in
Brooklyn and settled his father's small estate on 24 April 1890. He was
twenty-five years old and employed as a produce salesman.

The farm outside Atlanta had figured in the 1864 battle and was
visited from time to time by Union and Confederate soldiers who had
fought there and returned to reminisce. Among the Dahlgren papers in
Nashville there is a photograph of about fifteen older men, most of them
leaning on canes and wearing dark suits, in front of the two-story house
on the Dahlgren property. The photo is not dated but would seem to
be circa 1894—perhaps the thirtieth anniversary of the battle. Johnny
Dahlgren took a special interest in occasions of this kind—a chance to
act as guide, informant, and commentator on his family's history. On
the back of the photo, he noted (in 1933): "My beloved Mother standing
at the door of our house near Atlanta, Georgia, Grand Army of the
Republic friends visiting the battlefield. Col. Whitcomb of Nebraska, I
think, in foreground."[11] Although he was not born until five years after
the war, the conflict was vivid to Johnny Dahlgren. He delighted in
incidents handed down by his family—how Mary Edgar, her stepson
Bernard, and Mr. Dolan, the caretaker, had buried a "large tin box" on
the grounds of Llangollen before Vicksburg fell; how his father had
bought the Decatur property with 200 bales of cotton in 1863; how the
family had fled Atlanta when the battle began.[12]

As a dramatic finale to his remarks, Johnny would unfurl the 7th
Mississippi Battle Flag given to his father from the regiment of Col. W.

H. Bishop.[13] Another photograph, taken years later at the rear of the Decatur house, shows a bald Johnny in the foreground holding his beloved terrier by the collar and leaning against his trophy—an abandoned, ramshackle streetcar of the horsedrawn vintage. He had worked as a streetcar driver and managed to get the car pulled into the back yard—where it would remain as his summer house and shed—an attraction for visitors after the electric car outmoded it. In addition to tinkering, Johnny assumed the role of family historian, antiquarian, and public relations man.

As the sons grew older, interest in farming had waned by 1900; Johnny and Rowan were probably not productive managers. As a regular reader of the *Confederate Veteran,* Johnny placed the following advertisement in Volume 9, January 1901:

TRUCK FARM FOR RENT NEAR ATLANTA

At Dahlgren Station, near Atlanta, Ga., J.A. Dahlgren desires to rent a large, comfortable residence and twenty-four acres of land suitable for farm purposes. The place is suitable for dairy and truck farming. It is easily accessible by three lines of electric cars, and is on the way between Atlanta and Decatur. Address J.A. Dahlgren, Dahlgren Station, Atlanta, Ga.

Advertised as "The Famous Dahlgren Property Subdivision," it was finally divided into building lots by Van in 1910 and sold off in parcels.[14] Later, the home site was bought by J. G. Clark of Southern Builders on 23 January 1925, after Van had moved his mother, his sister Virginia, and his brother Johnny to Manchester, Tennessee.

ᘓᙠ

It was while she was still living in Atlanta that Mary Edgar learned of the changes at the Marydale plantation in Louisiana. The comic sequence had begun when the banker, David Urquhart from New Orleans, took over after Dahlgren lost Marydale. Urquhart had an ambitious daughter, Cora, who went on the stage in England and dressed in expensive and outrageous costumes.[15] Known as Cora Potter, she was a flamboyant actress who exhibited her limited talents in England and America in a variety of roles from Cleopatra to Juliet.[16] Her appearances from 1887 to 1910 actually became notorious. The reviews were either politely lukewarm or embarrassing. In 1889, at Palmer's Theatre in New York, Cora Potter's "attempt to act Cleopatra might fairly be made the subject of levity, but we have no disposition to ridicule the lady. It was a foregone conclusion that she would fail. To a woman of her meager acquirements the character is unattainable."[17] Another critic had spoken.

The reviewers noted Cora's magnificent costumes and all the trappings that dazzled the eye and drew attention away from Shakespeare's tragedy. Stories of those costumes and Cora Potter were remembered years later by a resident of Tensas Parish who composed a sketch for the *Tensas Gazette*: "Mrs. Potter's wardrobe, used in *Cleopatra*, cost her her [father's] valuable plantation property Marydale . . . which she mortgaged to her modiste, [Charles Frederick] Worth of Paris, internationally known dressmaker. . . . Mrs. Potter in her role as Queen Cleopatra required feathers of a certain bird of rare color native to Africa, and necessitating breast plumage of about eight hundred [sic] such birds and to acquire which hunters were dispatched to Africa. . . . Always living beyond her means, Mrs. Potter was unable to settle with Monsieur Worth." Marydale, valued at $14,035.72, was deeded to Charles Worth on 25 July 1893.[18] Mary Edgar Dahlgren was aware of the succession of owners of Marydale—from Charles Dahlgren to Charles Worth of Paris within a few years. If the general were still alive, she knew that his rage would have been heard all the way to Paris.

✃

Mary Edgar and her children followed the career of William de Rohan as best they could after General Dahlgren died in 1888. There are no letters to prove a correspondence between the Dahlgrens and de Rohan, but the genealogy complied by John Armfield Dahlgren in 1917 provides family details that were obviously gathered in Sweden by his Uncle

William Dahlgren (alias Count de Rohan). Another son of the general, Austin Mortimer, reported in *Goodspeed's Biographical and Historical Memoirs* that his uncle was "the celebrated Count de Rohan, who fought in every European war for the past forty years, and received the highest honors and titles from several crowned heads."[19] Like other members of his family, Mortimer was adept at embellishing hearsay.

After months of supporting the Risorgimento and carrying out Garibaldi's schemes in Italy, William lost favor and was relieved of duty with his revolutionary comrades. He referred to the breakup in a letter written in French some years later to Italian Prime Minister Marco Minghetti, who, he hoped, would help him get a pension from the government:

> I am convinced to the bottom of my soul that I always did faithfully and energetically what I undertook for Italy, without regard to my own interests. Perhaps in executing then what I thought was my duty, I may have been rather harsh [sévère] in my manner of acting, but this ought in no wise to lessen the merit of my acts.[20]

De Rohan did not supply the details, but an outburst of rage had obviously caused his rejection. In a moment of crisis, a flare-up of temper had followed hard on his weeks of ferrying the Red Shirts. Not succumbing to inaction, however, he joined the French during the Franco-Prussian War and later fought with the Turks, according to the genealogy.

By the time Mortimer was interviewed by Goodspeed's editor, the old soldier of fortune had fallen on hard times. His finances had dwindled, and his ploys and braggadocio could no longer sustain him. He remained convinced that his service with Garibaldi and the Red Shirts in 1860 merited full recognition and ample compensation from the Italian government. "I saved the Saviour of Italy," he boasted, but the Italians refused his pleas for a pension. He then went to the U.S. State Department in Washington for help with his claim and was turned down there, too.[21]

By 1888, William carried a light wallet and the weight of years. On 10 December, a week before Charles died in Brooklyn, William filed a claim in Washington for a Mexican War pension. He claimed service with Capt. N. Greusel's company, 1st Michigan Infantry, and noted both his birth name and his alias on the application. Here was the possibility of another ribbon to pin on the old man's chest, with a small check to go with it.

The claim was duly processed in Washington and the War Department sent a reply on 8 February 1889 that was signed by Assistant Adjutant General Thomas Ward: "The name William de Rohan or Thomas [Theodore] Dahlgren is not borne on the rolls of Company 'D' (Capt. N. Greusel), 1st Regiment, Michigan Vols. Mexican War." This minor scheme had ended in failure like many of William's larger ones, including the tin mines in Sardinia that he said he lost for lack of capital.

In Italy today, the names of de Rohan's fellows-in-arms attract the traveler's eye in streets, piazzas, and monuments: Garibaldi, Cavour, Victor Emmanuel, Mazzini, Minghetti, Depretis, and the host that backed the Risorgimento. A few historians, chiefly American, make passing references to William de Rohan. In a convincing paragraph about him in *America and the Mediterranean World, 1776–1882*, James A. Field concludes:

> . . . [T]his first reinforcing movement [9 June 1860] was of decisive importance: only the ammunition and the troops brought in by de Rohan enabled Garibaldi to continue the campaign and to extend his control over the island [Sicily] and pen the Neapolitans up inside the garrison towns. And even as late as early July [1860], two months after the sailing of the Thousand, more than three-fourths of the reinforcements that had left the mainland for Sicily had been carried by the "American" ships.[22]

Until his death, "Admiral" de Rohan claimed responsibility for Garibaldi's rescue at Gibraltar in 1849 and for his successes in Sicily and Naples in 1860. Historians now seem to have validated some of de Rohan's pleas for recognition.[23]

As an old man and near the end of his life, de Rohan concocted a final ploy. He went to his late brother John's house on Thomas Circle and asked for the help of Madeleine Dahlgren, his wealthy sister-in-law and priestess of old Washington society. There is no question that his scheme worked, for Madeleine took him in and provided for him in spite of the bitter rift between the admiral and William forty years earlier. Besides receiving bed and board and the amenities of a prosperous household, William received regular instruction in the tenets of the Roman Catholic Church. About his soul Madeleine was insistent and the old man surrendered.[24]

A contributor to *The Washington Post*, who had heard stories about de Rohan, remarked on his physical appearance during his prime:

He was broad shouldered and deep-chested, and in his prime of life must have been one of the most powerful men living. His head was Websterian in its proportions, while the cheekbones were high and the jaws wide, with the chin cut square across, so that the bush of English whiskers . . . reminded you of a desert lion.[25]

Both the admiral, with his thin angular face, and the general, with a tapered jaw and small chin, stood in contrast to their younger brother. Portraits exist of the older brothers, but none of William has come to light.

Early in 1891, his giant frame gaunt and his arm partially paralyzed from a stroke, William de Rohan was admitted to Providence Hospital in the District of Columbia and died there on 31 March. The city issued the usual permit for his burial on 2 April.[26]

There is no record that de Rohan left a child of his own body to mourn his passing. His twelve nieces and nephews—children of John and Charles—did not know him well and could not have felt a loss at the passing of the eccentric old man. His last words to Madeleine Dahlgren were, "Do not let Mrs. Read see me." He was determined to deny his estranged sister, Patty Dahlgren Read, a final condescending stare.[27]

Madeleine Dahlgren told Sargent Prentiss Nutt, a young lawyer from Natchez, when he came to console her, that Admiral de Rohan "died praying, etc., etc., etc." She was glad to share the finale with Nutt and to express her feeling of hope for de Rohan's redemption. Although she had been unable to convert Admiral Dahlgren to Catholicism during the five years of their marriage, she had successfully brought his philandering brother to the communion of the church.

Madeleine made arrangements for a funeral mass at Saint Peter's on Second Street, S.E., and saw to de Rohan's burial in Mount Olivet Cemetery. Atop the square gravestone is a heavy Roman cross, beneath which is the Dahlgren family motto in archaic Swedish: *What Heaven Creates Envy Cannot Destroy.* The letters carved on the base are simply "William Theodore Dahlgren, son of Bernard Ullric and Martha Rowan Dahlgren, born 1820, died 1891."[28] Fortune had marked him for a dignified resting place in consecrated earth. His nephews in the South would continue to tell stories of his exploits and moments of valor as a filibuster and mercenary in two hemispheres.

At times, William had been a skilled impersonator in presenting himself as an American captain, or as "Admiral" de Rohan, or as "Count" de Rohan. Joining the side of a conflict that might fill his pockets, he ingratiated himself with kings, commanders, prime ministers, and millionaires. He made a game of subterfuge and grabbed the spoils of conflict. He was an adventurer riding the ground swell of disorder, drawn to and savoring any clash of arms.

In a letter to George P. Marsh, U.S. Minister in Rome, de Rohan defended his role as an undercover agent in Italian affairs in 1860. He called what he did "left-handed transactions, as almost every government at times becomes a party to, a principle that is tacitly assented to in the quiet method of dealing with the agent employed. . . ." He defended the old argument that irregular tactics would eventually produce regular results. Playing by the rules of the game, openly, could be a waste of time and a hazard to success. He excused all his clandestine maneuvers like a well-seasoned pragmatist.[29]

Madeleine found de Rohan's will, had it recorded, and attended to the last formalities. He left his estate to her, a legacy of little value. He added that "Mr. Solomons, Gen. Ordway, and Mr. Roessle have medals, seals, etc. on which I have borrowed money. Redeem them after my death." So, if redeemed, to whom would the medals go? Did he intend them for his nephews at the end? There is no record of their disposition.

Madeleine did more for de Rohan, however, than getting his medals out of hock. She set about memorializing his career in the form of two accounts published shortly after his death. She was responsible for the long biographical obituary in *The Washington Post* on 10 April 1891 that recounted his eventful life over seven decades. Also, she saw to it that he had an entry in the *National Cyclopedia,* along with the admiral and the general. Madeleine, always busy with her claims on both time *present* and time *future,* wrote and paid for the family's history in print. She was intent upon keeping the brothers in public memory, adamant that the Dahlgrens would be memorialized as she fashioned them, determined to keep their fame inviolate, assured, perpetual because prepaid.

∝℞

Even though General Dahlgren lost the property at Beersheba Springs, as did the other cottage owners unable to pay off their notes, there was always the family's hope of returning to the mountain community in summer and meeting friends of happier days. For decades after the war, the hotel that Colonel Armfield had built and the cottages clustered around it remained a pocket of nineteenth-century culture. With a small, conservative population of local residents—subsistence farmers, herdsmen, hunters, and woodsmen—Beersheba was noted for its social stability, old-fashioned manners, and its close communion with nature. These attributes marked its character well into the twentieth century. Although the automobile made slow advances during the 1920s, it was not until the advent of electricity in the 1940s, the telephone in the 1950s, and city water in the 1960s that the community gradually embraced modern living.

Van Dahlgren arranged for his mother to stay at the Beersheba Hotel for short periods in summer and renew old acquaintances. Her niece, Laura Gardner Settle from Nashville, sometimes met her there. Mary Edgar's son Johnny, then thirty-five years old, worked at the hotel in 1905 and was on call as a handyman for the cottages. His help was recognized on 26 August when a collection was taken up and presented to him from "Hotel Guests and Cottages" with fifty-three signatures. The total was a sum of $44.50, including $2.00 from his mother. He preserved the names and later wrote: "In loving memory of these kind and true friends—John A. Dahlgren."[30]

In 1914, Johnny made a reservation for his mother and himself for rooms upstairs at the Beersheba Hotel, gift of brother Van. "If you can't give us upstairs, the two rooms adjoining at the [children's] sand pile will do," he wrote the manager. Always scrupulous about his debts, Johnny added: "Enclosed please find money order for my board in full, with 8% interest from Sept. 1, 1912."[31] This was a typical stance of Johnny Dahlgren, honest and mindful of his obligations. He was also serious about his guardianship of family relics and papers. He catalogued them after a fashion and gave them to the Tennessee Archives and Museum after the deaths of his mother and Van. Ridiculed by some of his contemporaries and shunned by others, Johnny, who looked like the general and revered him, had taken on the conscience of the family during his later years.

To express his appreciation for favors, Johnny Dahlgren made a point to jot down his thanks to the public officials whom he urged to name streets and roads for his family. In 1890, he wrote, "Kindness of Mrs. William H. Patterson, *Dahlgren Station*, Atlanta." The second courtesy was in Manchester, Tennessee, 1923, then Dahlgren Avenue, Beersheba Springs, 1932, "kindness of Mr. Isaac Smoot and Mr. R. T. Dykes." Next was Dahlgren Boulevard, Manchester, 1933, "Kindness of Mr. McCormack." There was also Vannoy Street, Atlanta, for his mother's family. Persistent and nagging, he was a determined promoter, and he nailed up Dahlgren signs that he ordered by parcel post.

ೲ

Van Dahlgren was eighteen years old in 1878 when Bernardina, the last of his siblings, was born in New York. As the chief wage earner among the boys in the Brooklyn household, Van took a protective interest in his mother and the little girl. He looked after them from the beginning of his career and to an even greater degree after his father died. Bernardina grew into a beautiful young woman who resembled Mary Edgar in her youth. Van, who later became a prosperous businessman in Saint Louis, never married. It was as though he chose to forgo a wife and family of his own in order to make Mary Edgar comfortable and to bestow favors on this charming young sister as she grew into womanhood. Thus Bernardina became Van's charge and his hostess for formal gatherings in his Saint Louis home.

Van also saw to it that Bernardina had pleasant holidays at a number of summer resorts when Saint Louis turned into a veritable furnace. He sent her to his friends in Pointe Aux Barques, Vermont, and Gloucester, Massachusetts. He wrote ahead to his cousin by marriage, Sargent Prentiss Nutt of Natchez, at that time a lawyer in Washington, when Bernardina was scheduled to spend some time there.[32]

In 1912, Van gave Bernardina a holiday in Grand Haven, Michigan, where she lived with a Judge Dyer and his family. There, she met William Berg, a hardy young man and lighthouse keeper. They fell in love, and, at age thirty-four, Bernardina married Berg on 11 December 1912. Van, crushed and disapproving, refused to see her again.[33] For years they were not in touch, for Van, like his father, could be stubborn and unforgiving. He withheld his patronage to Bernardina until a few days before her death in 1920 with the birth of her fourth child. After the births of her other children, Bernardina had written to her brother Johnny for notes on the Dahlgren families, and he had supplied her with the useful genealogy. She wanted her offspring, removed as they were, to grow up knowing their kin. Bernardina Dahlgren Berg died with the belief that her two sons and two daughters would extend the Dahlgren line into the twentieth century.

Inept as he was in daily affairs, Johnny Dahlgren had sat down with scattered notes, letters from home and abroad, Bible entries, and newspaper obituaries to record for his sister the genealogical record of the Dahlgrens and their related families in Sweden and America. His chronicle goes back to 1593 in Sweden and takes the family in America to 1917.[34] Johnny had obviously kept track of Admiral Dahlgren's issue from his two marriages, followed his erratic Uncle William Theodore Dahlgren, and corresponded with the children of his own father's two marriages. The seventy pages, in a small ringed notebook in Johnny's clear script, are a testament of the family's growth in nineteenth-century America. Thanks to the order and exactness, the family record was extended to include the Dahlgren marriages with the eastern houses of Astor, Drexel,

Lawrence, and others. Whatever else can be said about Johnny, the perpetual piddler, he had tried to fulfill his father's wishes to keep the family together. His inscription in the notebook reads: "Presented to Bernardina Dahlgren Berg from her affectionate brother, John A. Dahlgren, April 5, 1917."

◌◌

In 1922, at the age of eighty-two, Mary Edgar became adamant about leaving Georgia and returning to Tennessee. Her life had been spent in such a succession of moves that going home could be only easy. It was a wish that put the family on the alert, however, especially son Van in Saint Louis, who, at age sixty-two, felt responsible for carrying out his mother's wishes. He had helped her since he went to work at thirteen, so it was Van who made all the arrangements. On 9 September 1922, he wrote to Mary Edgar: "I selected a place on the Viola Road [Manchester] for your house and they have already commenced laying the foundation and digging the well. It will be back from the road and I am giving it my personal attention and you never will be as happy as when you come to Tennessee." Van went on to remark on the friendliness of the people in Manchester and their ties to Mary Edgar's late brother, McEwen Vannoy.

By April, the new house was finished and ready for occupancy. Van wrote to Johnny in Atlanta, outlined arrangements for the move, and instructed his brother, age fifty-three, about the details: "Mr. Floyd will attend to everything in Atlanta and send the cow by express, also Bobby. The former has to be crated and the latter muzzled." That part of the move was to cost more than a new cow and a new dog, but Johnny would not agree to parting with his friends. "You all will reach Manchester Saturday evening. You change cars at Tullahoma. *Please remember that.*" Then comes a barrage of instructions reminiscent of General Dahlgren: "Let me entreat you to be normal and not get excited, running around looking for Bobby and the cow . . . get into the car with Mother and remain there. Look at the scenery . . . act like any other white man . . . forget all about the cow and Bobby . . . do not try to find where they are. Help Mother, and do not bother your head about Bobby . . . when you get to Tullahoma . . . get off there and do not go on to Nashville."[35] In spite of Van's doubts about brother Johnny, the trip was apparently completed without incident. Once in Coffee County, Mary Edgar put the remaining family jewels in the Manchester bank vault, and Van was able to breathe some relief.

Van's career continued to prosper in the business world, and his mother took pride in his success. He had become a senior member of William Schotten and Company about 1900 in Saint Louis and had then joined the James H. Forbes Tea and Coffee Company about 1915. In 1909, while with Schotten, he had been honored with the appointment of colonel on the Governor's Staff of Missouri. Like his father, he had the reputation of being popular but "frank, and blunt spoken." He was nicknamed "Dahl." Among his social successes was election to membership in the prestigious Tennessee Society in Saint Louis.[36]

❧❧

Mary Edgar's second son, Rowan, lived in Atlanta and died there, apparently without issue, in 1920.[37] Edgar had remained in Brooklyn and worked as a produce salesman and streetcar operator. Later, he was caretaker for a cemetery at Hempstead, Long Island, and finally a guard in the bank vaults on lower Broadway. Married three times, Edgar was hit by hard luck in midlife. According to a grandson, when Edgar's second wife, Sophronia Beatty, was desperately ill and he had a small son to look after, he wrote to one of his affluent cousins, probably Eric Dahlgren in New York, and asked him to help with a loan until he could recover. The cousin refused, and thereafter Edgar regretted bitterly his connection with the admiral's side of the family.[38]

Charles Ulric Dahlgren worked as the manager of a mill in Gloster, Mississippi, and then in Oxford, Alabama. The mills processed peanuts for cooking oil, an industry in line with diversification in the South after the war.[39] Charles was happily married, had a son named Charles Gustavus, and enjoyed a position of leadership in several small Southern communities. Ira, Johnny's twin, remained in the East, apparently never married, and died in 1927.

During her last years, Mary Edgar suffered the loss of four of her sons and her daughter Bernardina. All of the general's sons by Mary Routh were already dead and lying in unmarked graves. The deaths had caught up with the births, and Mary Edgar must have had forebodings of her own last days when she wrote to Van after Rowan's death in 1920 and discussed her move to the Vannoy farm at Manchester.

There, in the little frame house on the Viola road, Mary Edgar Dahlgren lived out her allotted time and looked back on brighter days. She would recall memories of Nashville, Natchez, Llangollen, and Beersheba Springs. Then she might fall asleep and get the years out of order and try to put her nine children in sequence again. She had many happy times locked into memory, perhaps sometimes blocking the unhappy ones. Other nights were probably troubled. She would think of her beloved brother McEwen Vannoy, dead in 1909, never married. McEwen left her the 124-acre Vannoy farm, which had been their father's and their grandfather's. She knew from McEwen's will that he had been honorable toward his children by Clarissa, his mulatto mistress. He willed those children his town lots, household furnishings, and outstanding notes. McEwen had been forthright about his children and had tried to give them a start in life.[40]

During her last years, Mary Edgar had few visitors in the plain little house set on cedar posts. Three doors opened onto the front porch. The house was cold in winter and almost intolerable in summer. Her niece in Nashville, Mrs. Elizabeth Gardner Hall, and her daughters paid visits, brought her presents, and listened to her reminiscences.[41] They took snapshots of her standing with Johnny and Virginia on the steps of the house or in the front yard. At 85 pounds, Mary Edgar was too frail to stand for long. On 2 August 1928, at the age of eighty-eight, she died peacefully as Johnny read Scripture at her bedside. She was mourned by her children, Van, Virginia, and Johnny.[42] She had lived too long to expect much attention from others; her contemporaries had long since departed.

Mary Edgar Dahlgren was laid to rest at the city cemetery in Manchester. A year later, in the same plot, her beloved son Van was buried beside her. Both graves were marked by very small, upright slabs, their inscriptions simple and brief. With their limited means, Johnny and Virginia shared the cost of buying and setting the stones.

Ruth Kratz, the granddaughter of Johnny's elusive half brother Adolph (Pudge), was driving through Tennessee in the 1930s and asked her husband to stop the car when her eye caught a sign marking Dahlgren Boulevard out of Manchester. After inquiring, the Kratzes found Johnny and Virginia, reminisced about the family, and offered to buy some of Mary Edgar's jewelry that was in a Manchester bank vault. It was a well-meaning gesture, considering the state of finances on Viola Road, but Ruth said good-bye to her cousins after their polite refusal.[43]

The eccentric Johnny had become the frequent target of Manchester boys who teased him with their pranks. One Halloween, they stole his little pony cart from the shed behind his house, rolled it into town, and hoisted it onto the roof of the Manchester railroad station.[44] Townspeople laughed about this joke for years.

Sister Virginia, her hearing impaired by mumps as a young woman, suffered in later years from diabetes and lost her right limb below the knee. Both she and Johnny loved their mother and cherished the general's name. They referred to him as their "noble father." They were the last of his intended *aristokratia,* the shaken remnants of his dynasty in the South.

By 1928, General Dahlgren had already lain forty years in his iron casket at the Natchez Cemetery. When Johnny heard from friends that oxidation was eating away the Gothic spikes of the iron fence, he hoped to take arms as best he could against the decay:

Brother T. Wesley Flowers of Natchez [is] pastor of our Church of Christ. . . . I told him if he could get me a seat with any of his relatives or friends going to Natchez, please do so, as I wish to carry about one gallon of paint to paint my dear Noble Father's Cemetery fence. . . . Brother Flowers replied "Yes."[45]

There was no one to take the time or spend the money to mark the graves of Mortimer, who had been committed to the Meridian, Mississippi, Insane Asylum in 1906 and was buried in Biloxi, or Adolph, who deserted his wife and child in Nashville and probably died in California.

Only the little boulder in the pine grove beside the Dahlgren cottage at Beersheba Springs, like a mute epitaph, held intact the family's initials and silently evoked the memory of a long ago, nearly forgotten *annus mirabilis*. There, the day had been put in stone: "August 31, 1860."

❄ Twelve ❄

Postlude for a Patriarch

harles Dahlgren followed his family's *modus operandi* throughout his seventy-seven years. That is, Charles and his brothers
attracted the attention of their contemporaries and usually received the kind of scrutiny given public figures. With their bravado, the
Dahlgrens seemed to command all they surveyed. They were actors; they
assigned themselves roles; and they played their parts with confidence
and no lack of cunning. Each, for his own purposes, had written the
script and did not intend to depart from it. Each trod the boards with
lights on and curtain up, taking no counsel before the scene began and
no prompting as it played itself out.

Contemporaries who knew the brothers remarked on how they appeared. Some were struck by the manliness of the physique and the
confident stride. Others were put off by their calculating manner and
condescending replies. But nobody was indifferent to the bearers of the
Swedish name.

After his appointment as brigadier general of state troops in Mississippi, Charles Dahlgren saw himself as the defender of the Gulf Coast
against threatening Federal forces. He wore his uniform with dignity,
thereby commanding attention for the retinue that followed him: Mary
Edgar and the younger sons. He considered their proximity an indulgence
that went with his rank and was accepted at the time.

Two years later, when they retreated to Georgia, Charles and Mary
Edgar were cited by the patrician Mary S. Mallard of Atlanta and judged
"genteel, attractive persons in appearance."[1]

Many years later, when he was approaching seventy, Charles Dahlgren was interviewed in his office at 117 Broadway by a young journalist from Philadelphia who was struck by Dahlgren's powerful frame and the stories he told about the people whom he had known—many of them with legendary reputations.[2]

Brother John Dahlgren likewise learned to charm his contemporaries when he set out on his rise in the world. At age sixteen, his aim was an appointment as a midshipman in the U.S. Navy. His referee was the Honorable John Vaughan of Philadelphia, who wrote: "He is a good looking young man, and so passionately bent on the destination of the Navy of the United States that he cannot be diverted."[3] Not long after Vaughan sent this recommendation, the appointment was made and a distinguished career launched.

Brother William achieved instant notice with his warrior's stride and defiant jaw. He commanded attention wherever he appeared, sometimes like a strong gale barking orders to his crew, sometimes as a wily go-between in schemes of international intrigue. He knew how to get the upper hand of subordinates and when to flatter a general or a king. In 1860, with a volley of French and his fist pounding the counter in the office of the Piedmontese Governor of Caligari in Sardinia, William harangued the recalcitrant official into giving clearance to the mail ship carrying important papers for the revolutionary forces in Sicily. A close observer wrote:

> He [de Rohan] walked in and insisted on the great man [the governor] being sent for. After some few words, he said, "Are you an Italian in heart or only in name?" and then, advancing toward him [the governor] and pointing to a couple of decorations he wore, added, "Those decorations you wear have been given you by your country; will you now in turn betray her interests and disgrace those ribbons received from her?" The Governor jumped off his chair as if he feared he was going to be eaten, but when he found de Rohan had no such animal intention, recovered himself, and at length gave his word that she [the mail steamer] would leave as soon as her steam was up. . . . [4]

With his physical strength, William de Rohan had pummeled the Sardinian governor and shamed him into supporting Garibaldi. Yet, no international tribunal would hang de Rohan for his violations of international law. He was remembered as a noisy troublemaker and irrepressible soldier of fortune. Today, in spite of a volatile temper, he is credited with helping put Victor Emmanuel II on the throne of Italy.

ℭℬ

Charles Dahlgren joined the Rebellion in Mississippi when his investments in the agricultural economy were threatened. Taking the posture of an outspoken zealot, he became a defender of the South's right to govern itself in a Confederacy of States. Like many of his compatriots, he had read the English poet William Blake: "One yoke for the ox and the lion is oppression."

Dahlgren, like his neighbors, expected swift military victories. He counted on responsible commanders who had been trained at the U.S. Military Academy at West Point and were successful in the Mexican War or who had studied at the military schools in their respective states. Together, they would gain the South's independence and earn the world's acclaim for their struggle to throw off the "yoke" of national "oppression."

At the same time, Charles Dahlgren held on stubbornly to an image of himself in a pastoral landscape marked by cotton rows, river boats, and African labor. His vision stretched forward to the years ahead when his sons, and their sons, and even their sons would husband the earth and gather the yield of the black soil deposited under their feet by the Mississippi and its tributaries—a gift put there for their indulgence. No political sleight of hand, no threat of arms, no act of Providence would blind Charles to his vision of patriarchy. As a self-made man, his aggressive nature told him that he had earned the title of patriarch, along with its benefits, for himself and for his sons in perpetuity.

The day soon arrived, of course, when Charles failed to achieve the chivalric role that he had envisioned. His memory of the Hussars drilling in Natchez, smart in their colorful uniforms, was in sharp contrast to his observation of the arrival of raw troops, often surly and ill fed, on the Gulf Coast.

By fall, after several unpopular moves, he lost the confidence of the two regiments under his command. He made the fatal mistake of exercising a tight-fisted authority before first earning the trust required of a leader. As an appointee of Governor Pettus, he gave abrupt orders without first consulting the officers under him. The men became disgruntled and turned to support the popularly elected colonels. Rumors of their discontent soon reached the high command in Richmond, while Charles fought back with an editorial in a local newspaper: "I leave the judgment of my actions to the tribunal of time."[5] Unfortunately, the judgment had already been made.

☙❧

Plenty of evidence indicates that Charles was better suited to take command of his family and the business of the plantations than of the volunteers on the Gulf Coast. As a father and the head of a considerable domestic domain, he was prompt about carrying out his responsibilities. As soon as his sons were old enough, they followed their father's example of industry and found jobs after school to help with their support.

Whatever the sons might do to displease him, he would hold them accountable to his rules. Son John Armfield repeatedly referred to Dahlgren as his "noble father." Son Van, in contrast, was quietly critical of his father's dogmatic pronouncements. The other sons, as far as the record indicates, seem to have suffered them quietly. Perhaps they forgave him for his intractable ways because he had borne the responsibility of moral instruction for the six sons and two daughters whom he and Mary Edgar brought to maturity.

☙❧

During his many years in the public arena, Charles Dahlgren displayed his share of contradictions. He also perpetrated a number of eccentricities. These traits were recognized by his contemporaries but were not always apparent to him. Up to and through his middle years, while the children were growing up, his demeanor was stern and his edicts uncompromising; he seemed to eschew humor and any show of levity. Apparently, it was not in his nature as banker, planter, and litigant in the courts to recognize those ironic turns in his career that provoked smiles among his contemporaries.

After eighteen years in New York, however, removed from the South and daily reminders of his losses, he mellowed into a seriocomic figure. On lower Broadway, he adopted the persona to fit the tall tales that amused the commission merchants, lawyers, and young clerks on the Stock Exchange. They were drawn to the bombastic old general and amused by his stories about Admiral Farragut, President Johnson, Governors Wells and Sharkey, Generals Beauregard and Johnston, and scores of others. They listened with bemused attention while he detailed his wins and losses in the courts. The young reporter from Philadelphia fell in with Dahlgren's awed admirers: "Perhaps no man in New York is more rich in reminiscence and can at the same time make the story of what he has seen and experienced more interesting."[6]

So he had his recruits at last, his troops. They responded to his anecdotes and thunderous tales as young men can and will respond, especially when declaimed by a hoary bard endowed with the gift of old-time rhetoric. The young men compensated for the troops that Dahlgren had failed to engage twenty years before on the Gulf Coast, or those whom he could not rally to the defense of Natchez. They were caught up in the throes of a lost cause, comrades eager to hear his recollections of a fabled and fleeting past.

Dahlgren had finally found comfort in the role that he learned to play in the human comedy. Like Shakespeare's Sir John Falstaff, he turned his back on the pretensions of chivalry, but he did not fall into cynicism and dissipation. His stories, though certainly embellished, were not vainglorious lies. True, he had been in the wings of America's tragic stage, but not at the center. Ironically, the years of adversity had endowed him with the comedic incarnation. He reckoned that he had gloried long enough in trials and afflictions. Now he would teach his young listeners tales about the paradoxical forces at play in the world as he had known it.

It was perhaps during his journey to Washington, at the end of 1865, that the changes in Dahlgren began to take place. He knew then, standing with ten dollars in his pocket on the threshold of his brother's mansion, what it was like trying to move with his feet stuck in crossed stirrups, having to bow to John with hat in hand after nine years. That meeting was perhaps a prelude to his being able to see himself from outside himself, to begin the ironic turn, to engage in the bitter jocularity that enhances human perspective.

It was the humorous quality in his nature that Dahlgren's listeners would continue to applaud—that the young men would cheer and associate with his memory. Like the heroes of Shakespeare's comedies, he had demonstrated what is required for survival in a changing and turbulent world.

Appendix: Genealogical Charts

Dahlgren–Rowan

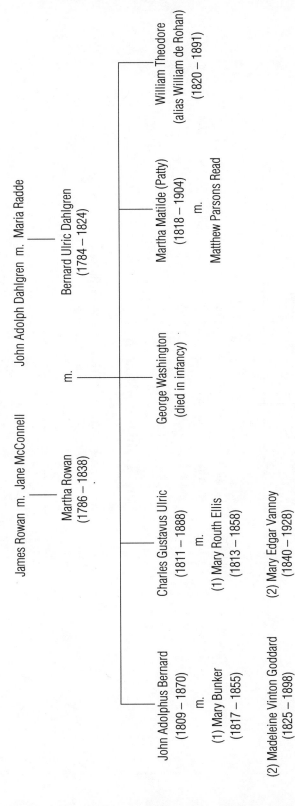

Source: Dahlgren Manuscript Genealogy by John Armfield Dahlgren

Dahlgren–Bunker

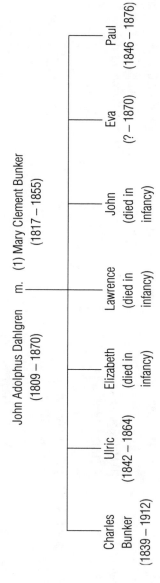

John Adolphus Dahlgren   m.   (1) Mary Clement Bunker
(1809 – 1870)   (1817 – 1855)

Charles Bunker (1839 – 1912)

Ulric (1842 – 1864)

Elizabeth (died in infancy)

Lawrence (died in infancy)

John (died in infancy)

Eva (? – 1870)

Paul (1846 – 1876)

Dahlgren–Vinton

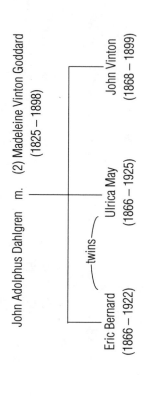

John Adolphus Dahlgren   m.   (2) Madeleine Vinton Goddard
                                                    (1825 – 1898)

Eric Bernard (1866 – 1922)

twins

Ulrica May (1866 – 1925)

John Vinton (1868 – 1899)

Source: Dahlgren Manuscript Genealogy by John Armfield Dahlgren

240

Dahlgren–Routh

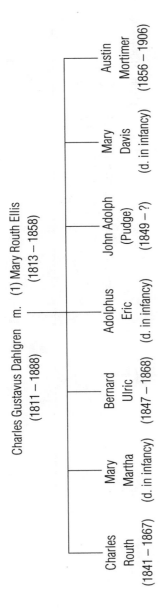

Charles Gustavus Dahlgren m. (1) Mary Routh Ellis
(1811 – 1888)   (1813 – 1858)

Charles Routh (1841 – 1867)

Mary Martha (d. in infancy)

Bernard Ulric (1847 – 1868)

Adolphus Eric (d. in infancy)

John Adolph (Pudge) (1849 – ?)

Mary Davis (d. in infancy)

Austin Mortimer (1856 – 1906)

Dahlgren–Vannoy

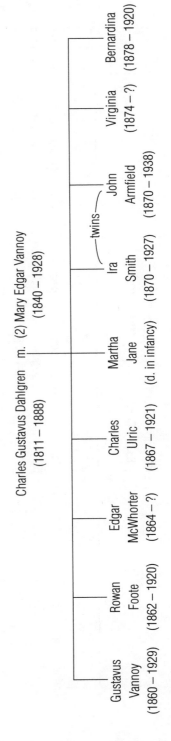

Charles Gustavus Dahlgren m. (2) Mary Edgar Vannoy
(1811 – 1888)   (1840 –1928)

Gustavus Vannoy (1860 – 1929)

Rowan Foote (1862 – 1920)

Edgar McWhorter (1864 – ?)

Charles Ulric (1867 – 1921)

Martha Jane (d. in infancy)

Ira Smith (1870 – 1927)

John Armfield (1870 – 1938)

twins

Virginia (1874 – ?)

Bernardina (1878 – 1920)

Source: Dahlgren Manuscript Genealogy by John Armfield Dahlgren

Drexel Genealogy (Simplified)

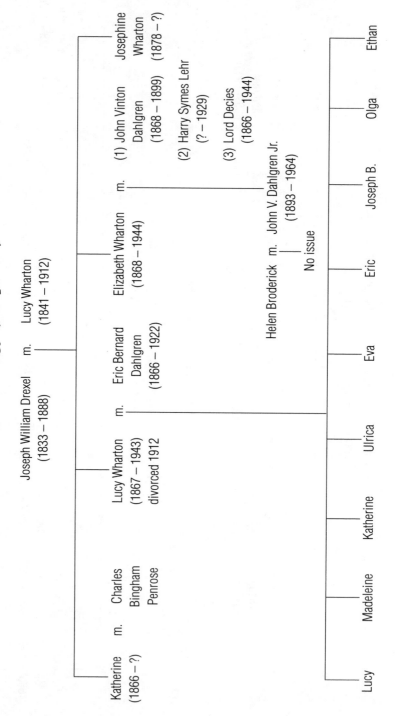

Joseph William Drexel m. Lucy Wharton
(1833 – 1888)   (1841 – 1912)

Katherine   m.   Charles   Lucy Wharton   m.   Eric Bernard   Elizabeth Wharton   m.   (1) John Vinton   Josephine
(1866 – ?)   Bingham   (1867 – 1943)   Dahlgren   (1868 – 1944)   Dahlgren   Wharton
                 Penrose   divorced 1912   (1866 – 1922)   (1868 – 1899)   (1878 – ?)

                                                                                                 (2) Harry Symes Lehr
                                                                                                     (? – 1929)

                                                                                                 (3) Lord Decies
                                                                                                     (1866 – 1944)

                                                                              Helen Broderick m. John V. Dahlgren Jr.
                                                                                                   (1893 – 1964)
                                                                                    No issue

Lucy   Madeleine   Katherine   Ulrica   Eva   Eric   Joseph B.   Olga   Ethan

Source: Bertram Lippincott, Newport Historical Society

Vannoy Genealogy

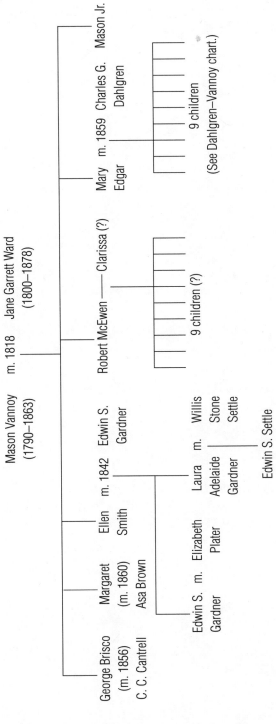

Mason Vannoy (1790–1863)   m. 1818   Jane Garrett Ward (1800–1878)

George Brisco (m. 1856) C. C. Cantrell

Margaret (m. 1860) Asa Brown

Ellen Smith   m. 1842   Edwin S. Gardner

Edwin S. Gardner   m.   Elizabeth Plater

Laura Adelaide Gardner   m.   Willis Stone Settle

Edwin S. Settle

Robert McEwen ———— Clarissa (?)

9 children (?)

Mary   m. 1859   Charles G. Dahlgren
Edgar

Mason Jr.

9 children
(See Dahlgren—Vannoy chart.)

m.   a union sanctioned by marriage

——— a union not sanctioned by marriage

Source: Edwin S. Gardner V.

243

ᘓ *Notes* ᘖ

1. Young Charles Dahlgren

1. Biographical notes are from the following: John Armfield Dahlgren, "Genealogy of the Dahlgren Family," Manuscript in DTSLA. Charles Bunker Dahlgren Journals, VWS; Madeleine Vinton Dahlgren, *Memoir of John A. Dahlgren* (Philadelphia: J. B. Lippincott, 1875), passim; "Heraldry in America, IV," *The Home Journal*, n.d., JAYJ.
2. Charles Dahlgren to Martha Rowan Dahlgren, 4 August 1824, Box 2, DTSLA.
3. Charles Dahlgren to John Dahlgren, at sea, 5 November 1826, Box 1, DTSLA.
4. Charles Dahlgren's diary, December 1865, indicates a continuing interest in ships and naval developments. He visited the Navy Yard at the invitation of his brother and recorded their tour of ships anchored in Washington, Box 2, DTSLA.
5. John Armfield Dahlgren to Natchez Chamber of Commerce, 16 March 1937, Armstrong Library MSS, Natchez.
6. John A. Dahlgren, *Macedonian Journal*, 18 March 1827, Box 32, DLC.
7. Recounted in undated clipping from *The Home Journal*, 84.
8. Ibid., 86.
9. *Encyclopedia Britannica*, 11th ed., s.v. "Swedish language and literature."
10. *The Home Journal*, undated clipping, 85.
11. Madeleine Vinton Dahlgren, *Memoir*, 8.
12. Charles G. Dahlgren to son John Adolph Dahlgren, Letterbook copy, ca. 1868, Box 1, DTSLA.
13. *Dictionary of American Biography*, s.v. "Biddle, Nicholas."

2. Banker, Planter, Husband, and Dynast

1. Minute Book, Bank of the United States. Notes from Richard Kilbourne, Clinton, La., referring to Dahlgren in the bank papers. Special Collections, Hill Library, Louisiana State University, Baton Rouge.
2. Hogan and Davis., eds., *William Johnson's Natchez*, 108; hereafter cited as *Johnson's Diary*.

3. Hennig Cohen and William B. Dillingham, introduction to *Humor of the Old Southwest*, rev. ed. (Athens: University of Georgia Press, 1964).

4. All quotations concerning the confrontation between Dahlgren and Stewart are from *Johnson's Diary*, 149.

5. John Armfield Dahlgren, Note, Box 2, DTSLA.

6. John Armfield Dahlgren to Natchez Chamber of Commerce, 16 March 1937, Armstrong Library, Natchez.

7. Charles G. Dahlgren, interview, [ca. 1 September] 1879, Philadelphia *Press*, transcription in Armstrong Library, Natchez.

8. Steinmetz, *Romance of Dueling*, 299. Mr. Hagan was probably John Hagan of New Orleans or his brother Richard. John was a rich New Orleans merchant who owned at least one plantation near Natchez.

9. John A. Dahlgren, *Macedonian Journal*, 1835, Box 32, DLC.

10. Schneller, *Quest for Glory*, 21–46.

11. William Dahlgren, letter to unidentified addressee, ca. 1838, Dahlgren Papers, DCHS.

12. Details of this episode from William's obituary in *The Washington Post*, ca. 10 April 1891.

13. Scarborough, "Lords or Capitalists?"; Taylor, "Southern Yankees." See also James, *Antebellum Natchez*, 43.

14. Muster sheets of Natchez Home Guards and the officers in each unit, MDAH.

15. Much of the information about the Rouths, Ellises, Percys, and related families comes from sources by Bertram Wyatt-Brown. The first is an early manuscript version of his chapter "Sarah Dorsey," which appears revised in Wyatt-Brown, *House of Percy*.

16. "Bank of the United States v. Estate of Thomas Ellis," MBBUS.

17. It is difficult to judge what Dahlgren was worth from year to year in land, slaves, and investments. See Wyatt-Brown, *House of Percy*, 122, for some estimates. It seems that figures were exaggerated by certain later historians. For instance, Dahlgren had only a small investment of $4,000 at Beersheba Springs and that not until 1859. The Federal Census for Tensas Parish in 1850 lists Dahlgren with thirty-seven male and thirty-six female slaves. For some reason, he is omitted in the Natchez census for that year but listed in the 1860 census as a farmer with real estate worth $75,000 and personal estate of $10,000. These were Mississippi holdings and did not include those in Tensas Parish, Louisiana.

18. Sarah Ker of Linden, Natchez, to Julia Williams Nutt, January 1841: "I suppose you have heard of Miss Dahlgren's arrival. I have not called on her, but intend doing so as soon as the weather will permit." AKC.

19. Mary Routh Dahlgren's will, 16 January 1858, credits Dahlgren with buying the slaves with money out of his own pocket, Adams County Courthouse. See also marriage agreement, 19 October 1840.
20. Wyatt-Brown, *House of Percy*, 121.
21. Ibid., 122.
22. John L. Goddard to Joseph L. Roberts, 1852, MBBUS.
23. Ibid.
24. Ibid.
25. Ibid.
26. Ibid.
27. Goddard to bank trustees, MBBUS.
28. Goddard to Roberts, MBBUS.
29. Ibid.
30. Handbill, Dahlgren file, MDAH.
31. Typescript attached to Sarah Dorsey's will, Armstrong Library, Natchez. See also Owens, "Burning of Lake St. Joseph," with an excellent map by the author.
32. James, *Antebellum Natchez*, 159. The plantation supply business was up against too much competition. Dahlgren advertised "the house and shed" for sale (Natchez *Daily Courier*, 10 March 1854) and sold them to E. B. Baker in 1855. Registrar's Office, Adams County. His financial difficulties in the early 1850s escaped the notice of the Natchez correspondents of R.G. Dun and Co. One of them reported in February 1852: "Married, of good business habits and character . . . deemed safe for all his engagements." In June 1854: "He is a farmer of great resources." RGD.
33. G. and D. Cook, *Illustrated Catalogue of Carriages* (1860; reprint, New York: Dover Publications, 1970), 5.
34. Ibid.
35. Invoice, Dahlgren file, NTC.
36. Invoice, Dahlgren file, MDAH.
37. Invoice, Dahlgren file, MDAH.
38. Wyatt-Brown, *House of Percy*, 121 ff. Dr. Stratton, a Presbyterian, took dinner with the Dahlgrens on 9 March 1853, a few weeks after the wedding, and reported in his diary: ". . . went out to Mr. Dahlgren's and dined with the family party. Found myself in a most uncomfortable position and have resolved to keep myself a stranger hereafter to places where the wine-cup is likely to circulate or those who love it constitute the company." AKC Papers.
39. This striking portrait by an artist famous in his time is now owned by the Telfair Museum, Savannah, and is on display in the Owens-Thomas house.

40. Dahlgren file, MDAH.

41. Joseph Buck Stratton Diary. Dahlgren's version of the fire is explained in a letter to the *Natchez Daily Democrat,* 24 January 1886: ". . . [The house] was struck by lightning and destroyed, in consequence of my wife desiring terra cotta chimney tops placed, which were elevated above the surrounding china trees, and so affording an object for the electric fluid."

42. Curator Pamela D. King, Telfair Academy, Savannah, in letter to author, 27 January 1992, remarks on the "black, soot-like film on the surface . . . and evidence of old water damage" before the canvas was restored by the Academy in 1987.

43. Wyatt-Brown, *House of Percy,* 123.

44. *Natchez Daily Democrat,* 25 January 1886.

45. Deed Book, 1859, Adams County Courthouse, Natchez. Routhland, after A. V. Davis and his wife moved there, is described by John Roy Lynch, a young slave at the time, in *Reminiscences.*

3. Riding the Crest

1. Owens, "Naming Plantations," 46–69.

2. James, *Antebellum Natchez,* 267.

3. Stratton, *Memorial of Quarter-Century's Pastorate,* 55.

4. Ibid., 244.

5. Tensas Parish Notarial Records, Saint Joseph, Louisiana, 6 June 1859.

6. Ulric to his father, John A. Dahlgren, 1 July and 10 November 1859, DLC.

7. Some of Ulric's survey notes are in the Dahlgren Collection at the Tennessee State Library and Archives. In small, pocket-size volumes, they were written in pencil and are now difficult to read. A second hand has written "Ully" on the first page, indicating Ulric as surveyor. Box 1, DTSLA.

8. Reported by Ulric to his father, 19 March 1859, UDIV.

9. Registrar's Office, Grundy County, Tennessee, Book D, p. 315.

10. Howell, *John Armfield,* 43.

11. Ulric to his father, 1 January 1860, DLC.

12. Both signed portraits hang today in a "Victorian Parlor" in the Tennessee State Museum, Nashville.

13. H. Emanuel to Charles Dahlgren, 4 January 1861, MS Division, DCHS

14. Ulric to his father, n.d., DLC.

15. John M. Daniel, U.S. Consul in Turin, to Lewis Cass, Secretary of State, 19 June 1860; dispatches from U.S. Ministers to the Italian States, 1832–1906, Microfilm, National Archives, Washington.

16. Agricultural Schedule, U.S. Census, 1860, Tensas Parish.

17. Mary Edgar Vannoy Dahlgren, "Some Recollections," recorded by John Armfield Dahlgren, Box 2, DTSLA.

18. Lucy Virginia French, *Darlingtonia: The Eaters and the Eaten,* novel serialized in *Detroit Free Press,* 27 April–17 August 1879. This quotation is from Sunday, 1 June. See also Gower, *Beersheba Springs Diaries.*

19. John Armfield Dahlgren, "Dahlgren Genealogy," DTSLA.

20. For a complete roster of the Tensas planters and the "literary" names they gave their domains, see Owens, "Naming Plantations."

21. Charles L. Dufour, *Gentle Tiger: The Gallant Life of Roberdeau Wheat* (Baton Rouge: Louisiana State University Press, 1957), 12–3.

22. Newspaper clipping (source unknown) in Dahlgren scrapbook, JAYJ.

4. A Civil War, a Family War

1. John A. Dahlgren to son Ulric, 18 December 1860, DLC.

2. Ibid.

3. John J. Pettus to Charles Dahlgren, 1861–62, DCHS.

4. Marchand, *Charleston Blockade,* 38–41.

5. *Daily True Delta,* 23 March 1862.

6. This and later conclusions are based on Dahlgren's correspondence with John J. Pettus, Governor of Mississippi, Governors' Correspondence, MDAH, and DCHS; see also Grady Howell, *To Live and Die.*

7. For more on Ulric, see Virgil C. Jones, *Eight Hours before Richmond,* and "The Kilpatrick Raid: Boldly Planned . . . Timidly Executed," *Civil War Times* 4 April 1965, 12–21. See also Schultz, *Dahlgren Affair,* and Sears, *Controversies and Commanders,* 232. For Charles Routh Dahlgren and Adams Troops, see Volney Daniel Fowler, "Memories of the Great War," DE.

8. Commander of Natchez Cadets to Bernard Dahlgren, 17 April 1861, DCHS.

9. Charlie Routh Dahlgren to his father, 17 June 1861, DCHS. There was surely a lively farewell party for Charlie Routh in Natchez on the order of the one given for David Holt of nearby Woodville and described by him in Holt, *Mississippi Rebel,* 60–6. Charlie left home with much of the same equipment: ". . . gun and accoutrements, haversack, set of underwear, two shirts, woolen socks, hat, cap, comforter, woolen gloves, knitted wristlets, handkerchiefs, and a large pocket knife . . . knife and fork, tin plate, a full copy of the Bible, a copy of Shakespeare, a portfolio complete with ink and paper, a tool chest, four bottles of medicine, a mirror, a small boiler for

coffee and some tea and tea spoons. I absolutely carried all that to Virginia." Charlie Routh's advantage was his horse.

10. Charlie Routh Dahlgren to his father, 29 August 1861, DCHS.
11. Quoted in a letter by James Huston of Percy's Creek, Mississippi, 3 September 1861, J. L. Power Collection, MDAH.
12. Howell, Grady, *To Live and Die,* 11.
13. Ibid., 12.
14. Owsley, *State Rights,* 9.
15. G. M. Davis to Dahlgren, 20 August 1861; 10 September 1861; 6 November 1861; 22 November 1861, DCHS.
16. Ibid.
17. Howell, Grady, *To Live and Die,* 43.
18. As quoted in ibid., 50.
19. Jones, Virgil C., *Eight Hours before Richmond,* 31; Schultz, *Dahlgren Affair,* 94.
20. Howell, Grady, *To Live and Die,* 53. See also Dahlgren to Pettus, 5 September 1861, Pettus correspondence, MDAH.
21. Dahlgren to Pettus, 15 September 1861, telegram, DCHS.
22. Quoted in Howell, Grady, *To Live and Die,* 57.
23. Pettus to Dahlgren, 10 October 1861, telegram, DCHS.
24. Pettus to Dahlgren, 11 October 1861, telegram, DCHS.
25. Quoted in *Daily True Delta,* 16 October 1861.
26. Ibid.
27. *OR,* ser. I, vol. 6, 742.
28. Howell, Grady, *To Live and Die,* 74. See also Governors' Correspondence, MDAH.
29. Howell, Grady, *To Live and Die,* 79. In his letter of 19 October to Adj. Gen. W. H. Brown, quoted by Howell, Dahlgren wrote: "I have nearly closed my action here and await the reply to my request for Court of Inquiry." He obviously wanted to be cleared of the current criticism.
30. *OR,* ser. I, vol. 6, 729–30.
31. Ibid., 746.
32. Ibid., 741.
33. Master's Mate Charles Bunker Dahlgren, USS *San Jacinto,* at sea, 12 November 1861, to Capt. Charles Wilk, *ORN,* ser. I, vol. 1, 138.
34. *OR,* ser. I, vol. 52, pt. 2, 216.
35. Howell, Grady, *To Live and Die,* 83.
36. Dahlgren to Pettus, 23 November 1861, telegram, Governors' Correspondence, MDAH.
37. Howell, Grady, *To Live and Die,* 85.

38. Marchand, *Charleston Blockade*, 38.
39. Quoted in ibid.
40. Ibid., 39.
41. Ibid.
42. Ibid., 40.
43. Ibid., 41.
44. D. T. Bisbie to Judah P. Benjamin, sent from steamship *Gladiator,* Nassau, 16 December 1861, *ORN,* ser. I, vol. 12, 835.
45. Copy of dispatch in John A. Dahlgren Scrapbook, De Golyer Library, Southern Methodist University, Dallas.
46. Dahlgren to Jefferson Davis, 23 December 1861, Jefferson Davis Papers, National Archives, RG 109.
47. Pettus to Dahlgren, 15 January 1862, DCHS.
48. Dr. H. Lyle to George Malin Davis, Natchez, 4 October 1862, DCHS.
49. *Daily True Delta,* 23 March 1862. The entire plan fills two long columns.
50. Ibid.
51. Ibid.
52. Ibid.
53. See Campbell, "Shiloh National Military Park," 301–5; Cooling, "Fort Donelson National Military Park," 121–6; Durham, *Nashville,* passim; and Durham, *Reluctant Partners,* passim.
54. Mrs. Irby Morgan, *How It Was: Four Years among the Rebels* (Nashville: Methodist Publishing House, 1892), 109.

5. Defeat at Vicksburg and Gettysburg

1. MB.
2. Cervantes, *Don Quixote,* trans. Walter Starkie (New York: Penguin Books, 1964), 148.
3. *OR,* ser. I, vol. 15, 736.
4. Quoted in Gresham, *Biography of General Gresham,* 243–51.
5. Yetman, *Life Under "Peculiar Institution,"* 74.
6. *OR,* ser. I, vol. 15, 317.
7. Note made by son John Armfield Dahlgren on photograph of Llangollen in *Natchez Old and New,* Box 2, DTSLA.
8. "The Dahlgren Family," *The Home Journal,* n.d., JAYJ.
9. *OR,* ser. I, vol. 15, 137.

10. Ibid.

11. *OR,* ser. I, vol. 15, 744.

12. Ibid.

13. Charles Dahlgren to Thomas Jordan, 8 June 1862, typescript from Donald Estes, Natchez. On 10 August 1862, B. L. C. Wailes of Jefferson College noted in his diary: "Part of the Dahlgren Rangers—oh cracky, what a name to fight under—have returned and are occupying rooms in the college." Wailes's sarcasm toned down when the cadets left three days later for service under General Breckinridge instead of Dahlgren. AKC.

14. Ibid.

15. Ibid.

16. Jordan to Dahlgren, 23 June 1862, *OR,* ser. I, vol. 15, 620.

17. Charles Dahlgren to J. C. Pemberton, 6 December 1862, *OR,* ser. I, vol. 15, 620.

18. Ballard, *Pemberton,* 110.

19. Ibid., 128.

20. Grant's maneuvers on the west side of the river and the destruction by his army are capsuled in Owens, "Burning of Lake St. Joseph."

21. Gower and Allen, *Pen & Sword,* 87–8.

22. *ORN,* ser. I, vol. 24, 306.

23. Charles Bunker Dahlgren Diary, VWS.

24. *ORN,* ser. I, vol. 25, 277. See Confederate Service Record for John Adolph ("Pudge") Dahlgren, National Archives.

25. Elder, *Civil War Diary,* 44.

26. Isaac Stier, in Rawick, *American Slave,* 142–7.

27. Ibid.

28. Ellen Shields, "Account of the Many Atrocities. . . . " Manuscript dated 1903, Armstrong Library, Natchez.

29. Frisby Freeland papers, archives, Beersheba Springs Historical Society.

30. Details of Mrs. Winston's encounter with General Gresham in Gresham, *Biography of General Gresham,* 261.

31. Ibid.

32. Harris, *Presidential Reconstruction,* 326.

6. The Flight to Georgia

1. Statement of Mary Jones Mallard, whose authority was very likely Dahlgren himself, in Myers, *Children of Pride*, 1157.
2. G. Griffing Wilcox, "War Times in Natchez," *Southern Historical Papers* 30:135–6; Natchez *Semi-Weekly Courier*, 16 October 1863; John S. McNeily, "War & Reconstruction in Mississippi 1863–1890," *Publications of the Mississippi Historical Society*, II, Centenary Series, 185.
3. Bertram Wyatt-Brown, "Sarah Dorsey," manuscript sent to author in 1992, later revised as a chapter in Wyatt-Brown, *House of Percy*.
4. Ibid., 135.
5. Copies of pertinent church records sent to the author by Liza Bishop, Crockett, Texas, 1993.
6. Owens, "Burning of Lake St. Joseph."
7. Liza Bishop, telephone interview, 25 June 1993.
8. Stone, *Brockenburn*, 135.
9. Ibid., 247.
10. Bernard Dahlgren to Mary Edgar Dahlgren, 13 April 1864, MDAH.
11. *Confederate Veteran* 5: 20.
12. Massey, *Refugee Life*, 83.
13. Fulton County Deeds, 1854–1880, Book 6, 247.
14. Quoted in Myers, *Children of Pride*, 1147.
15. Ibid., 1157. The Adams Troop of the Jeff Davis Legion, in which Charlie Routh served as second corporal, was a part of these engagements: Brandy Station, Upperville, and Gettysburg in 1863; Trevillion, Reams Station, Cavalry Battle near Raleigh, 1864, DE.
16. Confederate Service Record, National Archives.
17. See group photograph, Library of Congress Collection, in Jones, Virgil C., *Eight Hours before Richmond*, 58.
18. Ibid., 152.
19. Ibid., 37.
20. "The Eaters and the Eaten," a serialized novel, *Detroit Free Press*, 27 April–17 August 1879.
21. Real Estate Deeds and Mortgages, DeKalb County, 1840–1910, Book 6, 246. Dahlgren immediately transferred the property to son John Adolph ("Pudge") for reasons not explained. Beginning in 1869, the property was mortgaged several times when Dahlgren needed cash, once to William Edwin Osborn of Brooklyn but also to his son Austin.
22. John Armfield Dahlgren, Box 2, DTSLA.

23. Work Projects Administration, *Historical Background of Dougherty County*, 25.

24. Ibid.

25. Dougherty County Deeds, 714, but not recorded until 31 March 1865, presumably because of the war. Copy, courtesy of Walter R. Matthews, Albany.

26. Mary Edgar Dahlgren to Bernard Dahlgren, n.d., DMDAH.

27. Andrews, *War-Time Journal*, passim.

28. Myers, *Children of Pride*, 1278. This exploit was treated with sentiment in John A. Dahlgren, *Memoir*. A history of the raid, researched with damaging conclusions, is Virgil C. Jones, *Eight Hours before Richmond*, passim. A more recent study is David E. Long, "Lincoln the Assassin?" *The Lincoln Newsletter* 13, no. 2 (summer 1994). Long agrees with Jones and suggests that Lincoln was the instigator of the raid. Further discussion is found in Schultz, *Dahlgren Affair*. The notion that the orders found on Ulric's body were forged is still argued, but Sears, "Dahlgren Papers," makes the best case yet that they were genuine beyond a doubt and their validity incontestable. Sears refutes the stand taken by Schultz.

29. Quoted in Myers, *Children of Pride*, 1147.

30. Jones, Virgil C., *Eight Hours before Richmond*, 106.

31. Ulric to his father, 26 February 1864, DLC.

32. Catton, *Stillness at Appomattox*, 18.

33. Bernard Dahlgren to Mary Edgar Dahlgren, 13 April 1864, MDAH. DLC.

34. Jones, Virgil C., *Eight Hours before Richmond*, 134.

35. Reverend B. Sunderland, *Sermon in Memory of Col. Ulric Dahlgren* (Washington, D.C.: McGill and Witherow, 1864), DLC.

36. Seddon's remarks, *OR*, ser. I, vol. 33, 218.

37. Notes of John Armfield Dahlgren; photograph of Union veterans in front of Dahlgren home, ca. 1895, Box 1, DTSLA.

38. Robert E. Denney, *The Civil War Years: A Day by Day Chronology*, New York: Sterling Publishing Co, 1992, 488.

39. Work Projects Administration, *Historical Background of Dougherty County*, 40.

40. Charlie was probably referring to the admiral's letter of 24 July 1864, in a New York paper, not identified. The father tries to vindicate the son and declares the orders found on Ulric's body a forgery. His tone is indeed out of control. JAYJ.

41. Charlie Routh to Family, 4 December 1864, Box 2, DTSLA.

42. Andrews, *War-Time Journal*, 120–1.

43. *OR*, ser. I, vol. 52, pt. II, supple., 569–70.

44. Ibid., 568–9.
45. Andrews, *War-Time Journal*, 132.
46. Cornelia Peak McDonald, quoted in Sullivan, *War the Women Lived*, 228.
47. Ibid., 152. See also Thomas Daniel Young, *Gentleman in a Dustcoat: A Biography of John Crowe Ransom*, Baton Rouge: Louisiana State University Press, 1976, 1–6. Richard Polis Ransom was the grandfather of poet and critic John Crowe Ransom (1888–1974).
48. Andrews, *War-Time Journal*, 127.
49. U.S. Agricultural Census, Dougherty County, Georgia, 1860.
50. Dougherty County Deeds, Book 3, 715.
51. Confederate Service Record, National Archives.
52. F. A. W. Davis to Admiral J. A. Dahlgren, 11 April 1865, DNL.
53. Patty Dahlgren to brother John, 23 April 1865, DNL.
54. Dorsey, *Recollections of Allen*, 168.
55. *ORN*, ser. I, vol. 16, 282–3.
56. Schneller, *Quest for Glory*, 315–6.
57. Papers, VWS.
58. Jones, Virgil C., *Eight Hours before Richmond*, 74.
59. Dahlgren Genealogy, John Armfield Dahlgren, DTSLA.
60. F. A. W. Davis to Admiral Dahlgren, 11 April 1865, DNL; Dorsey, *Recollections of Allen*, 168.
61. Battle, *Battle Book*, 346; Ruth Kratz, Kansas City, Missouri, telephone interview by author, 16 January 1992; Mrs. Dwight W. Robinson, Westwood, Massachusetts, telephone interview by author, 8 February 1993.

7. Leading His Family Home by Wagon Train

1. W. Yearns, *From Richmond to Texas*.
2. Confederate Service Record, National Archives, Washington, D.C. Gordon Cotton, Court House Museum, Vicksburg, telephone interview by author, 21 July 1997.
3. Allardice, letter to author, 29 May 1997.
4. Edwin C. Bearss, *Campaign for Vicksburg*, vol. 2 (Dayton, Ohio: Morningside Press, 1986), 320; Bearss, *Decision in Mississippi* (Jackson: Mississippi Commission on the War Between the States, 1962), 469.
5. Bernard Dahlgren, letter to Mary Edgar Dahlgren, April 1864, MDAH.

8. Survival without Recovery

1. Volney Daniel Fowler, "Memories of the Great War," DE.
2. Reid, *After the War*.

3. C. Vann Woodward, quoting Reid in introduction to *After the War*, xix.

4. Whitelaw Reid to Miss Anna Dickinson, quoted by Woodward in ibid.

5. James T. Currie, *Enclave; Vicksburg and Her Plantations, 1863–1870* (Jackson: University Press of Mississippi, 1980), 56–7.

6. Ibid.

7. James E. Yeatman, "A Report on the Condition of the Freedmen of Mississippi presented to the Western Sanitary Commission, December 17, 1863," Western Sanitary Commission, Saint Louis, 1864, 148.

8. Morgan, *Yazoo*, (reprint, with a new introduction by Otto H. Olsen, New York: Russell and Russell, 1968), 127.

9. Harris, *Presidential Reconstruction*, 21.

10. Dorsey, *Recollections of Allen*, 122.

11. Gaston, *Hunting a Home*. See also Louis Agassiz, *A Journey to Brazil* (1868; reprint, with a new introduction by A. C. Wilgus, New York: Praeger, 1969). More recent studies include Douglas A. Grier, "Confederate Emigration to Brazil, 1865–1870" (Ph.D. dissertation, University of Michigan, 1968); and Harter, *Lost Colony of Confederacy*. Periodically, the descendants attract the attention of the popular press, the result being a plethora of articles and interviews.

12. See reference that Dahlgren made in his diary, following, under 24 November 1865, DTSLA.

13. This move is implied in Dahlgren's undated letter to son John Adolph (Pudge), in school in Toronto, ca. June 1868, DTSLA.

14. Charles R. Dahlgren, Jeff Davis Legion, Cavalry, 1861–65, Confederate Service Record, National Archives.

15. John Armfield Dahlgren, note, Box 2, DTSLA.

16. Ibid.

17. The tinted miniature on ivory is on display in the Tennessee State Museum but wrongly identified as General Dahlgren as a young midshipman.

18. John A. Dahlgren, *Memoir of Ulric Dahlgren*, 275.

19. Ibid., 276.

20. A bizarre case of nineteenth-century nostalgia centers on Ulric and the wound at Hagerstown. The bullet struck him in the right ankle and passed out through the top of his foot. When the wound failed to heal, his right leg was amputated just below the knee. Later, Dahlgren returned to service with a wooden leg, but the amputated member was put in a preservative and kept by the admiral. Eventually, it found a home in the wall of the new metal shop in the Navy Yard, with ceremonies marking its burial in 1863. The bronze tablet reads:

WITHIN THIS WALL IS DEPOSITED THE LEG OF COL. ULRIC
DAHLGREN USV WOUNDED JULY 6TH 1863 WHILE
SKIRMISHING IN THE STREETS OF HAGERSTOWN WITH
THE REBELS AFTER THE BATTLE OF GETTYSBURG.

The building has since been demolished. Workmen are said to have found
no evidence of the leg, but it might exist somewhere as a mute keepsake,
The New York Times, 24 April 1921.

21. See her application for widow's pension, 31 March 1871, U.S. Pension
Agency, Washington, D.C. Also see John A. Dahlgren's service record,
National Archives.

22. Wayne, *Reshaping of Plantation Society,* 10.

23. Dahlgren to Duncan, 20 February and 10 April 1866; Duncan to Dahlgren,
18 April 1866; Winchester Family Papers, Natchez Trace Collection, Center
for American History, University of Texas, Austin.

24. Wayne, *Reshaping of Plantation Society,* 17.

25. Journal of Bettie Ridley Blackmore, *Tennessee Historical Quarterly* 12
(March 1953): 48–80.

26. Lucy Virginia French, *The Beersheba Springs Diaries* (Beersheba Springs
Historical Society, 1986), 61.

27. See Amnesty Oath and Application for Pardon, approved 11 November
1865, Department of Justice. Original in National Archives.

28. John A. Dahlgren, *Memoir,* 277; *The New York Times,* 1 November 1865.

29. Diaries of Paul Dahlgren, Manuscript Division, Library of U.S. Military
Academy, West Point, New York.

30. Randall and Donald, *Civil War and Reconstruction,* frontispiece.

31. Diary of J. A. Dahlgren, Dahlgren Papers, vol. 13, box 4, Syracuse University, DS.

32. Dahlgren Papers, TSLA. The diary is contained in the second half of the
small leatherbound book that begins with the journey from Albany to
Rodney. The handwriting, although hurried and erratic, is in ink and easier
to read than the earlier section in pencil.

33. Nathaniel C. Hughes and R. P. Stonesifer Jr., *The Life and Wars of Gideon
J. Pillow* (Chapel Hill: University of North Carolina Press, 1993), 304.

34. Charles Dahlgren, Washington Diary, 19 December 1865.

35. Ibid., 18 December 1865.

36. Ibid.

37. Ibid., 20 December 1865.

38. Ibid., 23 December 1865.

39. Ibid., 26 December 1865.

40. Quoted in Sutherland, *Confederate Carpetbaggers,* 173.

41. Charles Dahlgren, Washington Diary, 30 December 1865.
42. Ibid., 29–30 December 1865, final entry.
43. Wayne, *Reshaping of Plantation Society*, 65.
44. Ibid., 63.

9. Another Move, Another Start at 60

1. Tax Books, 1850–1860, Tensas Parish Courthouse, Saint Joseph, Louisiana.
2. Dahlgren to Ellis, Deed Book E, 259, Saint Joseph, Louisiana.
3. Jeffrey Alan Owens, "The Civil War in Tensas Parish, Louisiana," master's thesis, Department of History, University of Texas at Tyler, 1992, 283.
4. John A. Dahlgren to Charles Dahlgren, 20 February 1866, Box 1, DTSLA.
5. Charles Dahlgren to son John Adolph ("Pudge"), ca. June 1868, Box 2, DTSLA.
6. "Dahlgren Genealogy."
7. Dr. Joseph Buck Stratton, diary, transcript in AKC.
8. Ibid.
9. Succession Record, 165, 166, and 206, Tensas Parish Courthouse, Saint Joseph, Louisiana.
10. "Dahlgren Genealogy."
11. Real Estate Deeds and Mortgages, DeKalb County, Georgia, Book 6, 247.
12. Deed Book, Dougherty County, Georgia, 1865, 714–5.
13. Dahlgren to John Adolph ("Pudge"), ca. 10 June 1868, Box 1, DTSLA.
14. Ibid.
15. Ibid.
16. Osborne, *Jubal*, 290.
17. Ibid., 404–10.
18. Writ of *Fi Fa*, 7th District Court, New Orleans, Sale of Property, 2 January 1869. Deed Book F, Tensas Parish, Saint Joseph, Louisiana, recorded 15 March 1869.
19. Deed Book F, Tensas Parish, Saint Joseph, Louisiana, 636–9.
20. John A. Dahlgren, Diary, 1 January 1869, vol. 15, Box 4, DS.
21. Charles Dahlgren to brother John, ca. January 1869, Box 7, DLC.
22. John A. Dahlgren to brother Charles, 3 March 1869, Box 7, DLC.
23. John A. Dahlgren, Diary, 26 March 1869, vol. 15, Box 4, DS.
24. John A. Dahlgren to Mary Edgar, 10 May 1869, DNLC.
25. "Dahlgren Genealogy."
26. John A. Dahlgren to brother Charles, 4 May 1869, Box 7, DLC.
27. Minute Book, Board of Aldermen, 1867, Adams County Courthouse, Natchez.

28. Gardner and Dahlgren correspondence, 1870, DTSLA.
29. Hemphill, *Fevers, Floods, and Faith*, 90–1.
30. As quoted in ibid., 254.
31. Gardner and Dahlgren correspondence, 1870, DTSLA.
32. Dahlgren Genealogy, DTSLA.
33. Gardner and Dahlgren correspondence, 1870, DTSLA.
34. Sutherland, *Confederate Carpetbaggers*, 41–2.
35. Charles Dahlgren, Account Book (Fragment), 1870, DTSLA.
36. "Dahlgren Genealogy"; U.S. Census, Brooklyn, New York, 1880.
37. Ruth Kratz, telephone interview by author, 8 July 1992.

10. Eighteen Years a Confederate Carpetbagger

1. MSS 1, E1 a 104, Ellis Family Papers, 1859–1889, Virginia State Library, Richmond. After perusing the letterhead, Edward W. Rose III of Dallas suggested: "It looks like your man Dahlgren is in the loan business. I think he tries to find places to put loans or investments and then scurries around and tries to find the money. Today he would be called an investment banker." Rose, letter to author, 12 December 1995.
2. Daniel E. Sutherland, letter to author, 20 December 1995.
3. Sutherland, *Confederate Carpetbaggers*, 148.
4. *Register of West Point Graduates and Biographical Sketches*, Library, U.S. Military Academy, West Point, New York.
5. Report of Dr. Lauchlan Aiken, 7 April 1876, in Dispatches from U.S. Ministers to the Italian States, 1832–1906. Microfilm from National Archives Regional Center, Forth Worth, Texas.
6. John Armfield Dahlgren, Notebooks, Box 2, DTSLA.
7. Pryor, *My Day*, 272.
8. Ibid., 278–9.
9. Quoted in ibid., 282–3.
10. Marriage Records, Diocesan Office, Nashville, Tennessee.
11. Battle, *Battle Book*, 345–6.
12. Wills, Recorder's Office, Adams County Courthouse, Natchez.
13. Letters of Mortimer Dahlgren, DTSLA.
14. Ibid.
15. Ibid.
16. Ibid.
17. Ibid.
18. John Armfield Dahlgren, Account Books, DTSLA.
19. John Armfield Dahlgren, Notebooks, DTSLA.

20. Quoted in Ross, *First Lady of South*, 238.

21. McElroy, *Jefferson Davis*, 641.

22. Austin Mortimer Dahlgren, interviews by *St. Louis Globe Democrat*, 1 August 1879, and *The New York Times*, 11, 18, and 24 July, 5 and 10 August, and 13 December 1879.

23. There is a photograph of Mortimer displaying boxes of cigars, Box 4, DTSLA.

24. Strode, *Jefferson Davis*, 495.

25. *Stephen Percy Ellis et al. v. Jefferson Davis*, U.S. Circuit Court, District of Louisiana, No. 8934.

26. Philadelphia *Press*, ca. 1 September 1879. Wyatt-Brown, *House of Percy*, chap. 12, passim, points out that Dahlgren was not a dependable genealogist.

27. Strode, *Jefferson Davis*, 495.

28. Philadelphia *Press*, undated clipping, ca. 1 September 1879, Armstrong Library, Natchez.

29. Quoted in Swanberg, *Sickles the Incredible*, 405.

30. Harrison, *Recollections*, 301–2.

31. Diary of Charles Bunker Dahlgren (1839–1912), who wrote, "Little did poor father imagine that only a short 2 mos. 13 days after [sister] Eva's burial that he also would lie there, in Ully's grave, placed there by Mrs. Madeleine Vinton Dahlgren, the Jesuit, who hoped to remove both" [presumably to the crypt of the private chapel that she was soon to build at South Mountain, Maryland].

32. "Dahlgren Genealogy."

33. Schneller, *Quest for Glory*, 362.

34. Quoted in Dahlgren's obituary, *Atlanta Constitution*, undated clipping. The von Moltke story is probably apocryphal.

35. Deed Book, Adams County Courthouse, Natchez, but not recorded until 22 July 1892.

36. Madeleine Vinton Dahlgren would not have accepted Charles as patriarch. Her biography of husband John does not mention either Charles or brother William. See Madeleine Vinton Dahlgren, *Memoir*.

37. *Brooklyn Daily Eagle*, 21 December 1888. Obituaries for General Dahlgren also appeared in *The New York Times*, 19 December 1888; *Natchez Daily Democrat*, 27 December 1888; Jackson *Clarion Ledger*, n.d.; and *Atlanta Constitution*, n.d. Each obituary perpetrated inaccuracies that were repeated in the *Twentieth Century Biographical Dictionary of Notable Americans*, especially the military record.

38. Van Dahlgren, quoted in John Armfield Dahlgren, Notebooks, Box 2, DTSLA.
39. Deed, Adams County Courthouse, Natchez.
40. John Armfield Dahlgren, Notebooks, Box 2, DTSLA.
41. Arrangements for the occasion were made by Donald Estes, Deposit Guaranty National Bank, Natchez. Estes is currently manager of the cemetery.
42. *Natchez Daily Democrat,* 19 January 1992. Representing the Civil War Round Table of Chicago was Bruce Allardice, who includes a sketch of Dahlgren in his *More Generals in Gray.*

11. The General's Relict and End of the Dynasty

1. "Dahlgren Genealogy," DTSLA.
2. Ibid.; also, notes on the Vannoy family provided by Edwin S. Gardner V, Charleston, South Carolina.
3. Hook and Ellen, *Vannoy Genealogy,* 139–42.
4. Edwin S. Gardner V, letter to author, 11 December 1992.
5. Phoebe Yates Pember, quoted in Sullivan, *War the Women Lived,* 268–9.
6. Registrar's Office, Adams County Courthouse, Natchez.
7. If Dahlgren had a will, it has not come to light after searches in Brooklyn. Disposition of his personal estate was made by son Edgar in Kings County Surrogate Court, 24 April 1890.
8. George Malin Davis, Natchez, to General Dahlgren, 19 October 1861, DCHS.
9. As quoted in Schneller, *Quest for Glory,* 358.
10. Gower, "Dahlgrens and Davis."
11. John Armfield Dahlgren, Photographs, Box 4, DTSLA.
12. Ibid.
13. Ibid.
14. *Atlanta Journal,* 8 May 1910. Real Estate Deeds and Mortgages, 1911–1930, Book 7. Fulton Co., Georgia.
15. "Marydale Plantation," *Tensas Gazette,* 30 March 1951, newspaper clipping about Cora Potter's extravagance in Tensas Parish Scrapbook, vol. 9, 18, Gladys Means Lloyd Papers, Special Collections, Louisiana State University.
16. *Who Was Who in the Theatre* (Detroit: Gale Research Co., 1992).
17. *The New York Times,* 9 January 1889.
18. *Tensas Gazette,* 30 March 1951.
19. "Dahlgren Genealogy"; *Goodspeed's Biographical and Historical Memoirs.*
20. William de Rohan to Marco Minghetti, Prime Minister of Italy, 25 April 1874, DUSM.

21. William de Rohan to George P. Marsh, U.S. Minister to Italy, 29 December 1880, DUSM.

22. James A. Field, *America and the Mediterranean World, 1776–1882* (Princeton, New Jersey: Princeton University Press, 1969), 304.

23. Eleven items pertaining to de Rohan are housed in the Library of the Risorgimento at the top of the Altare della Patria (Victor Emmanuel Monument) in Rome. In English, French, and Italian, they range from a broadside announcing the *causa nationale,* Milan, 1859, to letters from de Rohan to Victor Emmanuel II and Garibaldi that asked for compensation for his services. An early letter from Garibaldi to de Rohan, May 22, 1860, authorizes "Count" de Rohan's command of the *Washington* and is marked *Instruzione Segrete.* Edward Callahan of Pocasset, Massachusetts, kindly provided quotations from these materials. De Rohan's later letters reveal a man still struggling for recognition as youth, fame, and money fled from him through the neglect of an ungrateful world.

24. Sargent Prentiss Nutt, Washington, letter to his mother, Julia Nutt, Natchez, 3 April 1891, Nutt Family Papers, MDAH.

25. *The Washington Post,* ca. 10 April 1891.

26. District of Columbia Office of Public Records.

27. S. P. Nutt to Julia Nutt, 3 April 1891, Nutt Family Papers, MDAH.

28. Described by Richard Chenoweth, Silver Spring, Maryland, to author.

29. William De Rohan to George P. Marsh, Florence, 20 May 1868, DUSM.

30. John Armfield Dahlgren, Notebooks, Box 2, DTSLA.

31. John Armfield Dahlgren, letter to T. B. Northcut, 20 June 1914, owned by Frances Brown, McMinnville, Tennessee.

32. Vannoy Dahlgren, Saint Louis, to S. P. Nutt, Washington, n.d., MDAH.

33. Letter of Vannoy Dahlgren to mother, Mary Edgar Dahlgren, 1912, Box 3, DTSLA. Two letters have come to light recently that indicate Van relented and offered help to Bernardina a few days before her death when help was of no avail. Letters owned by Bernardina Berg Avdek, Mequon, Wisconsin.

34. The earlier years were recorded by his uncle William Theodore Dahlgren (alias de Rohan) after he visited Sweden during the early 1840s.

35. Vannoy Dahlgren to J. A. Dahlgren, 24 April 1923, Box 1, DTSLA.

36. The Tennessee Society honored Van's memory on 2 July 1930 with a resolution citing "his contributions to the fine results which have been attained by our city." Notes in Box 2, DTSLA.

37. Unidentified newspaper obituary, Box 2, DTSLA.

38. Alfred Charles Dahlgren, telephone interview by author, Andover, Massachusetts, 15 September 1992.

39. Unidentified newspaper clippings, Box 2, DTSLA.

40. Coffee County Court Clerk's Office, Manchester, Tennessee.

41. A few snapshots from the late 1920s are in the collection, Box 4, DTSLA.

42. Printed obituary written by son John Armfield Dahlgren, 8 August 1928, Box 3, DTSLA. The newspaper is not identified.

43. Ruth Kratz, telephone interview by author, 8 July 1992.

44. Statement of elderly male resident of Manchester, who asked not to be identified.

45. John Armfield Dahlgren, Notebooks, Box 2, DTSLA.

12. Postlude for a Patriarch

1. Myers, *Children of Pride*, 1147.

2. Philadelphia *Press*, ca. 1 September 1879.

3. Madeleine Vinton Dahlgren, *Memoir*, 15.

4. J. W. Peard, *Cornhill Magazine*, June 1908, 813ff.

5. *Daily True Delta*, 16 October 1861; *Weekly Mississippian*, Jackson, 30 October 1861.

6. Unsigned interview, Philadelphia *Press*, ca. 1 September 1879. Copy in Armstrong Library, Natchez.

◠ Bibliography ◡

Primary Sources

Archival

DCHS   Dahlgren Papers, Chicago Historical Society, Chicago, Illinois

DLC   John A. Dahlgren Papers, Manuscripts Division, Library of Congress. Washington, D.C., No. 41824

DNLC   John A. Dahlgren Papers, Newberry Library, Chicago, Illinois

DS   John A. Dahlgren Papers, George Arents Research Library at Syracuse University, Syracuse, New York

DTSLA   Dahlgren Family Papers, Tennessee State Library and Archives, Nashville

DUSM   Dispatches of U.S. Ministers to Italy, 1832–1906, microfilm, National Archives, Washington, D.C.

JDP   Jefferson Davis Papers, National Archives, Washington, D.C.

LR   Library of the Risorgimento, Altare della Patria, Rome.

MB   Minute Book No. 15, 1860–1872. Municipal Records Office, Natchez, Mississippi

MBBUS   Minute Book and Correspondence, Bank of the United States, Special Collections, Hill Library, Louisiana State University, Baton Rouge

MDAH   Subject files, Mississippi Department of Archives and History, Jackson

NTC   Natchez Trace Collection, Center for American History, University of Texas, Austin

ORA   *War of the Rebellion: A Compilation of the Official Records of the Union and Confederate Armies,* 128 volumes. Washington, D.C.: Government Printing Office, 1880–1901; cited as follows: series number, volume number, part number, page number

ORN   U.S. Department of the Navy, *Official Records of the Union and Confederate Navies in the War of the Rebellion,* Richard Rush et al., eds. 31 volumes and index, Washington, D.C.: Government Printing Office, 1894–1992; cited as follows: series number, volume number, page number

RGD   R. G. Dun & Company Collection: Louisiana and Mississippi, Baker Library, Harvard Graduate School of Business, Boston

Papers Privately Owned

AKC   Natchez (and Mississippi) Correspondence and Documents, Alma
         Kellogg Carpenter, Natchez, Mississippi
DE   Manuscript Collection of Civil War Memorabilia, Donald Estes,
         Natchez, Mississippi
DK   Family Portraits and Miscellaneous Papers, Frederick William Kratz,
         Santa Fe, New Mexico
JAYJ   Dahlgren Family Papers, Julie Ann Young Johnson, Belle Haven,
         Virginia
MH   Hollingsworth, Routh, and Related Family Correspondence,
         Marguerite Harrison, North Miami Beach, Florida
SC   Natchez Photographs and Miscellaneous Papers, Sim Callon Sr.,
         Natchez, Mississippi
THG   Photographs and Natchez Papers of Thomas H. and Joan Gandy,
         Natchez, Mississippi
UDIV   Dahlgren Correspondence, Ulric Dahlgren IV, Annapolis, Maryland
VWS   Dahlgren Family Papers, Virginia Wilson Severs, San Clemente, Cali-
         fornia

Books and Monographs

Andrews, Eliza R. *The War-Time Journal of a Georgia Girl.* 1908. Reprint,
    Macon: Ardwan Press, 1960.
Cockrell, Thomas D., and Michael B. Ballard, eds. *A Mississippi Rebel in the
    Army of Northern Virginia: The Civil War Memoirs of Private David Holt.*
    Baton Rouge: LSU Press, 1995.
Dahlgren, John A. *Memoir of Ulric Dahlgren.* Edited by Madeleine Vinton
    Dahlgren. Philadelphia: J. B. Lippincott, 1872.
Dahlgren, John A. *Sermon in Memory of Col. Ulric Dahlgren.* Washington, D.C.:
    McGill and Witherow, 1864.
Dahlgren, Madeleine Vinton. *Memoir of John A. Dahlgren, Rear-Admiral
    United States Navy.* Boston: James R. Osgood, 1882.
Davis, Varina. *Jefferson Davis: Ex-President of the Confederate States of America.*
    New York: Belford Co., 1890.
Dorsey, Sarah Ellis. *Recollections of Henry Watkins Allen.* New York: M. Doo-
    lady, 1866.
Elder, William Henry, Bishop of Natchez. *Civil War Diary (1862–1865).* Pub-
    lished by Most Reverend R. O. Gerow, Bishop of Natchez-Jackson, n.d.

Erwin, John Seymour, ed. *Like Some Green Laurel: Letters of Margaret Johnson Erwin, 1821–1863*. Baton Rouge: Louisiana State University Press, 1981.

Gaston, J. McF. *Hunting a Home in Brazil*. Philadelphia: 1867.

Goodspeed's Biographical and Historical Memoirs of Mississippi, 2 vols. Chicago: Goodspeed Publishing Co., 1891.

Gower, Herschel, ed. *The Beersheba Springs Diaries of Lucy Virginia French (1863–1864)*. Beersheba Springs Historical Society, 1986.

Gresham, Matilda. *Biography of General Walter Gresham, 1832–1895*. Chicago: Rand McNally & Co., 1919.

Harrison, Mrs. Burton. *Recollections Grave and Gay*. London: Smith, Elder and Co., 1912.

Hepworth, George H. *The Whip, Hoe, and Sword; or the Gulf Department in '63*. Boston: Walker Wise & Co., 1864.

Hogan, William Ransom, and Erwin Adams Davis, eds. *William Johnson's Natchez: The Ante-Bellum Diary of a Free Negro*. Baton Rouge: Louisiana State University Press, 1951.

Holt, David. *A Mississippi Rebel in the Army of Northern Virginia: The Civil War Memoirs of Private David Holt*. Edited by Thomas D. Cockrell and Michael B. Ballard. Baton Rouge: Louisiana State University Press, 1995.

Hook, James, and Virginia Ellen. *Vannoy Genealogy*. New Haven: Tuttle, Morehouse, and Taylor, 1925.

Jones, John B. *A Rebel War Clerk's Diary*. Edited by Earl Schenck Miers. New York: Sagamore Press, 1958.

Marchand, John B. *Charleston Blockade*. Edited with commentary by Craig L. Symonds. Newport, Rhode Island: Naval War College Press, 1976.

Morgan, Albert T. *Yazoo, or on the Picket Line of Freedom*, 1884. Reprint with a new introduction by Otto H. Olson, New York: Russell and Russell, 1968.

Northrup, Solomon. *Twelve Years a Slave*. Edited by Sue Eakin and Joseph Logsdon. Baton Rouge: Louisiana State University Press, 1968.

Paixhans, Henri Joseph. *An Agreement of the Experiments Made in the French Navy for the Trial of the Bomb Cannon*. Translated by John A. Dahlgren. Philadelphia: Dorsey, 1838.

Pryor, Mrs. Roger. *My Day*. New York: Macmillan Co., 1909.

Rawick, George P., gen. ed. *The American Slave: A Composite Autobiography*. Vol. 7. Westport, Connecticut: Greenwood Publishing Co., 1972.

Reid, Whitelaw. *After the War: Tour of the Southern States, 1865–1866*. 1866. Reprint, Harper Torchbook Edition, edited with an introduction by C. Vann Woodward, New York: Harper and Row, 1965.

Steinmetz, Andrew. *The Romance of Dueling in All Times and Countries*, Vol.

2 1868. Reprint with bibliographical references and index, Richmond, Surrey: The Richmond Publishing Co. Ltd.

Stone, Kate. *Brokenburn: The Journal of Kate Stone (1861–1865).* Edited by John Q. Anderson. Baton Rouge: Louisiana State University Press, 1972.

Stratton, Joseph Buck. *Memorial of a Quarter Century's Pastorate.* Philadelphia: J. P. Lippincott, 1869.

Strode, Hudson, ed. *Jefferson Davis: Private Letters.* New York: Harcourt Brace, 1966.

Sullivan, Walter, ed. *The War the Women Lived: Female Voices from the Confederate South.* Foreword by George Core. Nashville: J. S. Sanders & Co., 1995.

Sutherland, Daniel E., ed. *A Very Violent Rebel: The Civil War Diary of Ellen Renshaw House.* Knoxville: University of Tennessee Press, 1996.

Yearns, W. Buck, ed. *From Richmond to Texas: The 1865 Journey Home of Confederate Senator Williamson S. Oldham.* Dayton, Ohio: Morningside House, 1998.

Yetman, Norman R. *Life under the "Peculiar Institution": Selections from Slave Narratives.* Huntington, New York: Robert E. Krieger, 1976.

Newspapers

Atlanta Journal, 8 May 1910; 14 November 1918.

Brooklyn Daily Eagle, 17 and 21 December 1888.

Daily True Delta, 16 October 1861; 23 March 1862.

Detroit Free Press, 27 April through 17 August 1879.

Natchez *Daily Courier,* 1861–1863.

Natchez Daily Democrat, 24 January 1886.

Natchez Democrat, 19 January 1992.

Natchez *Free Trader,* January and February 1861.

Natchez *Semi-Weekly Courier,* 1863–1865,

Natchez Weekly Courier, 17 March 1858.

New York Herald, 26 September 1860.

The New York Times, 19 December 1888; 11, 18, and 24 July; 5 and 10 August; 13 December 1879.

Philadelphia *Press,* ca. 1 September 1879.

Richmond Daily Examiner, 5 March 1864.

St. Louis Globe Democrat, 1 August 1879.

Tensas Gazette, 30 March 1951.

The Washington Post, ca. 10 April 1891.

Magazines

Confederate Veteran, 1893–1932, Nashville, Tennessee.

Secondary Sources

Articles in Books and Periodicals

Campbell, Bernard T. "Shiloh National Military Park." In *Landmarks of Tennessee History* Vol. 1, edited by William T. Alderson and Robert M. McBride. Nashville: Tennessee Historical Society and Tennessee Historical Commission, 1965.

Cooling, B. Franklin. "Fort Donelson National Military Park." In *More Landmarks of Tennessee History,* edited by Robert M. McBride. Nashville: Tennessee Historical Society and Tennessee Historical Commission, 1969.

Gower, Herschel. "The Dahlgrens and Jefferson Davis." *Journal of Mississippi History* 55 (summer 1993): 179–201.

———. "The General Leads His Family Home." *Journal of Mississippi History* 60 (summer 1998): 123–45.

Hall, James O. "The Dahlgren Papers: A Yankee Plot to Kill President Davis." *Civil War Times Illustrated* (November 22, 1983): 30–9.

Hawks, Joanne V. "Julia A. Nutt of Longwood." *Journal of Mississippi History* 57 (November 1994): 291–308.

Jones, Virgil C. "The Kilpatrick-Dahlgren Raid: Boldly Planned . . . Timidly Executed." *Civil War Times* 4 (April 1965): 12–21.

Owens, Jeffrey Alan. "The Burning of Lake St. Joseph." *Louisiana History* 32, no. 4 (fall 1991): 393–415.

———. "Naming Plantations." *Agricultural History* 68, no. 4 (fall 1994): 46–69.

Owsley, Harriet Chappell. "Peace and the Presidential Election of 1864." *Tennessee Historical Quarterly* 18 (March 1959): 3–19.

Scarborough, William K. "Lords or Capitalists? The Natchez Nabobs in Comparative Perspective." *Journal of Mississippi History* 54 (August 1992): 239–67.

Sears, Stephen W. "The Dahlgren Papers Revisited." *Columbiad* (summer 1999): 1–18.

Stuart, Meriwether. "Colonel Ulric Dahlgren and Richmond's Union Underground, 1864." *Virginia Magazine of History and Biography* 72 (1964): 152–204.

Taylor, William Banks. "Southern Yankees: Wealth, High Society, and Political Economy in the Late Antebellum Natchez Region." *Journal of Mississippi History* 59, no. 2 (summer 1997): 79–121.

Thomas, Emory M. "The Kilpatrick-Dahlgren Raid," Part I. *Civil War Times Illustrated* 16 (February 1978): 4–9, 46–48. Part II, 17 (April 1978): 26–33.

Secondary Sources

Books and Monographs

Allardice, Bruce. *More Generals in Gray*. Baton Rouge: Louisiana State University Press, 1995.

Ballard, Michael B. *Pemberton: A Biography*. Jackson: University Press of Mississippi, 1991.

Bassett, John S. *The Southern Plantation Overseer*. Northampton, Massachusetts: Smith College, 1925.

Battle, Herbert B. *The Battle Book*. Montgomery, Alabama: Paragon Press, 1930.

Biographical Directory of the U.S. Congress, 1774–1989. Washington, D.C.: Government Printing Office, 1989.

Boatner III, Mark Mayo. *The Civil War Dictionary*. New York: Daird McKay Co., 1959.

Catton, Bruce. *A Stillness at Appomattox*. New York: Doubleday and Co., 1953.

Clayton, W. W. *History of Davidson County, Tennessee*. Philadelphia: J. W. Lewis & Co., 1880.

Cohen, Henning, and William B. Dillingham. *Humor of the Old Southwest*. Rev. ed. Athens: University of Georgia Press, 1994.

Coppinger, Margaret, et al. *Beersheba Springs, a History*. Beersheba Springs Historical Society, 1983.

Corlew, Robert E., Stanley J. Formsby, and Enoch L. Mitchell. *Tennessee, a Short History*. Knoxville: University of Tennessee Press, 1969.

Davis, William. *Jefferson Davis: The Man and His Hour*. New York: Harper Collins, 1991.

Dickson, John, ed. *National Cyclopaedia of American Biography*. 47 vols. New York: J. T. White, 1892.

Durham, Walter T. *Nashville: The Occupied City—The First Seventeen Months*. Nashville: Tennessee Historical Society, 1985.

———. *Reluctant Partners: Nashville and the Union*. Nashville: Tennessee Historical Society, 1987.

Editors of Time-Life Books, *Echoes of Glory: Arms and Equipment of the Union*. Alexandria, Virginia: Time-Life Books, 1996.

Field, Ron. *American Civil War: Confederate Army Uniforms*. London: Brassey's, Ltd., 1996.

Fontenot, Mary Alice, and Edith Zeigler. *The Tensas Story*. Newellton, Louisiana: Edith Zeigler, 1987.

Govan, Thomas Payne. *Nicholas Biddle*. Chicago: University of Chicago Press, 1959.

Gower, Herschel, and Jack Allen. *Pen & Sword: The Life and Journals of Randal W. McGavock.* Nashville: Tennessee Historical Commission, 1960.

Gragg, Rod. *Planters, Pirates, and Patriots.* Nashville: Rutledge Hill Press, 1985.

Green, Fletcher M. *The Role of the Yankee in the Old South.* Athens: University of Georgia Press, 1972.

Harris, William C. *Presidential Reconstruction in Mississippi.* Baton Rouge: Louisiana State University Press, 1967.

Harter, Eugene C. *The Lost Colony of the Confederacy.* Jackson: University Press of Mississippi, 1987.

Hemphill, Marie H. *Fevers, Floods, and Faith: A History of Sunflower County Mississippi.* Indianola, Mississippi, 1980.

Hook, Sidney. *The Hero in History: A Study in Limitation and Possibility.* New York: John Day, 1943.

Howell, Grady. *To Live and Die in Dixie: History of the Third Regiment Mississippi Volunteer Infantry, C.S.A.* Jackson: Chickasaw Bayou Press, 1991.

Howell, Isabel. *John Armfield of Beersheba Springs.* Beersheba Springs Historical Society, 1983.

Hughes, Jr., Nathaniel Cheairs. *Bentonville: The Final Battle of Sherman and Johnston.* Chapel Hill: University of North Carolina Press, 1996.

Ingraham, J. H. *The Sunny South; or the Southerner at Home.* Philadelphia: G. G. Evans, 1860.

James, D. Clayton. *Antebellum Natchez.* Baton Rouge: Louisiana State University Press, 1968.

Jensen, Leslie D. *Johnny Reb: The Uniform of the Confederate Army, 1861–1865.* Philadelphia: Chelsea House Publishers, 2000.

Johnson, Allen, and Dumas Malone, eds. *Dictionary of American Biography.* 20 vols. New York: Charles Scribner's Sons, 1928–1937.

Jones, Virgil C. *Eight Hours before Richmond.* New York: Henry Holt, 1957.

———. *The Civil War at Sea.* New York: Holt, Rinehart & Winston, 1960.

Jordan, Winthrop D. *Tumult and Silence at Second Creek: An Inquiry into a Civil War Slave Conspiracy.* Baton Rouge: Louisiana State University Press, 1993.

Lynch, John Roy. *Reminiscences of an Active Life.* Chicago: University of Chicago Press, 1970.

Marshall, Theodora Britton, and Gladys Crail Evans. *They Found It in Natchez.* New Orleans: Pelican, 1939.

Massey, Mary Elizabeth. *Ersatz in the Confederacy.* Columbia: University of South Carolina Press, 1952.

———. *Refugee Life in the Confederacy.* Baton Rouge: Louisiana State University Press, 1964.

McElroy, Robert. *Jefferson Davis: The Unusual and the Real.* New York: Harper and Brothers, 1973.

Myers, Robert Manson, ed. *Children of Pride: A True Story of Georgia and the Civil War.* New Haven: Yale University Press, 1972.

Osborne, Charles G. *Jubal.* Chapel Hill: University of North Carolina Press, 1992.

Ostrander, Stephen H. *A History of the City of Brooklyn and Kings County.* 2 vols. Brooklyn: 1894.

Owsley, Frank Lawrence. *State Rights and the Confederacy.* Chicago: University of Chicago Press, 1925.

Parks, Joseph Howard. *General Edmund Kirby Smith, C.S.A.* Baton Rouge: Louisiana State University Press, 1954.

Peltier, Jr., Corbett James. "Confederate Natchez." Master's thesis, Louisiana State University, 1948.

Randall, J. G., and David Herbert Donald. *The Civil War and Reconstruction.* Lexington, Massachusetts: D. C. Heath, 1969.

Remini, Robert V. *Andrew Jackson and the Course of American Democracy, 1833–1845.* Vol 3. New York: Harper & Row, 1984.

Ross, Isabel. *First Lady of the South: The Life of Mrs. Jefferson Davis.* New York: Harper, 1958.

Ryan, D. D., ed. *A Yankee Spy in Richmond: The Civil War Diary of "Crazy Bet" Van Low.* Mechanicsburg, Pennsylvania: Stackpole Books, 1996.

Sansing, David G., Sim C. Callon, and Carolyn Vance Smith. *Natchez: An Illustrated History.* Natchez: Plantation Publishing Co., 1992.

Schneller, Jr., Robert J. *A Quest for Glory: A Biography of Rear Admiral John A. Dahlgren.* Annapolis: Naval Institute Press, 1996.

Schultz, Duane. *The Dahlgren Affair.* New York: W. W. Norton, 1998.

Sears, Stephen W. *Controversies and Commanders: Dispatches from the Army of the Potomac.* Boston: Houghton Mifflin, 1999.

Sutherland, Daniel E. *Confederate Carpetbaggers.* Baton Rouge: Louisiana State University Press, 1988.

———. *Seasons of War: The Ordeal of a Confederate Community, 1861–1865.* New York: The Free Press, 1995.

———. *The Emergence of Total War.* Fort Worth and Boulder: Ryan Place Publishers, 1996.

Swanberg, W. A. *Sickles the Incredible.* New York: Charles Scribner's Sons, 1956.

Taylor, Joe Gray. *Negro Slavery in Louisiana.* Baton Rouge: Louisiana Historical Association, 1963.

———. *Louisiana Reconstructed, 1863–1877.* Baton Rouge: Louisiana State University Press, 1974.

Trefousse, Hans L. *Historical Dictionary of Reconstruction*. New York: Greenwood Press, 1991.

Warner, Ezra J. *Generals in Gray: Lives of the Confederate Commanders*. Baton Rouge: Louisiana State University Press, 1959.

———. *Generals in Blue: Lives of the Union Commanders*. Baton Rouge: Louisiana State University Press, 1964.

Wayne, Michael. *The Reshaping of Plantation Society: The Natchez District, 1860–1880*. Baton Rouge: Louisiana State University Press, 1983.

Who Was Who in the Theatre, 1912–1976. Detroit: Gale Research Co., 1992.

Willett, Jr., Robert L. *One Day of the Civil War*. Washington: Brassey's, 1997.

Wilson, J. G., and John Fisk, eds. *Appleton's Cyclopaedia of American Biography*. 7 vols. New York: D. Appleton, 1888–1900.

Wise, Stephen R. *Lifeline of the Confederacy: Blockade Running during the Civil War*. Columbia: University of South Carolina Press, 1988.

———. *Gate of Hell: Campaign for Charleston Harbor, 1863*. Columbia: University of South Carolina Press, 1994.

Work Projects Administration, compiler. *Historical Background of Dougherty County [Georgia], 1836–1940*. Atlanta: Cherokee Publishing Co., 1981.

Wyatt-Brown, Bertram. *Honor and Violence in the Old South*. New York: Oxford University Press, 1986.

———. *The House of Percy: Honor, Melancholy, and Imagination in a Southern Family*. New York: Oxford University Press, 1996.

Index

Dahlgren, Charles Routh
("Charlie") (C.R.D.), 21, 34,
45–46, 71, 88, 92, 141, 166, 204,
213; at Bentonville, 103; broken
spirit of, 107; death, 167; dis-
charge, 141; enlists in Adams
Troop MS Cavalry, 45; fights for
South, 44–45; friendship with
Ulric, 31–33; marriage to N. Holl-
ingsworth, 167; Natchez City
Cemetery, 175; photograph of
Ulric, 99, 141; picture of,
214–15; service record, 89–90, 91
Dahlgren, Charles Ulric, 230; birth,
167; buried Natchez City Cemetery, 206
Dahlgren, Clifford, 188
Dahlgren, Edgar McWhorter, 102,
113, 129, 229–30
Dahlgren, Elizabeth, 95, 206
Dahlgren, Eric Bernard, 175,
229–30
Dahlgren, Eva, 158
Dahlgren, Gustavus Vannoy
("Dahl"), 48, 88, 102, 113, 166,
204, 210, 219; birth, 38, 39,
215–16; at C.G.D. funeral, 205,
206; death, 231; family dependence on, 185, 218, 226–27; "little General," 217; moves M.E.D.
to new house in TN, 228–29; tea
and coffee broker, 198
Dahlgren, Ira Smith, 178–79, 230
Dahlgren, Johan Adolphus, 3
Dahlgren, John Adolph ("Pudge")
(J.A.D.), 21, 48, 81, 88, 141,
166, 167, 204, 206; birth Clifford D., 181; business acumen,
171–72; college in Canada, 168,

170; death, 107, 232; declared
major, 167; disillusionment and
instability of, 107; granddaughter
Ruth, 226; indispensable in return to Marydale, 112; land transferred to, 167–68; paroled at
Vicksburg, 79
Dahlgren, John Adolphus Bernard:
birth, 1; C.G.D. loans, 158, 166;
death, 185, 199–200; distinguished career, 49, 234; explosion aboard *Harvest Moon*,
105–6; grief over U.D. death,
95, 99; intercedes for Bernard
D., 104–5; invents cannon, 40,
42; marries Mary Clement Bunker, 240; marries Madeleine V.
Goddard, 142; physical appearance, 223; relationship with
C.G.D., 2; relationship with
W.T.D., 14; rumors of collusion
with C.G.D., 52, 89; sends
photo of U.D., 141, 214; surprise at C.G.D. visit, 146–47;
Union moderate, 41; youthful
temperament, 12–13
Dahlgren, John Armfield
("Johnny"), 10–11, 91–92, 206:
account of earnings 1885,
191–92; birth, 178–80; family
historian, 220–21, 226, 227–28;
later years, 231; memorializes
family name, 226; photographs
with M.E.D., 230–31; records
family churches, 192; recounts
family lore, 218–19; works at
Beersheba Springs, 225
Dahlgren, John Vinton: marries E.
Drexel, 175

food costs, 98; whiskey, 123
food riots, 120
Foote, Edwin, 71
Forbes, John Murray (capitalist), 162
Forbes, Robert Bennet (capitalist), 162–63
Ford, Dr. J. P., 114
Ford, Mr., 52
Ford, Washington, 70
Forrest, Nathan Bedford, 64, 120
Fort Donelson, TN, 63, 64
Fort Fisher, NC, 106
Fort Henry, TN, 63
Fort Panmure (Fort Rosalie), MS, 201
Fortress Monroe, VA, 170
Fort Sumter, SC, 44
4th Tennessee Cavalry, 141
Fowler, Volney Daniel, 135
Fowler, William, 152
Franco-Prussian War, 200, 221
Fredericksburg, MD, 90, 111
freedmen, 157; celebrate emancipation, 132; future of, 159; hiring, 151, 154, 166; unemployment among, 154
Freedmen's Bureau, 135, 151, 155
Freeland, Mrs. Frisby, 82
Freeman (on Albany-to-Marydale trip), 116, 123, 129, 132
Free Trader, 42
French, Lucy Virginia, 88; comments on U.D., 38, 91; observes vandalizing of C.G.D. cottage, 144

G. and D. Cook (carriage makers), 23

Gainey, J. J., 176–78
Gardner, Edwin Sumner (E.S.G.), 34, 175, 188, 212
Gardner, Elizabeth, 230
Gardner, Ellen Smith Vannoy (E.S.V.G.), 38, 39, 175, 214; assists in birth of M.E.D. twins, 178; assists in birth of Van D., 215–16; portrait done, 212
Gardner, Laura Adelaide (L.A.G.), 212, 214
Garibaldi, Giuseppe, 35–36, 57, 221, 235
Garner, Mr., 126
Gaston, Dr. J. McF., 139
General Sterling Price (ship), 79
George's Island, MA, 63
Georgetown, SC, 105
Georgia Bank Notes, 102
Gettysburg, PA, 92, 111, 136
USS *Gettysburg*, 106
Gibson, Dr. Tully Stewart, 113, 121; death, 176–78; family, education and service, 111–12
Gibson, Gibeon, 111
Gibson, Randal Lee, 55, 111
Gillespie, James M., 171
HMS *Gladiator*, 56–60
Glide (ship), 78–79
Goddard, John L., 19–22
Goddard, Madeleine V.: marries J.A.D., 142. *See also* Dahlgren, Madeleine V. Goddard
Goddard, Romaine, 158
Goddard, Vinton, 158
Goodspeed Publishing Co., 221
Goodspeed's Biographical and Historical Memoirs of Mississippi (Goodspeed), 16, 221
Gordon, Richard H., 148

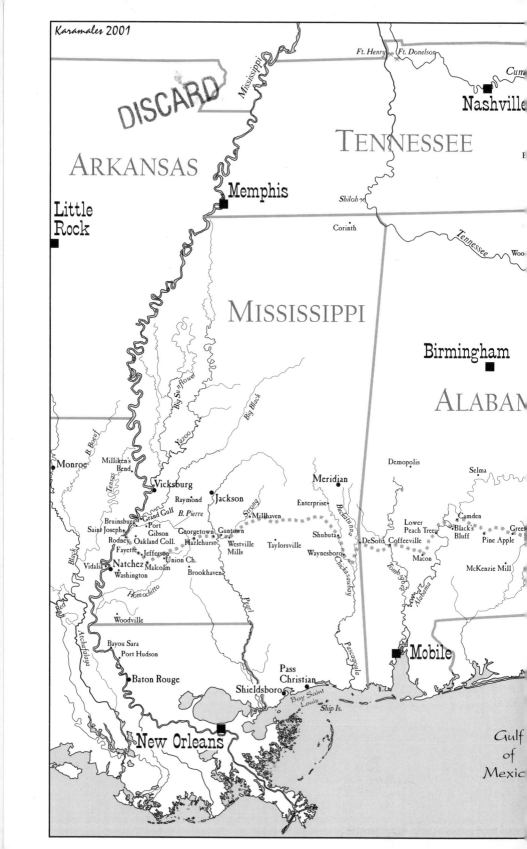